The Politics of Local Economic Policy

The Problems and Possibilities of Local Initiative

Aram Eisenschitz

and

Jamie Gough

150th YEAR

M

MACMILLAN

First published 1993 by
THE MACMILLAN PRESS LTD
Houndmills, Basingstoke, Hampshire RG21 2XS
and London
Companies and representatives
throughout the world

ISBN 0–333–52174–9 hardcover
ISBN 0–333–52175–7 paperback

A catalogue record for this book is available
from the British Library.

Printed in Hong Kong

Series Standing Order (Public Policy and Politics)

If you would like to receive future titles in this series as they are published,
you can make use of our standing order facility. To place a standing order
please contact your bookseller or, in case of difficulty, write to us at the
address below with your name and address and the name of the series.
Please state with which title you wish to begin your standing order. (If you
live outside the United Kingdom we may not have the rights for your area,
in which case we will forward your order to the publisher concerned.)

Customer Services Department, Macmillan Distribution Ltd,
Houndmills, Basingstoke, Hampshire, RG21 2XS, England.

Contents

PART II POLICIES AND DEBATES

Abbreviations

BiC	Business in the Community
BSC	British Steel Corporation
CBI	Confederation of British Industry
CLES	Centre for Local Economic Studies
DoE	Department of the Environment
DSS	Department of Social Security
DTI	Department of Trade and Industry
ERM	Exchange Rate Mechanism
EZ	Enterprise Zone
GLC	Greater London Council
IT	Information technology
LDDC	London Docklands Development Corporation
LEB	Local Enterprise Board
MSC	Manpower Services Commission
OECD	Organization for Economic Cooperation and Development
R&D	Research and development
TEC	Training and Enterprise Council
TUC	Trade Union Congress
UDC	Urban Development Corporation

Frequently Mentioned Programmes and Institutions

Business in the Community (BiC) A national body funded by the private sector which aims to promote the involvement of business in local economic and social regeneration.

City Grant, formerly the Urban Development Grant and Urban Regeneration Grant A grant paid by central government to developers on a discretionary basis for developments in depressed areas with economic or social benefits; the aim is to lever the maximum private sector investment for the minimum grant. The City Grant, unlike the Urban Development Grant, has no local authority involvement.

Community business or community enterprise An enterprise whose aims are to provide employment and to produce goods and services which the local community lacks. Such enterprises are controlled by bodies with local representation through which their profits are recycled, and are subsidised through grants and training schemes.

Economic development company Local agencies which carry out varied, sometimes wide ranging, economic policies. Mostly funded and controlled by District Councils, but sometimes with private sector participation.

Enterprise Agency or Enterprise Trust Local agencies set up by the private sector to support both conventional and Third Sector small businesses.

Enterprise Zone (EZ) A central government programme of areas within which various tax breaks are available to developers and occupying firms and within which land use planning procedures are streamlined. The areas were mostly derelict on designation.

Industrial Improvement Areas Old industrial or commercial areas within which property and environmental subsidies are concentrated. Pioneered by local authorities, they received statutory backing under the Inner Urban Areas Act.

Inner Urban Areas Act 1978 Provides powers for local authorities designated by the Secretary of State to give grants and loans for land, property and environmental improvements. The widest range of powers is available in 'partnership' and 'programme' authorities.

Innovation centres Agencies with mixed funding which provide information, training and resources for local technological innovation, transfer and diffusion.

Local economic agency Any body carrying out economic initiatives across a local area.

Local Enterprise Boards (LEBs) Provide loan and equity funding to private sector firms, and carry out property development and sometimes other functions. Controlled by local authorities, but since the mid-1980s obtain most of their funding from the private sector.

Science parks Properties designed for small, innovating enterprises. They are usually close to higher education institutions or research establishments, and sometimes provide training and other collective services.

Training and Enterprise Councils (TECs) The local arms of the government's programmes for training and small business development; there are eighty-two in England and Wales, coming under the Training Enterprise and Education Directorate, and twenty similar Local Enterprise Companies in Scotland under Scottish Enterprise. Their boards are government appointed and made up largely of business executives. They contract out training to public, private and voluntary sector agencies.

Training, Enterprise and Education Directorate, formerly the Manpower Services Commission (MSC), Training Commission and Training Agency Quangos appointed and funded by central government to carry out its training programmes. We sometimes refer to these collectively as the MSC.

Third Sector Organisations which are neither private nor public sector, neither profit oriented nor state controlled. Includes both production organisations like cooperatives and community businesses, and consumption organisations like housing associations and credit unions.

Urban Development Corporations Twelve corporations which have taken over local authorities' powers of planning land use and providing infrastructure and with extensive powers of land acquisition, aimed at regenerating largely derelict areas of cities. Central government appoints their boards and funds them. Named, e.g. Leeds Development Corporation.

Acknowledgements

We should like to thank Irene Bruegel and Allan Cochrane for their
generosity in reading the typescript and making many valuable suggestions. Our thanks also to our publisher Steven Kennedy for so patiently
steering us towards a focused text, and for his kind response to our
endlessly extended deadlines. The book's errors are of course ours
alone.

ARAM EISENSCHITZ
JAMIE GOUGH

Guide to Reading the Book

Local economic policy seeks to address economic problems within areas ranging from the neighbourhood to the subregion. Since the mid-1970s, local economic initiatives have burgeoned throughout the developed capitalist countries. They have helped to transform ideas about what a desirable economy is and how to achieve it: They have played an important part in changing notions about welfare and the relation between economy and society. They have reoriented the activities of local government. They have been developed and supported by all major currents in the political spectrum; and for each, a local level has become integral to their economic programme. The purpose of this book is to explore the origins, potential and problems of this remarkable movement.

A striking paradox is that the growth of local economic initiatives has taken place at a time when national governments in most capitalist countries have sought to withdraw from economic intervention. Why, then, has intervention grown at a local level? What are the limitations of local initiatives by virtue of their 'localness', and what issues can local policy address? What power does economic policy gain through being conducted at a local level? The effect of the localness of policy is the central theme of this book.

Our discussion is focused on Britain. However, we highlight the main differences between British and international experience, and how the specific economic, social and political structures of Britain have shaped local economic initiatives within it. This is a necessary basis for considering the lessons that can be learnt for policy in one country from successes and failures of initiatives in others. We are also centrally concerned with the implications for local initiatives of the increasing internationalisation of the world economy.

The spread of local economic initiatives has been based on their promise to stimulate enterprise, rebuild community, and re-establish some autonomy for the local economy – a 'Bootstraps' strategy for localities; this appeal is the focus of Part I of the book. Chapter 1 outlines the historical development of local economic policy and the

Bootstraps approach internationally and in Britain. It argues that a remarkable political consensus exists around this approach, albeit with varied motivations; in Britain this consensus has rested in part on the promise of local initiatives to address the causes of the long relative decline of the Britain economy. There is also a striking consensus around specific aims, strategies, and organisational forms of local economic policy, which are discussed in Chapter 2.

Although the consensus is real and important, there have been vital political differences in the implementation of the Bootstraps strategy. In Part II we present the principal policies which have been initiated by the Right, Left and Centre, looking at their stated aims, their historical evolution, the agencies involved, their success according to their own criteria, and the debates that have surrounded them. We find that the effects of policies have frequently been quite different from those intended, and that the difficulties encountered have often resulted in a given policy changing its aims and mode of implementation. The political complexion of many policies has been ambiguous and shifting. Over time there has been a convergence onto a Centre strategy which seeks to build a consensus between all groups in the locality and to combine increased competitiveness with welfare and greater equality. This mainstream approach has been pursued not only by local authorities and voluntary organisations but also, strikingly, by corporations and by some local agencies set up by the Conservative government.

In Part III we examine the economic, social and political underpinnings of local economic initiatives in order to gain a deeper understanding of their potential and limitations. In Chapter 5 we discuss what it means to speak of 'local economies' in a highly internationalised world economy. We examine the tensions involved in attempting to enhance local integration and local specialisation of production. Chapter 6 examines how local economic policy addresses 'locality' – the links between production, the local labour force, social life, and gender and ethnic/'race' relations. It looks at the diverse and problematic meanings of 'enterprise' and 'community' in local economic initiatives. Chapter 7 examines how and in what senses local economic policy can create greater local control of the economy and thus enhance economic democracy and local autonomy. We discuss the different ways in which the various political currents seek to deal with the tension between local control and regional and national policy, and their problems in using local control to carry out and exemplify their strategy.

A central theme of Part III is that, while local economies and local communities have a reality in the modern world, they are in tension with national and international mobility of capital and commodities. Localities are consequently both unstable and highly diverse, and there is no simple tendency for the economy to become 'more local', more decentralised or more fragmented. On the other hand, the coherence of localities is vital for their economic efficiency, and thus for the mobility of capital and efficiency of trade. There are therefore two complementary but conflicting processes, the mobility of capital and trade and the coherence of local economies, which local economic policy has to try to juggle. A second theme is that local economic initiatives are always integrally about social relations – the relations between capital and labour, between sections of business, and between parts of the labour force.

These themes form the starting point for our discussion in Part IV of the future of local economic policy. We examine how the socialist and the modernising Left, the Right and the consensus mainstream deal with the tensions around locality and community, and with the conflicts between and within the classes; we consider their past problems in these respects and the pressures and opportunities they are likely to encounter in the future. We argue that consensus local economic policy has both used the successes of the Conservative government *and* addressed some of its major failings; it has done so precisely by being local policy; this has underpinned the growth of the consensus approach. Nevertheless, in the final two chapters we argue that there are major tensions within mainstream local economic policy: its reproduction of inequality and economic instability, the difficulties and dangers of establishing active partnership between capital and labour in contemporary Britain, the relation of local initiatives to economic crisis, the internationalisation of capital, and Britain's place in Europe. The deep tensions within all approaches to local economic policy mean that its future is open.

A number of themes run through the book which are not specific to local economic policy: the dilemma for employers of how to combine discipline of workers and collaboration with them; the tension between the mobility of capital and the social organisation of production; the nature of 'the British disease' and the barriers to curing it; and the causes and limitations of 'flexibility' in contemporary economic organisation. Readers with a particular interest in these themes can use the index to trace our arguments.

Part I

The Promise of Local Economic Initiatives

1 The Emergence of an Idea

Successful urban regeneration on both sides of the Atlantic has been led by people pulling themselves and their communities up by their own bootstraps, not outsiders telling them what to do. As the experience of cities like Glasgow and Sheffield demonstrates, it requires local leaders with a wider vision of the community than their individual, sectional roles within it, and a community in which all sections are prepared to submerge their differences and work towards common goals (*Financial Times* editorial, 13 June 1991).

To look *within* a community for the resources and capacity to create new jobs ... [is] arguably the only sensible way forward for action on a local level ... It is the local authority's job – or rather the job of the entire community – to see that resources are devoted to providing individuals with the facilities which make the taking of individual initiative as easy as possible (Todd, 1984, p. 10).

When communities of active citizens band together, set their own agenda and embark on a course of common endeavour, we can begin to tackle the blight that hangs over so many of our communities ... [L]ocal communities can hold the key to their own destiny through personal and community enterprise (Civic Trust, 1989, p. 6).

Public sector intervention, working in positive partnership with the private sector, can save and create jobs and nurture enterprise in a way that builds on and works with the local community and respects the rights, opportunities and conditions of workpeople (Centre for Local Economic Studies, CLES, 1987a, p. 2).

Throughout the richer capitalist countries local economic initiatives are blossoming. There is enormous variety in the aims which they set themselves, the economic levers which they use, the scale of the pro-

3

grammes, and the roles of the private and public sectors and of national and local organisations. The geographical scale – the meaning of 'local' – is also varied: a derelict area of a few hectares, a neighbourhood, a town, a subregion. Yet across this variety there is a widely shared framework: the need for local control of the economy, the use of indigenous resources, the promotion of enterprise and the mobilisation of community cooperation. These are seen as the key to the health or revival of local economies, and indeed as an important means to national economic regeneration. One may speak of a movement of local economic initiatives, a new practice with a distinct ideology, popular appeal and considerable popular involvement. A role for local economic policy has become part of the common sense of the age.

Local economic policy has been seen as a means of addressing the problems experienced by the dominant capitalist countries since the late 1960s and, especially, since the world recession of 1974–6. As these problems have continued, there has been increasing scepticism about the ability of national governments alone to resolve them; the local level has presented itself as a possible terrain for action. Despite the high national and international integration of these economies, the new movement asserts the possibility and desirability of influencing economies from and at the local level. Local societies are no longer to be the objects of impersonal market forces but are to become active shapers of their destiny. To do so they have to make use of their indigenous resources rather than relying on the fickle decisions of private and public organisations based elsewhere.

The central way in which these local resources are conceptualised is as 'enterprise'. Enterprise denotes the initiative not only of business but also of workers, as workers or as would-be entrepreneurs, and of voluntary organisations and community groups. In an even wider sense, enterprise suggests the need to shake off past routines, to question past assumptions, to think and act radically; every local organisation, public as well as private, economic as well as social, is to be enterprising in this sense. All local social groups are to be involved, and their collaboration is to constitute the locality as a unified entity, a community, able to fight for its place within the hostile world outside. The movement, then, marches under the banners of local autonomy, enterprise and community.

It is this approach, more than the change in spatial scale, that distinguishes the new initiatives from the previously dominant form of spatial economic policy, regional policy. Regional policy presented itself as a means of influencing the distribution of resources, particularly mobile investment, between regions. Although this strand is still present, local economic policy is concerned not so much with the redistribution of resources between areas as with change within them, not with planning but with enterprise, not with influencing external actors but with mobilising internal ones. This distinctive ideology and promise of local economic initiatives have enabled them to gain political support and have been central to their development; this is the focus of the first part of this book, while succeeding parts examine their real effects. Our survey is initially international in scope; in the second half of this chapter we narrow our focus to Britain.

Historical threads: the ideas behind local economic policy

Local economic initiatives have been a particular kind of response to the long term stagnation of the world capitalist economy which began in the late 1960s and early 1970s (Mandel, 1978a). The growth rate of the OECD countries slowed from 4.8 per cent p.a. in 1960–73 to 2.6 per cent during 1973–9 and 2.8 per cent in 1979–89. Productivity increase showed a similar pattern. Underlying and propagating the slowdown was a falling rate of profit: for manufacturing in the leading seven capitalist countries at peaks of the cycle, it fell from 29 per cent in 1965 to 16 per cent in 1987. In the four leading European countries unemployment at the peak of the cycle rose from 2.6 per cent in 1970 to 5.7 per cent in 1980 and to 9.3 per cent in 1988 (Armstrong *et al.*, 1991). The impact of this stagnation has been highly uneven: while some regions and localities have maintained a fast growth rate and low unemployment, others, especially those dominated by traditional manufacturing and mining, have experienced sharp declines in employment, permanently high rates of unemployment and large-scale poverty.

These spatially uneven problems have been one motivation for local economic policy (Campbell, 1990a; Duncan and Goodwin, 1988, pp. 129–30 below); but the latter cannot be read off from the former. Severe local problems were widespread in the 1950s and 1960s, and, most tellingly, in the 1930s, and yet the predominant spatial economic strategy in those periods, regional policy, was, as we have just noted, quite different both in geographical scale and content. Local economic policy is a particular political and ideological response. We can trace its historical development in four practices: regional policy, local welfare programmes, land use planning, and support for enterprise. In each of these fields, indigenous local economic development has come to be

seen as offering solutions, and each has made a distinctive contribution
to the ideas of the movement.

 Regional development policy

Since the Second World War, regional policies have been carried out
either by government at regional level (USA, Canada, Australia, West
Germany), or in the rest of Western Europe and Japan by central
government; promotion and financial incentives have been used to steer
investment to the deprived regions, although often failing to solve their
problems. With the economic slowdown, a new strategy emerged:
rather than rely on redistribution, the region would take control over its
own economy (Holland, 1976). In some of the non-federal countries,
notably Britain, Belgium, France, Spain, movements for regional
autonomy emerged. Centrally directed regional policy, it was argued,
had exacerbated their structural problems. Incentives had been taken
up predominantly by large national and transnational companies, for
branch plants carrying out low-level work, with few local linkages, and
contributing little to the internal development of the region. Large firms
with their remote headquarters were branded as disloyal to the region,
liable to shift production to locations offering yet cheaper labour or yet
greater incentives. In Britain this mood was encapsulated in the rejection of Hitachi's plans for a TV plant in County Durham in 1977. A
close analogy was seen with Third World countries, their economies
dominated by transnationals and subjected to lopsided and unstable
forms of development (Hechter, 1975). The solution was to be similar:
autonomy.

In the 1970s and 1980s greater regional economic autonomy was
achieved, in Belgium and Spain as part of the creation of a regional level
of government, in Italy, France, Netherlands, Denmark and Greece
through devolution, and in Britain through the creation of development
agencies in Wales and Scotland. This increase in economic power of
the regional state was all the more remarkable given the retreat from
economic intervention by national governments of all political shades.
The new ideas developed at this level were subsequently transposed to
the local: the need to avoid reliance on externally-controlled firms and
institutions, and the importance of developing indigenous resources and
internal linkages (Weaver, 1982). As Windass (1982, p. vi) argued,
'many local initiatives are in areas which have been drained of local
resources by a centralised industrial and financial system. It is only just
that means should be found of returning resources to them or, at least,

of allowing them to retain more of what they generate, provided this [maximises] local self-reliance.'

Welfare policies

The 'rediscovery of poverty' in the 1960s conceived of poverty not as a failure of the productive economy but as a failure of distribution of income and public services, in particular their spatial distribution; accordingly, poverty programmes were locally targeted (Donnison and Soto, 1980, Ch. 3). The resilience of poverty was attributed to the mutual reinforcement of its different aspects at a *local* level – income, housing, education, family life, physical environment, which therefore needed locally coordinated action. Community organisations were increasingly involved, expressing and sometimes keeping in check the increasing demands for greater popular control over welfare provision (Cockburn, 1977). The local nature of these programmes was a precursor of local economic policy.

In the late 1960s and early 1970s, there was widespread concern with the interconnections of social and economic problems and for organisational coordination to match, reflected in the popularity of corporate and strategic planning, systems analysis, and in Britain the introduction of structure planning. As economic stagnation set in, the links between social questions and the economic could hardly be ignored. Strategic planning thus played a role in shifting local government towards economic concerns and inflecting all its activities with economic aims, even though the eventual form of local economic policy was far more fragmented and pragmatic than envisaged by strategic planning.

Neighbourhood poverty programmes also took a more economic slant, as the sharp rise in unemployment during the recession of 1974–5 underlined the importance of the local productive economy in creating poverty. On the left the Community Development Projects in Britain concluded that their remit to improve local distributional welfare policies had been misplaced because it neglected production, especially the activities of the transnationals (CDP, 1977). In the political mainstream it was increasingly proclaimed that 'it is necessary to create wealth before it can be distributed'. Thus both left and right helped to change the focus of local poverty programmes towards employment (for the US case see Donnel, 1984).

Not only were employment issues added to welfare ones, but the nature of welfare itself was being challenged. The right identified a 'dependency culture' in which individuals' responsibility for their own well-being was stifled. The left criticised welfare's authoritarian organisation and its insensitivity to diverse needs. They converged on self-help and self-management by individuals and communities; these were developed first in traditional welfare areas such as housing, and subsequently transferred to welfare-through-employment. In this way local job creation and enterprise came to be seen as alternatives to 'bureaucratic' welfare; redistribution of income and benefits gave way to redistribution of jobs. There was continuity in the means for achieving this, namely collaboration between local government and community organisations. Local economic policy has thus inherited the concern of the local poverty programmes for neighbourhood, community and self-management, but with their meaning shifted from the social to the interface of the social and the economic (Krumholz, 1986).

Land use planning

Land use planning has gradually incorporated explicitly economic aims into what formerly saw itself as an amenity and social movement. From the 1950s in the USA, central area redevelopment in old industrial cities has been explicitly presented as economic restructuring (Cook Benjamin, 1984), and much inner city renovation served the same aim (Castells, 1977, pp. 296–301). Land use planning in Britain since the mid-1970s has become increasingly concerned with encouraging higher rent uses in city centres as a means of economic regeneration.

A second thread has been the application of land use planning to benefit the poor and protect vulnerable parts of the economy. In the 1960s there was increasing awareness of how planning reinforced the regressive distribution of income and benefits created by spatial structures (Hall *et al.*, 1973). One reaction was for planning to support neighbourhood welfare programmes, particularly in defending low cost housing against commercial development and gentrification. In the 1970s this was widened to a defence of small businesses employing local people against displacement by higher rent uses. This current took up a critique of planning developed in the 1960s: that 'blueprint' planning had destroyed the variety, vitality and linkages within neighbourhoods that sustain both community life and small firms (Jacobs, 1965), a view which chimed with a developing aesthetic reaction against modernism. This strand of planning, then, pitted itself against large scale, comprehensive development, favouring pragmatism and flexibility in preserving and adapting buildings, and – what was thought to follow from this – the preservation of communities. These elements became central to the orientation of local economic policy towards community and grass-roots enterprise.

These threads have contributed to local economic policy two contrary views of large scale redevelopment. But both have fed into a central concern for the physical environment and for the integrity and inter-relatedness of local economies and local societies.

A third thread also sprang from the critique of land use planning as regressive. Some social democratic commentators responded to this discovery by proposing, not popular planning, but less or no planning (Banham *et al,* 1969). In the 1970s this strategy fed into and converged with the neo-liberal right, who argued that planning, through its distortion of land markets and bureaucracy, was destroying jobs. This concern with land use planning was the ideological starting point for the Right's local economic initiatives. We shall see that this kind of political cross-over has been characteristic of local economic policy.

Enterprise and small firms

A further strand has been the revival of enterprise, the entrepreneur, and the small firm. Interest in small firms revived in the early 1970s as the seemingly inexorable concentration of ownership began to falter. In a much-quoted piece of research, Birch (1979) found that net new job formation in the USA was taking place only in the small firm sector. Since then, the sector has expanded in most countries; in Britain the number of firms with fewer than 100 employees doubled between 1970 and 1986.

It was widely argued that these facts showed decisive advantages for small firms in the contemporary economy. Large firms lacked innovative capacity and flexibility required in fast changing markets; small firms had both the motivation and the ability to do these things, and the economic dynamism of localities depended on them. Moreover, this would also have social benefits. Self-employment would promote self-reliance and self-respect which had been smothered by large firms and the welfare state. Community enterprises could also replace inflexible welfare services. Small firms would help the community to cope with national economic turmoil, help to bring the poor into the economic mainstream, and supply a greater diversity of services. Support for enterprise needed to be delivered locally, both because actual and would-be entrepreneurs were geographically limited in their contacts, and because barriers to entrepreneurship were thought to be locally specific, being particularly severe in areas dominated by large work-places, branch plants and public sector employment. Support for enter-prise was thus a major impetus in developing local economic policy, and it promised to contribute to both economic regeneration and welfare.

'Bootstraps': the crystallisation of an idea

We find, then, that in a number of different fields – regionalism, neighbourhood welfare, land use planning, enterprise – a common solution emerges: indigenous local economic development. In each case the analysis involves similar villains: the internationalisation of the economy, the geographical mobility of investment and production, the large corporations and transnationals, 'bureaucratic' government, and, to some, the unions. Their effect has been to render the local economy unstable. Branch plants and large scale urban developments are seen as alien imports which have disrupted local economies, have failed to develop them organically, and have made off when the going got dif-ficult. The brains of the economy arc located outside the area, and large companies and welfare have sapped the capacity for initiative. The large organisations are uncaring and impersonal, ignorant of the details of the economies they control; they trample on communities whose skills, traditions and livelihoods can be destroyed almost inadvertently. These ills are reinforced by all levels of government, which maintain the attitudes of the boom years in their inflexibility and anti-enterprise orientation. This analysis and its novelty within the history of spatial policy reflect the fact that concentration of economic power has never been greater.

The solution was to be the antithesis of these forces: local autonomy, community and enterprise. As the quotations at the beginning of this chapter indicate, an *intertwining* of these themes produces a powerful vision of the desirable local economy. Small scale production and local ownership encourage greater initiative in employers and workers, and allow workers a greater sense of involvement with the enterprise; each economic unit then becomes both more of a community internally and more enterprising in external competition. Outside the workplace the disadvantaged are to find their own solutions through enterprise and community organisation. Local sources of investment and innovation are to be encouraged rather than relying on inward investment, and the area's existing industries and skills are to be developed. Through collaboration between firms and increased local trading, a community of local enterprises is to be formed. In this way, control of the economy is shifted to the locality; development becomes 'people based', rooted in the community. The locality becomes the subject rather than the object of development; its behaviour in the world, like that of individuals, is to be confident and 'proactive'. The locality becomes both more of a community, through collaboration between local institutions and interests, and more enterprising through competing more effectively with the world outside.

We may call this vision the 'Bootstraps strategy'. Within it local autonomy, community and enterprise take on multiple meanings, simultaneously economic, social and political; and each acquires its meaning in relation to the others – a 'Holy Trinity' of local economic development.

Some commentators have argued that the growth of local economic initiatives has caused a progressive replacement of the traditional welfare aims of local government by economic ones (Sabel, 1989). But a central part of the appeal of the Bootstraps strategy has been its promise to *integrate* welfare with economics, social justice with growth. By using community-based enterprises and basing development on local skills, the disadvantaged are to overcome their poverty through employment, while at the same time providing goods and services that their communities lack. This promises not only to improve the economic lot of the poor, but to enable them to achieve self-respect through their own enterprise. Destructive social pathologies and the anomie thought to be characteristic of modern society can be overcome through the economic creation of community. Thus Falk (1978a, p. 212) sees local economic initiatives as able to reverse the process whereby 'economic decline leads to physical decay which breeds apathy and neglect of community resources'. Enterprise, community and local control are to be both means to economic ends and desirable social-psychological aims in themselves.

The Bootstraps strategy, then, aims to construct the locality as a unified, organic entity, through reconciling the apparent opposites of enterprise and community, of efficiency and welfare, of economic means and social ends. As we shall see, it has many emphases, according to its implementation in different local political and economic circumstances and with different policy instruments; even the attraction of inward investment, large scale urban redevelopment, and action by central government and large corporations can be carried out in a Bootstraps mode.

The international growth of local economic initiatives

The involvement of local agencies, especially local government, in economic policy is often presented as wholly new (Centre for Employment Initiatives, 1985, section 6.5). Indeed, the notion that localities should make a radical break with past practice is part of the ideology of the new movement. But local economic policy has a substantial history. All local government activity of course has economic effects through its impact on local employment, on incomes via local taxes, and on local prices. But local government over the past hundred years or so has also undertaken a number of activities with more or less explicit economic *aims*.

First, it has operated municipal enterprises producing and selling goods and services, particularly utilities and transport services; these, and non-marketed services such as roads, education and housing, have sometimes been used to improve working conditions and promote economic growth. Similarly, the regulatory functions of local government in land use, environment and health, though usually seen as aiming to create a good environment, have at times been inflected towards economic aims.

Economic issues have always been central to local government's role in urban property development, although this is often presented simply as 'good planning'. Local government has played an essential role in town-centre development, sometimes presented as being about economic regeneration, and in regulating competition in retailing. In some countries local government has provided industrial land and advanced factories. For example, the West German Länder have used this as the principal instrument in strategies for relocating industry and attracting targeted new sectors. During the 1930s local government in several European countries and in the USA ran job-creation programmes, sometimes producing infrastructure of use to the local economy.

Business organisations and individual companies have long been involved in planning local economies. In West Germany the Chambers of Commerce and Chambers of Craftsmen have used compulsory levies to carry out indicative planning and lobbying, to provide credit, manage apprenticeship schemes, and to build and rent premises for small firms. In central Italy ('the Third Italy'), local employers' and artisans' associations in particular industries have provided collective services to their constituent firms. In north-eastern cities in the USA business-run development boards have coordinated large scale central redevelopments.

These precedents include most of the individual policies of the present movement. But contemporary local economic policy differs from its antecedents both in the number of localities in which it is practised, and in the variety of policies across and even within each locality. Whereas up to the 1970s local economic initiatives presented themselves as *ad hoc*, the ideology of the present movement gives an essential and specific place to local economic policy.

The growth of this more ambitious and comprehensive type of policy can be traced in institutional changes since the mid-1970s. First, the implementation of some central government economic programmes has been decentralised, particularly support for smaller firms, training and labour market policies. Second, central government has provided greater powers and funding to local government to carry out economic initiatives. In the USA, the criteria for dispensing the Federal urban welfare programme have been progressively switched towards economic aims, resulting in large funding of job-creating property development, infrastructure, and support to small, ethnic and community business. In Europe, regional decentralisation was followed by greater powers and finance for economic initiatives by both (small) regions and local authorities, notably in France, the Netherlands and Italy.

There remain, however, enormous differences between countries in the degree of autonomy of local government in carrying out economic initiatives. In Japan, Britain, Italy and Denmark local government can only carry out programmes specifically authorised by central government, and in the USA by the individual States. In contrast, in Germany, the Netherlands and Belgium, and since 1981 in France, local government is presumed to have a right to undertake any programmes which are not the specific domain of a higher level of government. Nevertheless, even in these countries local discretion is limited by effective veto powers by national or regional government.

Differences in local autonomy, however, do not explain the pattern of growth in local economic initiatives (Johnson and Cochrane, 1981, p. 97): Britain, with its strong central control of local action and narrow statutory basis for these initiatives, has been a leading country in their development, with much of the initiative for them coming from local government itself. The attitude of local government has been crucial since economic initiatives have everywhere been discretionary for local authorities, producing an enormous degree of local variation. In some countries *ad hoc* confederations of small adjacent local authorities have been formed so as to enable economic initiatives be undertaken (e.g. in France, Belgium, Italy and the USA).

The role of firms in developing local economic initiatives has been uneven between countries. Large firms have sponsored the formation of new enterprises within localities where they have been a major employer, and sometimes also supported nationwide bodies with similar aims (OECD, n.d.); these initiatives seem to be particularly prominent in countries such as the USA, Britain and the Netherlands with both concentrated ownership of the economy and rapid decline of manufacturing. In countries such as Germany and Italy where local business organisations have traditionally been interventionist their activity has tended to increase since the 1970s.

Initiatives have also come from intergovernmental organisations. The Organisation for Economic Cooperation and Development (OECD) and the European Community (EC) collaborated in the 1970s and 1980s on a programme of research and support for small and medium enterprises and unconventional forms of business; the EC set up a Directorate for Small and Medium Enterprises, and these are supported by the European Investment Bank. The EC's Social Fund has been an important support for local training schemes, small firms, R&D and tourism. The EC is now focusing some of its regional funding on to improving and integrating physical infrastructure within subregions.

The policy instruments used in local economic policy are extremely varied. This marks another difference with regional policy: whereas the latter used essentially two instruments – grants for fixed investment and infrastructure provision – local economic policy addresses every aspect of the economy, in line with the Bootstraps ideal of mobilising all the locality's resources and actors. A few policies, notably advice and property provision for small firms, are common to all major countries, but the others have been taken up unevenly. Some of these differences appear to relate to differences in the economic and social traditions of the various countries, with local economic policy correcting what are seen as specific national deficiencies. For example, enterprise has been emphasised in Britain and the Netherlands, while community has been stressed in the USA. The most innovative local initiatives are generally in areas of economic decline or, as in the case of many central city initiatives, threatened with such decline and experiencing rapid restructuring. But growth areas also have important economic policies, usually involving infrastructural provision and restraint and selection of incoming investment; policies in these areas have a greater continuity with those of the post-war boom. In some cases the main thrust of policy is anti-growth, under the influence of either residents or employers (Abbott, 1981).

Despite the growth of spending on local economic policy, in all countries it is still tiny in relation to the national economy. The contrast between the resources of the movement and its often fulsome promises has suggested to some that it may merely be a means for political propaganda and for obfuscation of harsh economic realities (Sills *et al*, 1988, p. 129); but it may also suggest that local economic initiatives are concerned not so much with quantitative changes as with change in the social organisation of local economies (Moynagh, 1985). Exploring this question will be a central theme of the book.

Political differences in Bootstraps

We have so far made little reference to political differences because the ideological shift we have been discussing has occurred right across the political spectrum. Our initial quotations show how enterprise, community and local autonomy have been accepted by Right (*Financial Times* and Todd), Centre (Civic Trust) and Left (CLES) as keys to local regeneration. Nevertheless, the paths by which different political currents have arrived at the Bootstraps strategy, and their interpretations of it, are diverse. We can distinguish three broad political–economic strategies which have been important in local economic policy, the Centre, Right and Left.

For the Centre, the state provides infrastructure and intervenes pragmatically to correct market failures. It provides welfare services and regulates working conditions, ensuring fairness to balance, and to promote, efficiency. The distinct interests of labour and capital are acknowledged but articulated into a consensus. This was the national political economy practised during the post-war boom in Western Europe and, with a stronger productive and weaker welfare role, in Japan. This approach has found a natural home in local economic policy. The details of production and labour markets can be best gauged at a local level. Because both sides of industry are seen as benefiting equally from a healthy local economy, they will collaborate in bringing it about. The relation between welfare and the private sector is best determined locally, not only because many welfare services have been the preserve of local government, but because the relation between production, labour supply and consumption is locally variable, and because welfare benefits can be bargained from local employers and developers.

On this basis, the Centre has formulated a particularly influential version of the Bootstraps approach: it is at the local level that the dynamism and individualism of enterprise can be balanced with the caring and solidarity of community. The different interests in the community unite in the project of local competitiveness; as 'citizens' their differences can be sunk. The local helps to create the consensus that the Centre seeks; as Johnstone (1985, p. 14) argues, whereas 'dogmatic views are more likely at a national level . . . at the local level a pragmatic approach supporting the need for intervention is more likely than a dogmatic ideological debate, as people see in their day-to-day lives the impact of unemployment and the fear of redundancy'.

At the national level, a Centre approach has tended to be displaced by neo-liberalism. But, strikingly, the Centre strategy has up to now been the dominant one in local economic initiatives in Western Europe; it has been important in the USA in community-based initiatives in poor neighbourhoods, and in ambitious restructuring initiatives for the old industries of the north-eastern Rust Belt.

The Right's strategy of neo-liberalism has been increasingly important at the national level in Western Europe since the mid-1970s, and in its purest form in Britain; it has been an important strand in the USA since the end of New Deal politics in the early 1950s, and dominant since the 1970s. Instead of collaboration of labour with capital, the Right proposes the untrammelled rule of employers. Within the firm, management is to have 'the right to manage', with trade unions playing a minimal role except in the discipline of their members. The role of the state is to be minimised in production, in welfare provision, and in the regulation of firms and markets. The competitiveness and transparency of markets are thereby increased, and collective responsibility replaced by individual responsibility. Local economic policy has been significantly influenced by this politics, primarily because the Right regards it as important to transform the local as the national state. Local government services are to be privatised, provided by voluntary organisations, or to be substantially controlled by industrialists though remaining in public ownership; some of these new bodies appear as local economic initiatives. These services thereby become *ad hoc* and more locally variable. Local government's regulatory functions, especially in land use and the environment, are to be weakened in the interests of the local economy. The Right also seeks to promote local rather than national pricing, especially of wages.

In this approach enterprise, community and local control again reinforce each other. Wages and local services become more locally variable, more responsive to local needs. Employers' roles in running collective services demonstrates that enterprise can also be concerned with the community. Local deregulation and support for enterprise ensure that it reaches disadvantaged groups, creating a decentralised, popular capitalism. Local government services are transferred to the control of the community, either through direct ownership (e.g. housing), control by local residents (e.g. education), or management by local business people (e.g. economic development). As we shall see, this strategy has been influential, though by no means dominant, in local economic policy in Western Europe; it has long dominated city-centre development in the USA, and is an element of community initiatives there.

The Left proposes stronger state regulation, and perhaps more public ownership, than existed during the post-war boom, to achieve greater productivity, better services and better employment conditions. Intervention should be informed by social accounting since the market only takes individual profitability into account. State control is to be more democratic than the bureaucratic forms characteristic of the post-war period, with workers and oppressed groups involved in decision making. The local level has a crucial place in this programme. Popular organisation is stronger at the local than the national level since people tend to see their main problems as the immediate, local ones. Small economic enterprises are potentially more democratic than large, national ones: it is at the local level that the creativity of ordinary people can most easily find expression, whether in workplace initiatives, reshaping welfare services to meet diverse needs, or developing new types of enterprise. Any alternative national plan for the economy also needs this local detail. We have here yet another version of Bootstraps: the democratisation of production and collective services is to be based on decentralisation and local control; and collective control can be as enterprising as the Right claims the private sector is provided it operates at the local level.

This strategy has not been implemented at the national government level. But some local authorities in Western Europe and Japan, and exceptionally in the USA (Chicago in 1983–7), have attempted to carry out a Left strategy against the national grain. In the USA some restructuring initiatives by Rust Belt States involve public equity holding. In many countries local trade union and community struggles have on occasion taken on a locality-wide nature and put forward elements of this alternative.

There is, then, wide political support for the Bootstraps approach; it is as if it solved problems within each of the political currents. This consensus has been noted in W. Germany (Johnson and Cochrane,

1981, pp. 133–6), the UK (Moore and Richardson, 1989, pp. 33–4, 127) and the USA (Bingham and Blair, 1984, pp. 15–17). A striking aspect of the consensus is the idea that welfare is to depend upon local profitability. For the Right, benefits are to be funded from local profits: the British Urban Development Corporations (UDCs), for example, finance their community schemes from the profits from land sales. On the Left, the Greater London Council (GLC) argued that improved conditions for workers were dependent on increases in firm profitability resulting from local intervention (GLC, 1985a, pp. 38–9). All political currents support the disadvantaged improving their incomes through training and the formation of new conventional or unconventional enterprises. In producing this degree of consensus even on the contentious issue of welfare, the Bootstraps approach shows its power.

The particular appeal in Britain of local economic policy

The particular problems of the British economy have given local economic policy a strong appeal. Because of the long-term weakness of much of Britain's manufacturing industry many of its localities have suffered particularly severely from global stagnation. Crisis has also renewed the hundred-year-old hunt for 'the British disease', putting economic, social and political practices under radical scrutiny. The British economy is uniquely internationalised, concentrated, urbanised and proletarianised, and it has floundered; surely then the solution must lie in reversing these qualities – in localising, in fragmenting, in community and in enterprise?

This appeal of local economic policy in Britain appears within each of the streams which fed it – regionalism, local welfare, town planning, and small firm policy. There has been pressure for economic autonomy in Scotland and Wales and the English regions. The partial conversion of demands for regional autonomy into ones for local autonomy was propelled by the de-industrialisation of the cities, which has been more rapid than on the continent (Cheshire and Hay, 1988). The local – and neighbourhood – targeting of welfare programmes has been encouraged by severe fiscal problems. Community policies have promised to provide social cohesion in a long-urbanised society with an individualistic culture.

Large, externally controlled firms were a particularly obvious target in Britain: ownership of industry and commerce is more concentrated there than in any other OECD country. Manufacturing investment in the regions during the boom had been concentrated in branch plants of

British and overseas corporations, Britain having the largest number of US-owned factories in Western Europe. In the cities, conflicts around the displacement of lower rent uses from central area fringes were identified with the particularly prominent position in Britain of property companies and financial institutions (Ambrose and Colenutt, 1975).

Many of the commonly-identified causes of the British disease – the split between finance and manufacturing, lack of training, weak technology transfer – could be addressed by local policies. A favourite culprit, a British anti-enterprise culture, and the low weight of small firms in the British economy, gave particular appeal to policies for enterprise. Finally, the equation of a good physical environment with a good society has a strong tradition in Britain, reflected in a strong legislative basis for land use planning; the evolution of ideas within land use planning towards economic concerns was therefore particularly significant.

The powerful promise of local economic policy in Britain, then, arose not only from the acute symptoms of economic crisis but from conviction that it could address some of the structural problems of the British economy.

Agencies and powers

Local government has played a central role in developing local economic initiatives in Britain. A general statutory power for economic development was first introduced by the Local Government and Housing Act 1989. This replaced a wide variety of powers which local authorities had used, particularly for land use planning, land and building supply, and provision of information to the public. A power which enabled innovative policies had been section 137 of the Local Government Act 1972, which allowed spending up to the product of a 2p rate for the benefit of local people; in the mid-1980s around two-thirds of spending under this power was devoted to economic initiatives (Widdicombe Inquiry, 1986). Fifty-seven authorities in poor areas have been able to use powers and central government funds under the Urban Programme, and some of these can use property and environmental powers under the Inner Urban Areas Act 1978. Home Office funds are available for economic initiatives by authorities with substantial black communities. The 1989 legislation and directives by the Secretary of State restrict local authority control of and funding to economic development companies and enterprise boards, particularly those taking equity in companies; however, it is not clear how much this inhibits resourceful local authorities in practice; authorities with below-average unemployment are also restricted in their spending on individual projects. Spending on specifically economic policies by English local authorities was estimated as £280–400m in 1985/6 (Widdicombe Inquiry, 1986); this was less than 1 per cent of their total spending, but of the same order as central government regional spending.

A 1988 survey found that 90 per cent of local authorities had at least one officer engaged on economic policy, with Metropolitan Districts on average employing the most (twenty-nine) and Non-Metropolitan Districts the least (three) (Coulson, 1990, p. 176). The range spans the big city council, such as Birmingham with 300 staff in the mid-1980s, able to undertake varied and large scale programmes, to the majority of councils with a few officers and inexpensive policies. Among Metropolitan Districts in the mid-1980s funds to firms, premises and business advice were provided by the majority, while around half funded training schemes, Information Technology Centres, and cooperatives; Non-Metropolitan District activity was less but still substantial (Association of District Councils 1987).

Central government has also carried out programmes directly, through the Scottish and Welsh Development Agencies, the UDCs and Enterprise Zones (EZs) set up in the 1980s, and through a succession of spatially targeted property grants. The largest area of spending on local economic initiatives, training schemes, is dominated by central government funding but implemented by local agencies. There is a major non-state element too. The voluntary sector has been active in community business and training, and grew enormously in the 1980s as central government training funds were channelled through them. British Coal and British Steel have job-creation programmes for areas in which they are making closures. Since the late 1970s business has funded local Enterprise Agencies, now numbering over 300, to help new and small firms; it has also supported Business in the Community (BiC), which encourages both commercial and unconventional initiatives, often working with voluntary organisations. There are now many initiatives that involve local government and the private and voluntary sectors in *ad hoc* local networking.

The phases of British local economic policy

Since their expansion from the mid-1970s, local economic initiatives in Britain have undergone major changes. These have been partly associated with national economic and political change, but they also reflect problems encountered within the local initiatives themselves.

Local economic problems were initially conceptualised primarily through the built environment. As part of the strengthening of regional policy in the 1960s, greater powers had been granted to local authorities for land and premises policies. In the 1970s it was the physical decay of the inner city which attracted particular attention, despite ample evidence that similar problems of employment and poverty existed in other areas. Policy centred on the replacement, conversion or improvement of premises and physical infrastructure in industrial zones. This approach was pioneered by a few local authorities, and in 1978 given statutory muscle and central funding by the Inner Urban Areas Act.

The 1974–6 recession and the austerity policy of the Labour government in 1975–9 encouraged many local authorities to become more accommodating towards businesses in their land use planning and land assembly programmes. The idea of revival through small firms was born in this period; aid was centred on property, but local authorities also began to open small firm advice centres and to provide funding. Some authorities created specialist economic development departments, concentrating on property and promotion. More comprehensive approaches using special Acts were pioneered by Labour councils such as Tameside and Newcastle-upon-Tyne, which included training, school-industry links, and housing policies for labour mobility, as well as ambitious land, property, environmental and infrastructure policies (Muller and Bruce, 1981). In 1977 these initiatives were reflected and further encouraged by the Department of the Environment (DoE) Circular 'Local government and the industrial strategy' (71/77), which urged local authorities not only to become more accommodating to the private sector but to integrate economic development into all their activities.

The victory of the Conservatives in 1979 led to major changes. In the recession of 1979–81 manufacturing output dropped by 20 per cent and unemployment rose from 1.3 to 2.9 million; in the worst hit districts manufacturing employment fell by a third or a half and unemployment rose to 20–50 per cent. The recession provoked sharp debates on economic strategy and intensified interest in local initiatives. In the summer of 1981 there was widespread rioting in inner city areas, led by black male youths whose rate of unemployment in these localities was 60–80 per cent. The acute local forms of the crisis and the spectre of anarchy increased support for spatially and socially targeted schemes with a strong community content, articulated forcibly by liberal opinion (Lord Scarman, 1981; Archbishop of Canterbury, 1985).

The most direct response of the Conservatives was in their training programmes. Between 1980 and 1990 central government spending on training nearly tripled in real terms to £2.7bn per annum. The ever-changing schemes were targeted overwhelmingly on young people and the long term unemployed. Many schemes were make-work; some provided skills but of a low level. Recipients of social security were pushed on to training schemes or the self-employment of the Enterprise Allowance, shifting welfare towards 'workfare'. The Manpower Services Commission (MSC) and its successors worked through local managing agencies, including training workshops, local authorities and voluntary organisations; because of the lack of interest of employers and paucity of local powers for training, these depended on the MSC for most of their funds.

The Conservatives launched an ideological crusade in support of small firms and enterprise, enacting numerous measures to ease regula-tion and administrative responsibilities of small firms, and promoting entrepreneurship through the Enterprise Allowance; an enterprise element was incorporated into many training schemes. The most prominent central government initiatives under both the Labour and Conservative administrations – the Inner Urban Areas Act, the EZs and the UDCs – have shared an extreme spatial selectivity. This was adumbrated by the community welfare initiatives of the late 1960s and early 1970s, such as the Housing Action Areas and the Education Priority Areas, which were carried out in selected small areas. In both periods this approach has been justified by their experimental nature, although in the event none of these programmes was generalised. In both periods a major motivation has been to concentrate limited re-sources on to areas small enough for there to be a visible impact.

The Conservatives' area initiatives, despite their presentation as radical, adopted the traditional strategy of physical renovation. The EZs use tax exemptions and streamlined land use planning to demon-strate that the removal of state impositions results in a blossoming of business. The UDCs embody a strategy of land and property manage-ment and infrastructure provision in the tradition of the New Towns; this approach to the inner cities has also been supported by social democrats (Couch, 1977).

The pattern of local economic initiatives as a whole did not follow the limited degree of redistribution embodied in central government pro-grammes. By the mid-1980s nearly every locality, including those with strong local economies, had some form of economic policy in place. Unconsciously, the priority to the inner city had been abandoned.

The 1979 election also influenced the Left. A substantial Left current had emerged in opposition to the monetarist policies of the Labour government. This current used its position in local government to develop alternative economic policies both to the Conservatives and to the Labour leadership. The appeal of the local level to the Left was enhanced by the localist and decentralised tradition of British trade unionism. The Left located the country's economic ills in a lack of productive investment; this was addressed through creating Local Enterprise Boards (LEBs) and through high quality training initiatives. In opposition to the government's programme of freeing the labour market, these authorities pursued equal opportunities policies and declared their intention to strengthen the bargaining power of labour, using LEB investment to promote workers' rights and participation, placing conditions on the authorities' purchasing contracts, and supporting union and community campaigns.

The subsequent electoral victories of the Conservatives undermined the Left's aim of carrying out an 'exemplary' economic policy at the local level. The strategy of linking economic policy to strong union organisation was weakened by successive union defeats. In 1986 the Conservative government turned the knife by abolishing the flagship of Left initiatives, the GLC, and the Metropolitan County Councils. These defeats fed a 'new realism' in the labour movement and in Labour's local economic initiatives. The adoption in 1987 by Sheffield City Council, previously a bastion of the Left, of a mainstream 'partnership' with the private sector was a milestone.

During the second half of the 1980s, mainstream local initiatives underwent important metamorphoses. In 1982–9 the British economy experienced strong growth in output on the basis of inflationary fiscal and monetary policy and the worldwide expansion fuelled by the US deficit. In 1983–9 the number of full time jobs increased by 6 per cent and of part time ones by 11 per cent, and unemployment calculated on the 1979 basis fell from 3.4 to 2.9 million (Unemployment Unit Index). Despite this rather modest impact on the labour market, skills shortages intensified; the government reacted to employers' criticisms of its training programmes by further decentralising them to local Training and Enterprise Councils (TECs).

The uncritical admiration for small firms of the early 1980s had been punctured by the experience of aiding them: high rates of failure, displacement effects, and meagre job-creation. One reaction was to target particular types of small firm: established firms rather than start-ups; firms engaged in design, crafts, or high technology; or firms in significant local sectors. The choice of these targets was often informed by wider theories popular at the time: demand was shifting towards varied, special and designer-labelled products; the 'industrial district' of a linked community of firms was being reborn. Accordingly, support for small firms widened to include technology transfer schemes, managed workspaces and technical facilities, collective services to local sectors, and management training.

A second important change was the establishment of a broader consensus that special policies were needed for disadvantaged groups. Members of these groups had not become entrepreneurs in any numbers. The mid-1980s boom left high unemployment among them, and the new, largely service sector, jobs which they took were low paid. One response was to convert enterprise into a welfare strategy. Encouragement to start-ups shifted from the redundant skilled workers of the early 1980s' recession to disadvantaged groups, including support for forms of enterprise such as worker cooperatives and non-profit community businesses which are sheltered from excessive market forces. A second response was to incorporate positive action into existing initiatives. The UDCs, for example, have sponsored training schemes to enable local people to be employed in their new developments. Local economic initiatives and poverty policy became increasingly fused.

A third reaction to the limitations of previous initiatives was to relax the focus on local ownership and re-emphasise inward and corporate investment. The mid-1980s saw a boom in consumer services, most dramatically in large scale projects – hypermarkets and mega shopping centres, sports, leisure and cultural facilities, theme parks and heritage. Strong growth of the financial and business services sector further fuelled the boom in central area property investment. Though these sectors were less spatially mobile than most manufacturing, they had considerable locational choice, particularly within regions, and local agencies rushed to attract them. Many agencies outside the conurbations, particularly New and Expanded Towns with greenfield sites and heavy infrastructure investment and towns in assisted regions, had never stopped trying to attract inward manufacturing investment; some newly devastated towns like Corby and Consett have successfully adopted this policy. The Development Agencies have provided a much-admired model for attracting manufacturing investment from overseas using targeted marketing and aid packages.

Local policy now therefore uses both development through small, locally controlled enterprises, and externally controlled investment in manufacturing, business and consumer services. This is not a simple dualism. Many large agencies hedge their bets by using both approaches. Inward investment strategy has not been limited to indiscriminate grabbing of mobile investment through financial inducements, but increasingly targets sectors on economic and social criteria, using indigenous resources as the competitive edge; it has thus incorporated the essence of the Bootstraps approach. There are also now major redevelopments in which local institutions coordinate packages which combine inward property investment with social uses, manufacturing and small business. There is thus a considerable convergence between indigenous and externally controlled development strategies.

During the 1980s there was also a political convergence in local economic policy. The Right increasingly acknowledged the need for policies targeted at the disadvantaged, for land use planning, for sectoral targeting, for infrastructure investment, and for winning community support. On the other hand, the Left was not simply destroyed; many of its policies, such as LEB investment and equal opportunities policies, have come into the mainstream, albeit in modified form. This convergence has complex roots, which we shall explore. But our account already suggests one of its underpinnings: the political consensus around Bootstraps.

The rapid rate of change of local economic policy over its short history is remarkable. Particular policies have had periods of fashion; their inertia means that many agencies have an archaeology of policies of different vintages. Change has also come through metamorphoses of policies: their implementation has changed; their aims have shifted; and different political currents have interpreted them in different ways. These ambiguities will be a theme of Part II.

The evolving institutional framework: a suppression of local government?

Privatisation and restriction of local government have been major Conservative policies. It would be tempting to see these as the main trends in local economic initiatives; but the reality has been more complex.

In the late 1970s the field was dominated by the local authorities. In the 1980s, though their economic spending was constrained by other pressing demands, this was counterbalanced by an inflection of their traditional activities towards economic ends, particularly in education, land use planning, environmental services and culture. The 1989 legislation was intended to inhibit large scale funding of the private sector, to prevent escalation of competition between localities, and to inflect policy further towards the expressed demands of business (HMSO, 1988); it is not yet clear what effect the legislation has had in practice.

While local authority activity has been constrained, since the early 1980s other agencies have been increasingly active. First, in the EZs, UDCs and Simplified Planning Zones central government has initiated programmes under its direct control or through nominated boards which replace local authority action. Though it is too early to predict their evolution, the TECs may take over most of the small firm assistance of both the local authorities and Enterprise Agencies, and may become the key coordinators of local economic policy. Second, central government has increased its influence over councils' economic policy. Whitehall's leverage has increased with the squeeze on local government finances, which has pressured local authorities into bidding for discretionary economic funds and into tailoring their policies to Conservative priorities so as to avoid penalties. Centre–local partnerships through the Development Agencies, the Inner Urban Area Act partnerships and the Task Forces have also influenced local authorities' strategies.

Third, much of local authorities' economic policy has been devolved to semi-independent agencies such as community business trusts and Enterprise Agencies; around seventy Economic Development Companies carrying out finance, property, and training policies have been set up as arms-length organisations. Fourth, the private sector has taken up some initiatives pioneered by local authorities, for example small unit conversions. Because of resource starvation, local authorities have had to select high leverage projects, and have come increasingly to rely on extracting employment benefits from developers in exchange for planning permission, though real concessions have been rather meagre (Brownill, 1990, p. 154ff). Fifth, corporations have expanded their own initiatives such as the Enterprise Agencies, Livewire and Phoenix. Their executives have been given majority control of the UDCs and TECs. The *Financial Times* (editorial, 4 May 1988) commented that there has been:

> a return to ... the late Victorian [age] where business leaders and entrepreneurs saw no dividing line between their duties to shareholders and to communities ... [T]he 1950s, 1960s and 1970s saw ... a withdrawal from a dense network of local and community ties and reciprocal obligations, as the state assumed a larger hegemony over private lives and companies merged, closed and retreated from the

headquarters office in provincial towns and cities. ... The caring, involved, enabling corporation is now becoming a central focus of contemporary capitalism.

These changes do not constitute an absolute decline in local authorities' economic initiatives, but rather a relative decline as central government and the private sector have expanded their initiatives. Total central government spending on local economic initiatives has increased enormously if one includes the training programmes, the EZs, and tax relief for business's initiatives. Central government and the private sector have not so much taken over from local government initiatives as added to them.

Similarly, the principal trend has not been a change from public to private control, but rather a continuation of public–private 'partnership' – the buzz word of the late 1980s (Moore and Richardson, 1989). The UDCs and TECs may be dominated by local executives, but they rely on public money and are staffed by civil servants, while the Enterprise Agencies are jointly financed. Integrated area and town regeneration initiatives are typically undertaken by public–private consortia, composed of various combinations of the local authority, Enterprise Agencies, local business bodies, private companies and nationalised industries, the Development Agencies and central government's local agencies. This 'balanced' institutional form fits with the increasing political convergence over strategy.

The local authorities have nevertheless changed their methods significantly. Whitehall and fiscal constraints, and the *ad hoc* networks involved in most initiatives, have produced a pragmatic style. BiC and many Enterprise Agencies have seen it as their mission to break down local government's 'bureaucratic' habits. The dominant model for organising local economic initiatives is now, as Prince Charles (1986) puts it, 'a partnership between the public and private sector, between local politicians, community groups and non-public sources of finance ... We must sink our differences and cut great swathes through the cat's cradle of red tape which chokes this country from end to end.'

Political debate in British local economic policy

We have noted a political consensus around local economic initiatives internationally, and in Britain an increasing consensus over time. This has been missed by the many commentators who see only their contrasted political–economic intentions (Benington, 1986; Church and Hall, 1989). Many policies have been supported by all political currents, though they do so with different aims and implement them in different ways; the next chapter examines these consensus policies.

Nevertheless, local initiatives have been a field on which wider debates on economic policy have been played out, such as the degree of control to be exercised by capital, labour and the state, and how these interests can be articulated. The nature of Britain's specific economic problems has also been in contention: while the Right has attributed them to excessive powers of the state and the unions and to a long-standing anti-enterprise culture, the Left has located the problem in institutional barriers to long term investment. But as we shall see, the political colour of policies has in many cases changed over time or been ambiguous; they are, after all, under the common banner of Bootstraps.

Local economic policy has been a field of experimentation for these competing political prescriptions; but, increasingly, it has become integral to them. One can see this evolution on both Right and Left. The Conservative government saw its early initiatives as *exemplifying* its economic philosophy: an aim of the UDCs, for example, was to show how inner city development would flourish if taken out of the hands of 'anti-enterprise' Labour councils, and was undertaken on a local scale as an experiment. In contrast, for the TECs, the government's major initiative in the late 1980s, the local level is *integral*, since in principle it enables training to be provided and enterprise encouraged according to local demands.

Similarly, the Left local initiatives of the early 1980s were seen as limited in themselves, useful principally as propaganda for a Left government. Yet from the mid-1980s it was increasingly argued that local policy has an integral place in Labour's economic strategy precisely by virtue of its local scale and the detailed knowledge, variety, innovation and democratic control that this could make possible (Batkin, 1987; Labour Party, 1991a). Localness had turned from being contingent, even a hindrance, to being a virtue. The appeal of Bootstraps, then, has meant the increasing integration of the local dimension into the different political–economic programmes.

Further reading

An invaluable source of information on local economic initiatives in Britain is the *Local Economic Development Information Service*, published since 1982 by the Planning Exchange, Glasgow; its series on UK initiatives covers most of the examples given in this book. Two British journals are dedicated to the subject, *Local Economy* and *Local Work*; the latter is published by CLES, which also produces reports, information briefings, and *Local Economic News* and *Local Economic News Training Quarterly*. Relevant articles can be found in *Built Environment, Community Development Journal, Environment and Planning C: Government and Policy, Local Government Studies, Planning, Policy and Politics* and *Regional Studies*. More theoretical articles, generally on the left, are carried in *International Journal of Urban and Regional Research, Society and Space, Antipode, Work, Employment and Society* and *Capital and Class*.

Book-length studies of local economic policy in Britain are Chandler and Lawless (1985) on local authority initiatives, Morison (1987) mostly on central government programmes, Moore and Richardson (1989) on local public–private partnerships, and Keating and Boyle (1986) on Scotland, all from a Centre or Centre–Left perspective. There are also collections of articles with diverse viewpoints in Young and Mason (1983), Hausner (1986 and 1987a), Wilmers and Bourdillon (1985) and Campbell (1900b). Lawless (1989) describes the range of inner city policies. Quantitative data on the activity of local economic agencies are given in Camina (1974), Mills and Young (1986), Sellgren (1987) and Armstrong and Fildes (1988).

The OECD has produced a series of documents on developments internationally. Within the vast literature on policy in the USA, the volumes of articles in the Sage *Urban Affairs Annual Reviews* are a useful reference; Conference of Mayors (1986) gives an overview. Local economic initiatives in the EC are reviewed by Todd (1984), CEI (1985), Johnstone (1985) and Martinos and Humphreys (1990); detailed information is electronically published by ELISE, Brussels. On Germany see Johnson and Cochrane (1981) and Bennett and Krebs (1991); on Sweden Moore and Pierre (1988), and on the Third Italy Brusco (1980). On local economic policy before the 1970s, see Chandler and Lawless (1985) and Ward (1990) for Britain, and Beauregard (1989b) for the USA.

Illich (1973) was a politically ambiguous and influential proposal for self-help and self-management in welfare. Aside from Birch, the most influential author in the fashion for small enterprise was probably Schumacher (1973). The peculiarities of the British economy are analysed in Gamble (1981), Ingham (1984) and Fine and Harris (1985); their impact on its spatial economic problems is discussed by Massey (1987a). The uneven geography of recent economic change is explored in Massey and Meegan (1982) and Martin and Rowthorn (1987).

2 Consensus Strategies and their Ambiguous Politics

A number of widely used strategies have been pursued by local economic agencies of different political complexions; these are examined in this chapter. The crucial choices in local economic policy are often seen as choices between these favourite strategies, and they structure debate on policy. Each strategy focuses on what is seen as a crucial weak link of the local economy. We shall examine in turn:

- *Targeting types of firm* Three popular strategies focus on particular types of enterprise: conventional small firms; unconventional forms of ownership such as cooperatives and community business; and, in contrast, inward investment.
- *Targeting types of input* Many strategies concentrate on a particular type of input to production in the locality: labour, finance, technology, or property.
- *Targeting sectors* Some agencies attempt to breathe new life into long-established local sectors; others attempt to import new, especially growth sectors.
- *Targeting areas* A favourite strategy is to concentrate resources on to a neighbourhood or smaller area of the locality, typically one of physical dereliction.

These targets are politically uncontroversial. The promotion of small firms, new technology, growing service industries, or renovation of a decaying area as such are apolitical goals, since they specify a subdivision of the economy rather than the approach to be used towards it. Consensus around these targets is reinforced by their being widely seen as weaknesses of the British economy as a whole. They can therefore be espoused by agencies of all political persuasions, and policy makers can use the apparently consensus nature of the strategy to gain support for it.

The political consensus around each strategy hides differences in implementation by each political current. During the 1980s, however, there was also a tendency for these approaches to converge and combine: distinctively Right and Left strategies were abandoned and a consensus approach to each policy was woven. In this chapter we shall look at the consensus appeal of each strategy, the political divergences in its implementation, and convergence where this has taken place. The chapter thus serves to introduce the policies of the different political currents in Part II. Our focus here, then, is on the ideologies of the favourite strategies which enable broad support to be built for them. Their mechanisms of implementation and their economic effects vary with political approach and are therefore discussed in subsequent chapters.

The consensus in local economic policy has included not only economic targets but certain forms of organisation and employment aims, which we consider in the remainder of the chapter. All political positions have supported the decentralisation of local decision-making to multiple agencies. There has been a consensus around two distinct aims on jobs and unemployment. The first accepts that there is a permanent deficit of jobs; it seeks to share available work and blur the distinction between work and leisure. The second seeks to reduce unemployment by creating jobs. We examine the nature of the consensus and the political divergences around decentralisation and work sharing. Our discussion of job creation is rather different. We shall argue that local economic policy may redistribute, but does not create, jobs, and that this is so for all the political approaches. This is obviously of central importance to an assessment of local economic initiatives. In this final section of the chapter, then, we shall be concerned not with political differences in approach, but with the effectiveness of the consensus aim.

Targeting types of firm

Small firms and enterprise

Support for established small firms and start-ups has been a major thread in the development of local economic initiatives (pp. 9–10). Small firms promise indigenous, diversified, innovative enterprise, rather than the routine of mass production and the stifling practices of the large firms; as Jane Jacobs (1965) portrayed it in the 1960s, they offer the creative chaos of Birmingham as against the deadness of Detroit or of Kodak-dominated Rochester. Small firm policies thus have particular appeal in areas like the north-east which have been dominated by large scale workplaces (Hudson, 1987): local authorities such as Cleveland, where the density of small firms relative to population is only a third of the British average, have been most active. The popularity of these policies is enhanced by the idea that the British economy as a whole is hampered by shortage of small firms – among Western European countries their weight in the economy is the lowest, and their profitability in relation to that of large firms is the lowest for countries for which there are statistics (Burns and Dewhurst, 1986a, p. 195); this popularity is despite evidence that there is no correlation between small firm density and national economic performance (Storey and Johnson, 1986).

Small firms thus promise both economic and social benefits. They can be supported in ways which are well within the resources of local economic agencies. There is a consensus repertoire of policies: management advice and education, small loan funds and guarantee schemes, and the provision of property, but without the agency attempting to influence the firms' strategies. An indicator of the consensus is the universal support for managed workspaces which offer various services to the occupiers and encourage internal linkages – Bootstraps in one building; these have been supported by the Conservatives through English Estates, by the corporately funded Inner City Enterprises, by numerous centrist local authorities, and by the GLC.

A similar consensus exists around support for small businesses owned by black people and members of ethnic minorities. In countering discrimination by the banks, this policy appeals both to the Right, since it eliminates an imperfection in the market for money, and to the Left, in opposing racism (GLC, 1986b, pp. 132–5). For the Right, it helps to expand the middle class and increase integration especially among Afro-Caribbeans; as the Conservative minister for small firms said on a visit to Brixton, 'it gives them a stake in the country, er, that is, in the economy' (Hirst, 1988, p. 25). For the Centre and Left black entrepreneurship provides a new avenue for social mobility.

There are, however, some political differences in approach. Because entrepreneurship is important for the Right as an illustration of neo-liberal philosophy, it lays particular emphasis on teaching enterprise in education and training. It is also cautious about funding, though not opposed to it. The Left, on the other hand, has tended to be suspicious of support to small firms that does not exert some influence over their operations. It questions the efficiency, dynamism and employment conditions of many small firms, and therefore either excludes them from certain of its policies, as did the West Midlands and Greater London Enterprise Boards in the early 1980s, or provides aid to them in directive ways. Problems encountered in indiscriminate small firm policies resulted in the late 1980s in greater selectivity, so that some of the Left's criticisms have been incorporated into the consensus approach. This evolution is examined further in Chapter 4.

Community business and the Third Sector

One way in which the limitations of small firms have been addressed is through support for small enterprises with unconventional forms of ownership, particularly cooperatives and community businesses, sometimes called the 'Third Sector' (Newman, 1989). Community businesses are non-profit bodies which often receive revenue support through subsidised premises and wages partly paid by training schemes. Their work is typically in producing consumer services for poor communities which the private and public sectors fail to provide, such as graffiti removal, landscaping, insulation, and furniture and appliance repairs, mostly on contract to local authorities.

The Third Sector tends to be more stable than conventional small firms because there are no dividends to be paid, because reinvestment takes place only in the existing business and workplace, and because they may be subsidised by local agencies. They are also strengthened by commitment from the workforce, sometimes resting on a high degree of job satisfaction (Hodgson, 1984, ch.9), and by political support from consumers. These strengths mean that they can employ people who would not be employed by a conventional small firm because of their lack of skill or experience, or because of discrimination. The Third Sector therefore provides a relatively stable way in which new businesses can be formed, disadvantaged groups of workers employed, and a spirit of enterprise encouraged among them.

Part of the attraction of the Third Sector is the way in which it combines, and blurs the distinction between, employment and entrepreneurship, with workers taking managerial roles and directly facing the pressure of markets. This fusion is embodied also in integrated employment and enterprise centres, which combine counselling for the unemployed, training and support for enterprise as well as community facilities. They provide a supportive environment by being clearly geared to manual workers and by blurring the distinction between would-be worker and would-be entrepreneur; this crossover is facilitated by their local, community basis. This linkage and ambiguity have gained them wide political support: in the early 1980s the Stonebridge project in Neasden, located in an area with a 70 per cent black population, was supported by the Department of the Environment (DoE), the GLC and the borough council.

Unconventional enterprises promise to square another circle: to operate in the market, even in weak local economies, while helping disadvantaged groups, thus combining economic regeneration with welfare. Perhaps more intimately than any other local policy, they incorporate the consensus themes of enterprise, community, welfare and local control, and thereby find support across the political spectrum. For the Right and Centre, they are vehicles for spreading enterprise to groups which would not undertake conventional entrepreneurship, typically in Labour Party heartlands; they shift income maintenance on to a new basis where it is achieved through employment; and they deliver welfare services without the state. The Centre supports them also for providing a model of market-based cooperation between management and workers, and for providing a quality of employment that is higher than in government training schemes. For the Left, on the rebound from traditional nationalisation, the sector provides 'new forms of social ownership', involving worker participation, socially responsible products, and a degree of local political control. For those on the Left who support a stronger market orientation and decentralisation of public services (Hall and Jacques, 1989), the Third Sector shows how socially useful services can be marketed and produced by small enterprises. The strong targeting of the Third Sector on to local people and disadvantaged groups appeals both to the Right, since welfare is thereby made selective, and to the Left, because of its egalitarianism. The Third Sector also appeals to Green sensibilities in its small scale, local control, its socially useful production, and its apparent avoidance of growth for its own sake. The Third Sector is thus a good example of the combination of local control, community responsibility and enterprise in the market forming a consensus around a strategy.

Inward investment and promotion

At first blush, pursuing inward investment appears to be the antithesis of the indigenous development strategy. However, both strategies require the locality to become more competitive, and both have to deal with the national and international mobility of capital. Internal development can increase the confidence of external investors (Guild, 1988). Conversely, the growth of locally controlled firms often requires resources from outside, such as finance, managers, business services, property developers or skilled labour. Indigenous development may be stimulated by inward investment, particularly if the incoming firms support local enterprises and have political clout in Whitehall. The locality, then, may have to promote itself even if it wishes to use its indigenous resources better. Moreover, the process of selling the locality to external investors propagates internally the Bootstraps ideology of everyone pulling together ('Corby Works').

This link of the locality's competition for investment to its internal qualities is reflected in the bases on which British localities have promoted themselves, which differ from those which dominate State and city promotion in the USA. The latter rely heavily on comparisons of the prices of wages, premises and energy, implying that investors seek to compete above all through reduction in factor costs. Promotion in Britain also uses cost comparisons, particularly the price of premises and the availability of subsidies (wage and energy cost differences are not cited since they are much smaller than in the USA, though currently increasing). However, promotion typically emphasises the *qualitative* strengths of the locality, in such aspects as industrial relations, skills, communications, consumption, culture, environment, and above all 'enterprise' and 'self-confidence'.

Targeting sectors for inward investment can also have a Bootstraps quality. In the second half of the 1980s, the larger local authorities and the UDCs increasingly emulated the Scottish and Welsh Development Agencies by seeking inward investment in selected sectors. In particular, they have sought to exploit synergies by reinforcing existing local sectors or developing new specialisations. This again differs from indiscriminate competition through factor prices.

Changing the locality's image has been central to the 'place marketing' of old industrial areas. Following a tradition going back to the Garden City, the quality of both production and consumption are highlighted and linked. The dominance of both spheres by the male manual working class is said to have gone. Sometimes the area's gender image is changed to correspond to new sectors with a large female workforce, though high tech may be marketed as 'masculine' (Watson, 1991). Architectural style also speaks: post-modern buildings to denote a post-industrial economy, or, as in Swindon (Basset *et al.* 1989), modernism to denote high tech. Facilities for high culture are used to attract professionals; central area renewal aims to convey that the town is a vibrant and exciting place to live; in Montpellier and Rennes, high tech media are used to promote high tech industry; at a smaller spatial level, neighbourhood cultural festivals are used to show that a 'bad' area has been pacified (Bianchini, 1991); a cultural face lift is used like an environmental face lift. Cultural renewal both offers attractions to mobile labour and acts as a token of economic regeneration. Changing image through advertising has the attraction of relative cheapness; but changing cultural and leisure facilities can require very large investments.

The distinction between cost and quality competition between localities is a divide between the Right and the Centre. Neoclassical economics sees competition as operating exclusively through price, through minimising input prices and maximising final price. The Centre on the other hand emphasises the imperfections of markets and the importance of the quality of both factor inputs and final products. It puts great stress on the way in which its internal interconnections give the local economy as an integrated whole a particular quality. Thus Thompson and Thompson (1987) have argued for comparative locational indices which incorporate qualitative strengths as well as costs. We shall return to this distinction many times. The attraction of inward investment in competition with other localities might appear at first sight to be a strategy of the Right, and this was one reason why the Left in the early 1980s rejected promotion. But the typical form of local promotion in Britain, focused on the qualitative features of the locality and its overall coherence, is of the Centre rather than the Right.

Targeting inputs to production

There is a high degree of consensus around local intervention into each of the major inputs to production.

● All currents have central policies for improving *premises and environment*: the Right through EZs, UDCs, City Grant, the Centre and Left through the Inner Urban Areas Act, grants for improvements and relocations, provision of small units, and specialist property like science parks. A strong consensus exists around the built environment because its problems are so visible, and because provision of property largely avoids sharp choices about economic strategy; moreover, British common sense puts great store by the built environment. This bias is strongly evident in community enterprise initiatives, the majority of which are directed towards improving housing and public spaces and constructing buildings for community activities. A property focus has come to be considered almost axiomatic (Civic Trust, 1989); it is widely assumed that a better environment 'shows that something is being done', lifts morale, improves image, and is thus the key to economic and social improvement.

A focus on environment can create consensus around activities which might otherwise be controversial. A good example is seen in the twenty or so local Groundwork Trusts. These organise voluntary labour to reclaim derelict land by low cost methods in order to provide the basis for long term regeneration; they are backed by central and local government funds as well as donations from local firms. They have shifted responsibility for infrastructure provision from government to the voluntary sector, pushed it towards a more explicit pro-business stance, and have involved local people in self-help. These highly political changes have been facilitated by the view of environmental improvement as an obvious and apolitical good.

• There is widespread agreement that the level of *training* in Britain, well below that of other EC countries, is insufficient. The consensus about training reflects its promise to benefit simultaneously both profitability and the life chances of the disadvantaged, both capital and labour, both efficiency and welfare. All political positions agree on the need for local training schemes 'for the needs of production' (though there are differences as to what these are), and for training targeted on the disadvantaged.

There is a broad consensus that *education* should be more strongly geared to employment: for the Right this tames a public service which had developed too strong an autonomy from the needs of business; for the Left it helps working-class youth to get a job. Thus compacts between schools and local firms were pioneered in Britain by the Inner London Education Authority (later abolished for its left politics) in partnership with the CBI and the TUC, and have subsequently been funded by the Conservative government. Similarly, there is wide political agreement that higher education should shift from intellectual priorities to become more closely involved with and dependent on industry, a change seen as an essential part of British 'modernisation' (Robins and Webster, 1985).

• There is wide agreement about *technology*: that there is need for more of 'it'. Faster technical change in processes and products is seen as the key to competitiveness and a high wage economy. The consensus tends to regard technology as a 'thing' which can be input into production, as one would put oil into a machine: in this way it can ignore the politically divisive questions – the social nature of its uses, and the way these shape the technologies themselves. The consensus on technology incorporates a strong emphasis on training and higher education

(OECD, 1987). As an article in BiC's magazine argued, 'Cambridge and Massachusetts are perhaps the most successful examples of local economic development in the world. The experience of both areas leads to the same conclusion: higher education – especially in science and technology – is a driving force behind genuine economic revival' (Wray, 1987, p. 21). This strategy is often supported by a vision of a coming 'information economy' in which the new information technologies (ITs) eliminate much manual and routine work and create more skilled and interesting jobs; we examine this thesis in Chapter 5.

● There is considerable agreement that the supply of *finance* should be improved, especially to smaller firms, and that it should become more locally rooted. The Centre and Left see British finance as having weak ties with industry, as risk averting and internationally oriented, and as too centralised. Although the Conservatives are more cautious in criticising the City, their deregulation of finance, particularly of retail banking and savings, was partly prompted by recognition that the clearing banks' oligopoly led to risk aversion and contradicted the Right's crusade for enterprise. Moreover, in the USA, which is generally the Right's favoured model, finance is strongly local, with State and city-based banking and local individual investors providing a large amount of equity capital to small firms and start-ups. Thus all currents favour a larger proportion of savings being invested locally, especially in locally owned enterprises, as a necessary condition for a locally rooted, indigenous capitalism.

The wide support for intervention into each type of input, then, rests on a view that it is a key, perhaps *the* key, to the British disease. Since both the supplies of and demands for these inputs are highly differentiated by locality, it is agreed that policies for factors should have a local dimension.

Despite this consensus, each political position has a different approach to intervention in factor markets. The tension between cost and quality competition, mentioned in relation to promotion, appears here too. The Right focuses on reducing the prices of inputs, using as little subsidy as possible. The Centre places greater emphasis on the quality of the inputs; and since the market alone frequently fails to deliver this, active intervention can be required. Thus the Right's training schemes are aimed at reducing the price of low skilled labour, while the Centre aims to provide higher quality skills. The price–quality contrast, however, is never simple. A Centre programme to supply an input of higher quality tends to reduce its price; and its attempts to overcome inadequacies in quality can be very similar to the Right's policies to increase supply and reduce cost, for example, their shared support for fiscal incentives for small unit construction.

While the Centre seeks to provide inputs according to the expressed wishes of local firms, both the Right and the Left are more prepared to form an independent view of what is needed. For the Left, firms have a tendency to skimp on the production of general inputs, skilled labour being the classic case. The Right seeks to make input markets freer, even if, as in its provision of low quality training, this is opposed by sections of business. We shall see, however, that the difference between the demands of business and policy makers' theories has been a tension for all political currents, and has changed its resolution over time. A related dilemma is the extent to which inputs should be developed in isolation from each other. The Left attempts to coordinate policies for them, especially around sector strategies, while the Right and Centre focus on market imperfections and therefore treat each input in isolation. In recent years, a belief in the need for some degree of coordination between policies for different inputs has gained the upper hand (pp. 85, 94–5).

In the early 1980s parts of the consensus on factor markets were challenged by the Left: it recognised the social construction of technology, proposed to use finance to change industrial relations, and opposed some forms of profitable land development. However, we shall see that these policies subsequently shifted into the mainstream.

Targeting sectors

New sectors for old?

The choice between support for existing sectors and encouragement of new ones is no longer a politically charged one; the criteria used in this decision are largely consensus ones. In the early period of local economic initiatives, the Left and Centre gave priority to manufacturing on the grounds that it had the greatest problems and (more dubiously) that it provided more and better jobs for manual workers than services; for the Left the strong union organisation in some old manufacturing sectors was an additional motivation. In the early 1980s the Conservative government was thought by the Centre and Left to have a positive aversion to manufacturing and a project of encouraging new services, denounced as the 'candyfloss economy'. But since the mid-1980s, this debate has faded. For the Centre and Left, local policies to sustain manufacturing often seemed to face insuperable odds, and it appeared more realistic to pursue service industries, especially the glamorous business services and media sectors. Jobs for local manual workers were to be sought through negotiating quotas from new service sector employers and through retraining. On the Left there was also increasing concern, not to promote services, but to intervene to improve the many low paid service jobs, the predominant employer of women (Bruegel, 1987). On the other side, it became clear that the Conservatives did not in fact have an anti-manufacturing, pro-services *policy*. The closure of much manufacturing capacity and the boom of consumer and financial services was in part an effect of government policies, but it was not a sectoral choice. Indeed, the Right has eschewed policies for particular sectors, or any strategy for the sectoral composition of the national or local economies, in favour of policies which allow *investors* the maximum freedom to make sectoral choices. It loosens regulation of factor markets that might prevent sectoral change (e.g. weakening land use planning), and provides inputs which can be used by any sector (e.g. training schemes to swell the unskilled labour pool). Further, the government has allowed the Development Agencies and the UDCs to target manufacturing sectors if those seemed to be in line with investors' preferences. There is therefore now little political division in the choice between sunset and sunrise industries.

It might be thought that the Bootstraps reliance on indigenous resources would produce a preference for reviving existing sectors rather than attracting new ones. In the early period of local economic initiatives manufacturing was indeed defended in the name of local tradition and local skills, against services with their rootless, cosmopolitan image. But new sectors can be attracted in ways which use the locality's indigenous resources. High technology, for example, is pursued through encouragement to local entrepreneurs, training schemes for local people, and strengthing links between higher education and local firms; historical features such as canals and wharves can give distinctiveness to a leisure and tourism industry. New or growth sectors, then, do not necessarily mean submerging all inherited distinctiveness but can be pursued in a Bootstraps mode.

Back to basics: reviving old sectors

Most local agencies support firms in traditional sectors, but fewer do so on the basis of a sectoral strategy. This is, in part, because such strategies are more complex than strategies for types of firm or inputs, and raise difficult questions about why the sector has failed. This complexity also explains why sectoral strategies show more political variety than other favourite strategies.

Most sectoral approaches, of all political stripes, have tried to minimise this complexity and its attendant political difficulties by abstaining from influencing firms' strategies. An approach with wide political support is to improve the quality of supply of an input on a sectoral basis. The Centre-Right has sought to attract external investment in targeted sectors on the basis of existing advantages of the locality. Up to the mid-1980s the Left attempted to preserve old industries by subsidising ailing firms, by showing that plants really were profitable, or by opposing changes in land use.

There have, however, been attempts actively to influence firms' strategies and the structure of the sector. The Left sometimes put forward alternative plans for major plants. From the early 1980s a different Centre-Left strategy emerged, which argued that a key weakness of British manufacturing is a lack of coordination within industries (Best, 1990); local agencies therefore need to arrange new networks and forms of collective action within sectors. A successful strategy of this kind has been the conversion of the Detroit car components industry not merely to high tech components but to the production of robots and machine tools for the industry, through collaboration involving the State of Michigan, industry research institutions and engineering colleges (Neill, 1991). In Britain, this strategy has taken the form of provision of collective services to the sector, and using funding by LEBs to influence firms' strategies and rationalise capacity. This approach was initiated by the Left; but over time it has taken on the complexion of the Centre, and, though it is limited by resource constraints, it is now part of the consensus repertoire.

A fundamental distinction is often made between 'sunset' sectors and 'high tech' or 'informational' sectors. But the Detroit example shows that this is misleading: mature sectors are constantly changing technologically and organisationally, now typically using IT; the notion of the product cycle is unhelpful. Detroit shows also that, on the basis of given production methods or given customers, active sectoral strategies may actually change what the sector does. It may switch between stages of production of a given product; the strategy of the Greater London Enterprise Board for the furniture and clothing sectors involved the manufacturers increasing their design and marketing activity, thus repositioning themselves in relation to wholesalers and retailers. Manufacturers are incorporating an increasing 'service' element into the product in the form of software and maintenance and updating contracts. Radical transformations of 'sunset' sectors in effect create 'sunrise' sectors; it is the active sectoral strategies which address this possibility.

Local support for traditional manufacturing sectors, then, is not politically controversial; but the means of doing so are.

Sunrise sectors

The past twenty years have seen some major shifts in the relative weight and profitability of sectors. Local economic agencies have increasingly sought to capture a part of the high profit or high growth industries. The main targets are:

● *High tech manufacturing*   In most cases this means electronics, internationally the fastest growing area of manufacturing. This is composed of two quite different parts: highly differentiated electronic capital goods, and mass produced consumer electronics; the former involves webs of local interdependencies, of which the Sun Belt is the leading British example, while the latter is largely a branch plant industry (Morgan and Sayer, 1988). The main local approach is provision of sectoral inputs: the ubiquitous science parks, innovation centres and electronics training schemes. Only the LEBs have attempted to enter more actively into the innovation process, to make choices about which subsectors to target, at which stage of their emergence to intervene into innovative subsectors and firms, and which stages of production to support.

● *Software, design, cultural production and crafts*   These knowledge producing sectors are high value added, risky but with potentially high profits. Cultural and craft production can be based on indigenous skills and traditions, and can help to develop a sense of local identity. Many local agencies see themselves as able to play a role in these sectors since they contain small enterprises and because coordinated intervention is required to provide infrastructure and build up the local interconnections which are important in knowledge sectors. This potential local rootedness of the sectors has produced a strong consensus around them, represented most obviously in the ubiquitous craft and design workshops. But within this consensus there are important distinctions: concentrating on indigenous skilled labour or attracting new professions; bidding for investment by large firms and institutions or building incrementally from small units; providing different degrees of collective infrastructure, and whether to set up new channels of distribution (McKellar, 1988).

● *Finance and producer services*   This sector experienced a spectacular expansion in the 1980s, doubling its real output; ironically, this was a result of economic stagnation, which increased the demand for credit and for the competitive edge given by specialist producer services. Cities and large towns have sought to attract the sector not only as a growth industry but to provide a locally rooted financial and business infrastructure. Exhibition and conference facilities, town centre renewal and culture are used as magnets. As with high tech, the sector is strongly internally differentiated: most of the higher functions can only be captured by cities, while routine back office work is mobile.

● *Retailing, leisure, sport, culture, tourism*   Expenditure on these areas increased rapidly in the 1980s on the back of credit expansion and regressive income redistribution. But new leisure investment also reflects the changing spatial form of the sector: concentration of capacity on to large, greenfield sites, and a resurgence of town centres which compete by creating a place specific ambience through 'heritage' and cultural facilities; local agencies have promoted both of these forms. Many see these sectors as a new export base: capturing shoppers from the next town, getting a slice of the region's retail and leisure spending, or attracting national and international tourists. They also help to change the area's image, and provide a better quality of life for local people. This combination of benefits has produced a strong consensus around these sectors. For example, new cultural facilities have been promoted by the Conservatives in their Garden Festivals and decentralisation of arts funding, by the Centre in new concert halls and theatres and in town-centre renewal, and by the Left in facilities for popular or locally based cultural production.

● *'The post-industrial city'*   This combines the last two elements into an appealing cocktail – a business, finance and conference sector, together with mid-to up-market consumption facilities, hotels and luxury housing to attract executives as residents and visitors, as well as tourists and regional shoppers. The international city rests on the increasing spatial centralisation of these sectors and increasing integration between them. Of all the sunrise strategies, this involves the greatest degree of spatial coordination of different sectors. Accordingly, the key elements of strategy concern land, property, and physical infrastructure – above all, water! The integrated nature of the international city also requires the greatest effort to change the image of the locality. Following two decades of this strategy in the cities of the US Rust Belt, it is now being pursued by most British cities with population of over half a million.

These sketches suggest that the changes producing the sunrise industries are diverse. Some of these changes are permanent, for example the rise of IT; others, such as the burgeoning of the financial sector and higher income consumption, are more episodic; some such as retailing are *local* sunrise sectors only because of spatial redistribution (p. 126). But the consensus around the sunrise sectors often uses sweeping, totalising views of the future: the 'post-industrial', 'knowledge', 'wired', 'leisure', or 'information' society. These formulations are arbitrary abstractions and extrapolations of some current trends. They are silent on, or explicitly deny power relations (Mulgan, 1988). They thereby provide an impression that, whatever the concrete local and sectoral conditions, a sunrise strategy is both unavoidable and socially desirable; this eases the enormous political and technical problems of these strategies.

Despite bland futurology, there are a myriad ways of attracting new sectors. All the approaches for reviving old sectors can be applied to expanding new ones. The Right again emphasises the freeing of factor markets and sectoral choice by investors, while the Centre emphasises the need for sectoral targeting and for coordination and pump-priming at least until critical mass and investor confidence are created.

Sunrise strategies often require a tough political stance. The post-industrial city is a clear example: it is politically sensitive because of the extensive physical changes required, the need for large public subsidy for infrastructures and 'magnets', the contrast between the glitter of the central areas and the surrounding poverty, the destruction of neighbourhoods adjacent to the central area, and the limited benefits to the inner area and its labour force (Giloth, 1990). The Conservative government has dealt with these problems by using agencies with no local accountability – the UDCs and EZs; though these have been denounced by the Centre-Left as undemocratic, they are scarcely less so than their precursors, the New Towns. But the post-industrial city has also been implemented by 'growth coalitions' of business and local government, with varied balance between the two and varied organisational forms. These have sought to build a local consensus for the transformation, using despair of regenerating old industries, the promise of improved facilities for local people, and training schemes to help working class people to get some of the new white collar jobs. Again, the different political currents use different means to deliver the same strategy and deal with its problems.

Targeting areas

Area policies have a long lineage in the coordinated physical redevelopment of towns characteristic of capitalist urbanisation. As economic and social policies, they have an obvious problem: areas of physical dereliction have no necessary economic coherence, and labour markets typically extend far beyond them. However, their promise is of *visible* regeneration through physical renovation, and the latter is usually taken as the principal measure of their success. They also reflect a hope that limited resources can have a demonstrable impact by being spatially concentrated.

There is consensus around a number of different types of area project: the upgrading of functioning but run-down industrial and commercial areas; the redevelopment of large derelict areas; community projects for estates and small derelict sites; property led, community based projects for the industrial, commercial and social renaissance of the cores of small or medium towns, such as those in Halifax and Wirksworth; and regeneration of retailing and leisure in town centres.

Particularly ambitious are area projects which aim to act as catalysts for the renaissance of the whole locality, an approach which stretches politically from the Conservative's UDCs and EZs and Garden Festivals to the GLC's 'exemplary' Community Area projects. Regeneration is to spread not so much through its economic linkages, as in the traditional growth pole approach, but through changing image and expectations (Confederation of British Industry, 1988). Accordingly, this approach depends on prestigious 'flagship' projects: the Cardiff barrage, Glasgow's Burrell Museum, Liverpool's Albert Dock, Manchester's 1996 Olympics, Corby's WonderWorld, Gateshead's Metrocentre. While support for flagships as a short cut to the entrepreneurial city has extended across the political spectrum, so has opposition to them, on the grounds that they do nothing for organic, indigenous development and often displace traditional activities.

There is a broad consensus, which includes the Right, on using large initial public funding on the basis that it will eventually attract much greater private investment. Equally, there is a consensus, which extends to the Left, on private developers and institutional funding playing a central role. But there have been distinctive political emphases. Some area programmes, such as the London Docklands Development Corporation (LDDC) and the Integrated Area Projects of the Scottish

Development Agency, have selected relatively easy areas with obvious commercial potential. There has been varied willingness to carry out 'rounded' programmes incorporating lower profit uses and redistributive policies; these have been pursued most strongly in Left policies to protect areas with traditional sectors threatened by central area expansion. However, over time a consensus form of area policy has evolved. Early strategies – both Industrial Improvement Areas and early UDCs and EZs – used only the levers of premises, land and physical infrastructure. But it became evident that this narrow approach often failed even in physical regeneration, that other economic aims were not met, and that political opposition could emerge. From the second half of the 1980s area projects therefore tended to incorporate strategies for old and new sectors, enterprise, training, and housing with a social mix, and combined commercial redevelopment with employment and consumption policies for the poor; in other words, a Bootstraps strategy within a small area.

A favourite form of organisation: the decentralised agency

The growth of local economic policy represents a decentralisation of national decision-making; it has been accompanied by a second level of fragmentation, a proliferation of quasi-independent agencies within each locality, 'qualgos'. These have been promoted by all political currents. The Conservative government, despite rhetoric against quangos, set up the UDCs, City Action Teams, Task Forces and TECs; implementation of its training programmes has been delegated to a myriad public, private and voluntary agencies. The Left set up as independent bodies the LEBs, sectoral organisations like the Fashion Centres, and the Technology Networks. It grant-funded not only existing autonomous organisations, but also organisations set up through, and often wholly dependent upon, local government funding. The private sector has organised its initiatives through new agencies, principally the Enterprise Agencies, and these have found broad political support. Of the initiatives examined by Sellgren (1987, pp. 54–6), only a quarter were run by the organisation that initiated them; half the local authority schemes were decentralised. This proliferation of agencies has given rise to the 'social entrepreneur' who, for a particular initiative, can put together a coalition of agencies and a funding package from disparate sources; Sellgren's initiatives had an average of 2.3 funding sources each.

Because of the potential political sensitivity of local economic policy, qualgos have been used to insulate national and local government from controversy while enabling them to take credit for successes. They are supported by all as being non-bureaucratic, flexible and speedy, fitting with the Bootstraps ideology of decentralisation, local specificity and pragmatism. But, as always, Bootstraps is marked by varied politics. The Right presents qualgos as the 'contract state', where government activities are put out to quasi-independent agencies with defined aims and central finance. Though this may not differ substantially from creating internal divisions within the state with clear objectives and autonomy in implementation, the Right presents it as a weakening of the state. For the Left, on the other hand, qualgos respond to a perceived lack of democracy and legitimacy of local government. Qualgos have been a means for putting particular social groups in charge of state-funded activities: business executives by the Right, trade unionists and representatives of oppressed groups by the Left, technocrats by the Centre. They have also been a means of sidestepping control of parts of the state by political rivals, one reason that the Right set up UDCs and EZs, the Centre the Development Corporations, and the Left LEBs. Thus although justified as consensus decentralisation, the shift to qualgos involves divergent political projects.

The jobs deficit and new patterns of work and leisure

An important impetus for local economic initiatives has come from the idea that industry is following agriculture into becoming a small minority of employment and that service jobs are unlikely to absorb those seeking work, resulting in a chronic oversupply of labour; there has been widespread concern about the social and political problems of the resulting permanent 'surplus population'. This epochal shift is seen as resulting from the destruction of jobs by particularly rapid technological change; it is assumed that the volume of consumption is fixed or rising only slowly, and that technological change does not itself help to stimulate economic expansion. This is a weak theorisation of high unemployment (see pp. 265–9); but the latter's persistence worldwide over decades and with different government policies has lent plausibility and support to this kind of fatalistic view.

There is a wide political consensus, exhibited within local initiatives, on policies to address excess labour. In order to avoid a permanently unemployed population the misery is to be shared by cutting paid labour hours, through policies such as later schooling, early retirement, a shorter working week, part-time working, and job sharing. Measures are to be taken to soften the cut in income: for the Centre and Left a minimum wage; for the libertarian Right an equal distribution throughout the population of shares in privatised enterprises; and from Right to Left support for worker share ownership. On the other side, the unemployed are to be drawn into work, but not necessarily of a conventional kind. Community enterprises and self-help are to provide jobs of a kind while also producing goods and services for communities to compensate for lack of earnings. Self-employment and enterprise are to enable people to create their own jobs, sidestepping the formal economy. The informal economy has been increasingly accepted as a necessary blurring of the boundaries of paying work: the Conservatives have encouraged it, for example, through, relaxing statutory control of small business, through the DSS allowing claimants to hold their earnings in trust, and through the Enterprise Allowance scheme; the local Centre and Left support small business in sectors where non-registered work is the norm, and there have been proposals for legislative change to take the informal economy out of its ghetto (Bown, 1986). A final consensus element is to make free time more 'productive' and to enable people to find a sense of achievement outside paid work. This has been pursued through incorporating voluntary work in community employment and welfare initiatives, and by supporting the expanding forms of self-improving free time through sports and leisure facilities. In Cortonwood, a mile from the pit where the 1984 miners' strike started, a leisure centre is now to be added to the managed workspace and youth club already built.

The local level of policy has been important in developing this approach, and not coincidentally. Unemployment, the labour market, patterns of working hours, the informal economy and the need for community welfare are all highly variable by locality. Community enterprise and self-employment require support at a local level. Welfare provision, whether for basic services or leisure, has traditionally been the ambit of local government. We have noted that local economic initiatives span production and social life; within this strategy they tend to merge them. Local and community control can legitimate what might otherwise be unacceptable changes in expectations.

There have, of course, been political differences in how to deal with the supposed permanent deficit in paid work. The Right has sought to use high unemployment to discipline labour, and its emphasis on commercial leisure facilities and cuts in public spending have undermined the development of alternative forms of work and leisure for the poor.

Across the political spectrum there has been some support for loading the cuts in paid work on to oppressed groups rather than sharing them, by encouraging women to 'return' to the home and by excluding or repatriating immigrant workers; the effective labour force in West Germany was reduced by 1.7m between 1973 and 1979, largely by these means, and they have enabled Switzerland to achieve 'full employment' (Therborn, 1986). The policy of all political currents of inflecting welfare and education towards the supposed needs of production is in tension with supporting satisfying and creative leisure. Nevertheless, there is a remarkable consensus for local policies to redefine and blur the boundaries between paid and unpaid work.

The complex politics of consensus strategies

The favourite strategies we have discussed have a contradictory political layering. First, there is consensus around them, based on widely shared ideas about national and local economic weakness such as lack of enterprise or excessive centralised control. This is reinforced by their promise of being based on local implementation and on indigenous development – which we have seen can be true even of inward investment and new sectors.

Yet, second, the strategies are implemented in politically diverse ways, and the choice of implementation can be more significant than the choice of basic strategy. This is disguised by the way in which most local economic agencies, even local authorities, try to present their policies in apolitical terms (see pp. 113–14). The focus of policy on a discrete aspect of the economy such as a form of firm ownership or a sector can create a consensus around it because the method of implementation is not specified. But these aspects of the economy are in reality connected to others, and the different ways of handling these connections is a source of political divergences. Similarly, the consensus around decentralisation, work sharing and blurring the boundaries of labour disguise vital differences in how they are implemented. The importance of these differences is the reason for structuring much of this book by political project.

However, third, within many favourite strategies there has been a convergence on to a consensus mode of implementation. Over time the distinctly Right and Left approaches have fallen away or metamorphosed into Centre forms. The nature and roots of this convergence will be a major theme of Part IV.

Finally in this chapter we examine a key part of the consensus, job creation. In contrast to the discussion so far, we shall focus not on political ideologies but on the effectiveness of pursuing this aim.

The illusory consensus on job-creation

A negative-sum game

Although there is a consensus to share and to blur unemployment, all political currents claim that their principal aim in local initiatives is to create jobs, or at least to save or sustain them. In a time of high unemployment it is not surprising that this claim is made; but it is unfounded (James, 1984; Gough, 1986a).

The claim rests on the ability of initiatives to increase the competitiveness of local enterprises and encourage the formation of new ones. But such policies cannot increase final demand, or, therefore, the total output and jobs in the relevant sectors; any job increases are at the expense of jobs in other enterprises. Indeed, increases in competitiveness nearly always mean fewer labour hours per unit of output, so the effect is usually to decrease the aggregate number of jobs. To show that increases in competitiveness or productivity do create jobs, one would need to show that this occurred at the macro level, a question to which we return in Chapter 11. The only other way in which local economic initiatives might create net jobs is through the impact of increasing public expenditure; this takes us into theories of fiscal and monetary stimulus which are beyond the scope of this book (see Layard *et al.*, 1986).

One way in which this depressing conclusion has been sidestepped is to claim that, while competitive attraction of inward investment is a zero sum game carried on at the expense of other areas, 'indigenous development' is not. The Bootstraps strategy is seen as putting unused local resources to work, with no aggressive intent towards other areas; thus some Left local authorities argued that because they did not try to attract inward investment they were not competing for jobs (GLC, 1983a). But indigenous development, no less than inward investment, does not increase demand; it displaces jobs elsewhere, but in a less obvious manner. Similarly, product innovation is sometimes claimed to be a non-competitive policy through creating its own new market; but this demand is necessarily diverted from other goods and services.

In reply, most local economic agencies would say that their responsibility is to increase the number of jobs *in their territory*; displacement of jobs elsewhere is not their affair (Davies, 1988). But even this aim is often not achieved. Aid to an enterprise often increases labour productivity by more than it increases the enterprise's output, resulting in the enterprise losing jobs. Much support is to enterprises in consumer services, jobbing sectors, and fragmented manufacturing industries which compete with other local workplaces. Other displacement takes place outside the agency's territory but within the same labour market; it does something for 'the locality' but nothing for its workers. A further problem is that jobs now are sometimes at the expense of jobs in the future: support to weak firms can perpetuate lack of investment in local sectors by undermining the better firms, and in the long term contribute to the sector's decline (p. 92). Finally, job-creation in one sector can displace jobs in another through the operation of the land market (pp. 68–9). Local economic initiatives thus often fail even to increase jobs for local people.

The spiral of spatial competition

Some local aid does succeed in displacing job loss to outside the locality, particularly through concentrating aid on firms which do not compete locally or which export from the locality, as Gudgin *et al.* (1986) have urged. But this raises a political–moral problem: are the jobs more needed here or in the location where they are displaced, whether it be in Britain or abroad? This is a particularly pertinent question when, as is often the case, the losing locality has a higher unemployment rate. Local economic agencies, however, usually remain ignorant of the locations from which their policies displace jobs, so that this difficult question is scarcely ever asked.

More taxing for most agencies is a practical problem in competing for jobs: the other areas hit back. One of the reasons for the spread of local economic initiatives has been localities defending themselves from the initiatives of other areas: if Peterborough advertises, so too must Milton Keynes; since the Scottish Development Agency has overseas offices to attract inward investment, Northern England sets up a Development Corporation to do likewise. But as local initiatives have become more widespread, their ability to shift jobs spatially has declined. There are still, of course, large differences in the subsidies available in different localities; but many types of policy – information and advice, advertising, small-unit provision – are now so common as to have little geographical leverage.

Increasing competition has put pressure on local agencies to increase their inducements, paralleling the international auction to attract transnationals. In the USA since the 1960s the competition of State and city governments has resulted in a spiral of subsidies of diminishing returns (Goodman, 1979); but a location which eschews these subsidies is not only out-competed but seen as positively anti-business (Smith, 1988, pp. 212–14). In Britain this process has been inhibited by local authorities' limited powers for economic competition. Nevertheless, a competitive spiral can be seen in the race to become a post-industrial city. The local authority focuses the activities of all its departments towards this aim; large property, area and transport developments are undertaken, levering central government funds. The sums spent on cultural and leisure facilities in order to change the city's image can be very large. Competition for tourism, in particular, has become intense and increasingly expensive: Edinburgh has been told that it must spend £100m on infrastructure over the next ten years in order to hold on to its share of the tourism market.

Some of the local authorities with the greatest economic problems have relatively low spending on economic policy because of the constraints of local taxation and pressure of other spending priorities; conversely, many local authorities in relatively prosperous areas have high spending. Peterborough advertises itself on TV; Barrow-in-Furnace advertises itself on the side of six articulated lorries. In this way, the apparently progressive aim of local job creation becomes spatially regressive. To the extent that attempts at spatial competition for jobs are mutually cancelling, their most direct effect is to transfer resources from local and central government to the private sector.

Creating what jobs and for whom?

If local economic initiatives are a negative sum game with respect to job numbers, then their quality and social distribution should be of paramount importance. The Centre and Left have criticised the Right for assuming that increases in local jobs would automatically trickle down to the most needy (Miller and Tomaskovic-Devey, 1983), and they have put more emphasis on redistributing jobs towards disadvantaged groups. Certainly, many local initiatives, even those that increase local jobs, have no impact on local working class unemployment, either because they are middle class jobs or because they are taken by people from outside the area. The Right's argument, however, can be true under certain conditions. If unemployment declines across a whole region or subregion, and inward migration is not too fast, then jobs will trickle down: the disadvantaged are much better off in Hampshire than in Tyneside (Buck and Gordon, 1987).

Though the Centre and Left have adopted policies for job redistribution, considerations of who gets the jobs and their quality have taken second place to 'job creation', which has the political attraction of being quantifiable. Wages and conditions were considered in early policies: priority was given to manufacturing because, for manual men, job quality tends to be higher than in services. The Left's intention was to use improvements in competitiveness to achieve better wages and conditions. But policies for increasing competitiveness have seldom *integrated* considerations of who gets the jobs, their wages, conditions and stability, or the quality of the work involved. Policies for redistributing jobs towards disadvantaged groups have generally been separately planned and executed from policies for increasing competitiveness. This criticism has been articulated forcibly by the 'people based strategy' (Royal Town Planning Institute, 1985; Howl, 1985; see further pp. 243–4).

As a result, many policies tend to worsen the qualitative aspects of employment. Since most aid is provided to enterprises which are relatively unprofitable, a high proportion of aided jobs have wages and conditions inferior to the average for their industry: Nottingham's support for its local dying and finishing firms, for example, has put pressure on firms with generally better wages and unionisation in West Yorkshire. If the aid is successful in sustaining the enterprise, it is likely to displace jobs of superior quality elsewhere. Improvements in job quality *might* follow, but local economic agencies seldom attempt to ensure that this occurs. Even policies concerned with aspects of job quality or equal opportunities ignore other aspects. Printing cooperatives, for example, supported because of their participatory work relations, generally have wages inferior to those of their competitors. Training schemes for disadvantaged groups have been undertaken with no consideration of the impact of more trainees on the wages and conditions of existing workers. As with job creation, the knock-on effects through product and labour markets are not thought through. Different regard to these wider effects often lies behind divergent assessments of policy success. Local economic 'miracles' such as Massachusetts, Glasgow and Consett may fail to benefit those most in need (Heafey, 1989), and may displace problems from one group, sector or area to another. This points to the very real political and analytical difficulties in assessing local economic initiatives.

'Cost per job'

Given the consensus on 'creating jobs', comparison of the cost per job created appears as a politically objective measure of policy effectiveness. Our discussion above already suggests some major problems with this measure. It abstracts from who gets the jobs and from their quality. It ignores the benefits of increases in competitiveness which do not create, or which lose jobs (Turok and Wannop, 1989). Since local policies displace an equal (or greater) number of jobs elsewhere (known as the 'substitution' or 'displacement' effect), the question of cost efficiency should be rephrased as 'cost per job gain *in area x*'; as we have seen, for a given initiative the choice of area '*x*' can have a crucial effect on this quantity, including its sign. Thus 'cost per job' figures for local initiatives cannot be compared with those for national government policies, though this is often done. When cost per job figures are given, one should always ask: within what boundary?

There are other difficulties in estimating cost per job. Multiplier effects, where aid generates spending and more jobs, are not easy to gauge. Time scale presents problems: resources and jobs are lost when aid comes to an end, while some policies take a long time to have beneficial effects. Not all job growth in aided enterprises can be attributed to the aid, and much aid is wasted since the jobs would have been created anyway, the 'deadweight' effect. It is often difficult to find a comparable non-policy situation against which the policy effects can be measured. The impact of a policy varies according to the phase of the economic cycle. Finally, when different policies combine, it is often impossible to disentangle the effects of one policy alone.

Though local economic agencies are fond of quoting cost per job figures for their policies, there have been few investigations which deal convincingly with even a subset of these problems (Coulson 1990; *Local Economy*, vol. 4, no. 2, 1988). We shall therefore be very sparing in our use of this measure.

We have seen, then, that enthusiasm for job creation depends on limited monitoring of effects: an increase in competitiveness and numbers of enterprises is often counted as job creation even where it results in fewer local jobs; the spatial and social displacement of jobs is ignored; and quality, distribution and stability take second place to job creation. This narrow view is politically convenient. It disguises the losers and the beneficiaries of policy. It enables conflicts between different goals – job numbers, quality, distribution, stability – to be ignored. It sidesteps difficult choices about the control and conditions attached to aid, and minimises the differences between policies of the Right, Centre and Left. The stress on job creation, like the presentation of the favourite strategies, thus helps to construct the consensus around local economic policy.

Further reading

Gerry (1985) shows the long history of support by right and left for small enterprise. Joseph (1976) argues for their promise from the Right, while from the Centre-Left Sabel (1989) emphasises their potential for the local economy and Falk (1978b) their promise to solve local social, political and environmental problems. The ability of community business to change social relations in consensus fashion is evangelistically set out in OECD (1984a), Knevitt (1986), Civic Trust (1989), from a CBI–Church of England point of view in Moynagh (1985) and from the Left in Whyatt (1988). Panet-Raymond (1987) shows the political ambiguities and consensus around community. The large literature on worker cooperatives mostly presents their merits from a Centre-Left point of view; for a sophisticated argument, see Tomlinson (1982). The consensus on a major role for the voluntary sector is explored in Wolch (1989). The political tensions of transition from a manufacturing to a service based strategy are discussed by Graham and Ross (1989) and Cochrane (1991). The need and possibility for policies for the sunset sectors, including rapid technical change, are argued by Kantrow (1985) and Totterdill (1990a). Because targeted strategies for particular sectors, other than through property, are Centre or Left, most of the sectoral literature is of this stripe. Texts which argue for the 'local promise' of the sector are Wiggins and Snell (1986) on food, Greater London Council (1986c) on textiles and clothing, Hall and Markusen (1985) on electronics and software, Marshall (1988) on producer services, Hendon and Shaw (1987) on culture, Bianchini *et al.* (1991) on town centres, Totterdill (1990b) on retailing, and Hoyle *et al.* (1988) on waterfronts. Castells (1989) analyses the 'post-industrial' city, while Cheshire and Hay (1988) give an upbeat account of its promise. Good critiques of the technological determinism and political evasiveness of the 'post-industrial society' can be found in *Science as Culture* journal; Allen (1988) gives a guide to the debate. Vivid accounts of the appeal and illusions of a local 'high-tech future' to different social groups are Robins and Webster (1988) and Ruggiero (1989). Critical but generally supportive views on organisational decentralisation in local government are Hoggett and Hambleton (1987b) on the left and Bennett (1990) on the right. Jenkins and Sherman (1981) discuss the blurring of work and leisure.

Part II

Policies and Debates

Introduction

In this part of the book, we present three broad strategies which have been implemented in local economic policy, 'the Right', 'the Centre' and 'the Left'. These are in essence political projects, systems of linked ideas about how British local economies should be changed. None has been implemented in a pure form; many local economic agencies have carried out initiatives informed by more than one of the political strategies; and the strategies and the policies flowing from them have changed over time. In Part IV we shall see that these 'impure' forms of implementation reflect contradictions inherent in the strategies. But despite tensions and ambiguities, the three projects have been vital reference points in the construction of local economic strategies and policies, and therefore form the next stage of our presentation. Policies are discussed under the political current with which they were initially most strongly associated.

3 The Radical Alternatives: the Right and the Left

THE RIGHT

The recession of 1974 produced a sharp turn towards neo-liberal policies throughout the dominant capitalist countries – as well as the present wave of local economic initiatives. Britain was no exception: in 1975 the Labour government inaugurated the present era of neo-liberalism with a policy of deflation through control of the money supply, cuts in public spending and a reorientation of the welfare state. This was continued by the Conservative government, which gave it a more explicit ideological basis: to restore the disciplines of the market and the dynamism of enterprise, and as far as possible remove the state from economic and social affairs; we term this the strategy of the Right.

This strategy has had a number of key elements. Through fiscal and monetary policy, it has aimed 'to restrain inflation'; in practice this meant a high level of unemployment to contain wage inflation. It has aimed to cut public spending 'to reduce the burden of taxation on enterprise'. Taxation of high and unearned incomes was reduced 'to increase the rewards of enterprise', while total taxation of low incomes was increased. Nationalised industries, and many central and local government services, were privatised 'to increase their efficiency' and to subject their workers to 'market realities'. Many public services, notably education and the National Health Service, have been fragmented into small units each of which is responsible for its own budget, mirroring corporations' setting up of profit centres; the centre provides funding for each unit under a contract setting out its tasks, and the units can then be in the public, voluntary, or private sector. Business executives were given an increased role in running public and semi-privatised agencies 'since they are the experts'. Some responsibilities of the welfare state were transferred to individuals or the voluntary sector 'to increase individual responsibility'.

The government declared its intention to withdraw from an active industrial policy in order to 'let the market work': most subsidies were reduced, employment legislation was weakened, and statutory compulsion on industry to train was reduced. In their sharpest departure from the policy of the Labour government, the Conservatives eschewed incomes policies and agreements with the unions, relying on unemployment and deflation to restrain wages. In some fields where markets were regulated – privately rented housing, buses, telecommunication, TV and radio – controls have been weakened. The government promoted self-employment, individual economic enterprise and small-firm formation as a 'dynamic' and 'free' sector of the economy.

There have been some inconsistencies in the Conservatives' strategy, for which it has been criticised from the right. Monetary targets were abandoned in the mid-1980s and credit relaxed, fuelling the boom of the late 1980s. Some subsidies have been sacrosanct: those to agriculture and owner occupation, and the extensive tax perks of the rich. Privatisations perpetuated monopolies, and the shares were not dispersed in the egalitarian fashion that neo-liberalism would suggest. Nevertheless, the Conservatives' programme has had a consistent thread.

Local government has been a major area of change. The proportion of local government spending funded by central government fell from 60 per cent in 1979/80 to 33 per cent in 1990/1. The new money produced for innovative projects in needy localities was clawed back by reductions in mainstream funding: the poorest local authorities lost 20 per cent of their rate support grant in real terms between 1982 and 1986; for local government as a whole increases of £2bn in Urban Programme money between 1981 and 1987 were offset by £10bn lost in block grant (Colenutt and Tansley, 1989, p. 11). The ability of local authorities to make up for these reductions through increasing local taxation was countered by increasing central government control over spending and borrowing. Particularly severely hit were council house construction, which virtually stopped, and public transport subsidies. Local government services were fragmented and privatised through legislation; some, such as the polytechnics and contracted-out schools, were appropriated by central government. Central funding became increasingly dependent on the politics of the local authority or the particular project. The local government system, then, experienced fragmentation at the bottom and increasing control at the top, paralleling organisational changes within corporations.

The Conservatives' local economic strategy

The core of the Conservatives' local economic strategy has been to free local factor markets. The key obstruction has been pictured as local government itself, seen as a stultifying bureaucracy which delays projects, 'leaves jobs in filing cabinets', frightens off inward investment, and drives jobs out of the cities through high taxes and anti-business attitudes. This attack neatly combines neo-liberal anti-statism with a more mundane criticism of the Labour Party. Through removing local authority, central government and trade union interference in markets, factor markets and welfare services are to become more locally responsive. This strategy has been pursued through cuts in local government spending; increased central control over local taxation and spending; compulsory contracting out of services; and by by-passing the local authorities through increasing the role of business and the voluntary sector in local economic policy and through local initiatives directly controlled by the government. Implicit in this is a local industrial policy: to open up new industries to the private sector via privatisation. Implicit also is a welfare policy for dealing with localised poverty without strengthening the local authorities. This approach has been applied in a range of policy areas.

Decentralisation of wage bargaining has been of central concern. Large employers have been abandoning national wage bargaining and tailoring wages to the profitability of the workplace and to local labour market conditions. The Right has sought to reinforce this policy through deflationary policies and weakening of the unions, which are intended to feed through to more differentiated local labour markets. Changes in wage bargaining in local government have been seen as crucial, since in most localities the local authority is the largest single employer; greater wage 'flexibility' has been pursued through privatisation, sponsorship of community and voluntary welfare agencies, the use of 'trainees' in welfare work, and moves towards relating pay to the particular market in the skill and to 'results'. Bargaining has thus both been decentralised from the national to the regional or local level, and decentralised within each locality.

A second strand in the Right's labour market policy has been *to reduce wages, conditions and security at the lower end of the labour market*. This was pursued partly through cuts in social security levels and entitlements and weakening of protective employment legislation. A key instrument has been the MSC and its successors, whose programmes have been implemented in an organisationally decentralised way through public, voluntary and profit-making training agencies. The Conservatives' view has been that training in substantial skills is the responsibility of individuals and firms; the MSC has therefore essentially been concerned with labour markets, not with substantial training. It has aimed to keep the adult and youth unemployed within the ambit of the formal waged economy and thus of potential use to employers. Its youth training schemes sought to integrate youth as a cheap workforce with basic skills and acceptance of work discipline. Employers were subsidised to take on youth as, effectively, cheap labour; in the Young Workers Scheme low wages were actually encouraged by making subsidy conditional on wages being below £40 per week. These schemes have helped to recrcate the 1930s pattern where youth are employed as long as low wages can be paid, and then join the long term unemployed. These measures served and reinforced the move by employers to casualised and low paid employment (Finn, 1987). This effect of MSC schemes can be very large in areas of high unemployment, where those in such programmes can outnumber those employed in local government and effectively counteract the positive effect of the latter on local wages and conditions. The Right justifies this strategy as creating jobs through cost competition, and as providing a reserve workforce with basic skills which can respond to the rapid qualitative and quantitative changes in the demand for labour required to shake out local economies.

The Conservatives moved towards 'workfare' – requiring work for social security payments – without formalising it, using incremental changes in training schemes and social security legislation. Strong pressure has been put on the uncmployed to take a job or go on a training scheme; it is no longer permitted to refuse a job which is below your qualifications and experience. Allowances for training and work schemes have been progressively reduced, in some schemes to just over benefit level. The Enterprise Allowance is self-employed workfare, and has had an increasing take-up as pressure on claimants has risen. The low paid work in community businesses sponsored by the Urban Programme is also close to workfare. However, creeping workfare has been opposed by unions and by private employers threatened by unfair competition.

From the mid-1980s, with increasingly serious skill shortages, the Conservatives came under strong pressure from sections of business to provide real training. Partly in response, from 1990 the government further decentralised its training programmes by creating the TECs, two-thirds of whose boards are local business executives. Central control, however, remained strong and in some ways intensified, with

90 per cent of their central funding earmarked for national programmes. They were to be funded according to output measures, putting them under pressure to carry out cheap training in easy-to-fill high turnover jobs, and jeopardising the higher quality and equal opportunities schemes previously funded (Peck, 1991). Since they are also required to offer training to anyone under 25 and unemployed for over six months, training programmes are being shortened and cheapened for groups unlikely to get a 'positive outcome'.

The Conservatives' *education reforms* have had a similar direction: to focus education on employment, but with low-grade skills. The national curriculum has sought to instil discipline rather than originality; increased parental choice has been intended to reinforce a focus in schools on preparing students for employment; and, through Local Management, schools were expected to respond to their specific labour markets, in particular through increasing differences between working class and middle class schools. Vocational further education was privileged compared with higher education (though not consistently); and funding for non-vocational adult education was slashed.

The government sought to *reduce local taxation on business* which was claimed, with little evidence (Kirwan, 1986), to have played a major role in the decline of city manufacturing; in 1988 the business rate was 'nationalised' by being set at a nationally uniform rate poundage and appropriated by the Treasury. Cuts in local taxation were also the central mechanism of the EZ programme, initiated in 1981. Twenty-three EZs were designated, located in largely derelict urban areas. Developments, of whatever type, pay no rates for ten years, building costs can be set against tax over 25 years, and this right can be sold on to companies seeking tax losses. A further local tax-cutting initiative was the Freeports, six of which have been opened since 1984, in which imports used to make exports are free of customs duty.

The Conservatives have seen *local authority regulation of land markets* as an acute problem. Land use planning is said to have destroyed jobs, through intolerance of non-conforming uses, long delays and imposition of petty conditions in planning applications. The Conservative government urged local authorities to be 'less restrictive', and increasingly overturned refusals of planning permission on appeal. The Use Classes Order was changed to allow the conversion of manufacturing space to mixed uses including offices and storage, thus freeing much space previously zoned for manufacturing. Streamlined planning procedures were an element of the EZ package, and these have been extended through the Simplified Planning Zones which, in a characteristic privatisation, can be declared by the Secretary of State at the request of a developer. The Conservatives claimed that local authorities and nationalised industries were preventing development by holding on to unused land; it was hoped that tighter financial controls over them, and 'shaming' the councils through a public Derelict Land Register, would encourage them to sell unused land. The UDCs were set up to by-pass 'anti-business' local authorities. The London and Merseyside UDCs were designated in 1980 and ten others in 1987–91; they have an expected life of 15 years, cover 40 000 acres in total, and in 1981–90 received £2.0bn in 'grant in aid'. They are located in largely derelict areas of cities, assembling and preparing land for development and providing physical infrastructure. They usually spread risk by disposing of land at low, even below cost, prices at early stages, and then setting higher prices and reaping development gains as confidence grows. The greater power of land purchase of the UDCs has been an important advantage over large scale developments carried out by local authorities.

The Right favours what it presents as *'market-led' forms of subsidy*. By this is meant subsidies which are selective rather than of right, and whose amount is determined to be just sufficient to enable the particular project to be undertaken; in this way it is hoped that the maximum amount of development can be leveraged with the minimum assistance. Regional grants as of right were criticised for their large deadweight (Robinson *et al.*, 1987); the Conservatives reduced these sharply and increased the use of selective powers, with large developments levered with *ad hoc* grants. The government maintained the standard incentives system of the Inner Urban Areas Act. But in 1984 they introduced the Urban Development Grant, modelled on the Urban Development Action Grants, the mainstay of the US Federal urban programme. Targeted on the same fifty-seven authorities as the Urban Programme, it was available for private sector projects alleviating deprivation whether through jobs, housing or environmental improvements. The grant was just enough to give the developer a profit sufficient to pro-ceed, as evaluated by secondees from business at the DoE. While the local authority organised the Urban Development Grant for the developers and contributed a quarter of the cost, in 1988 the govern-ment introduced a revised version, the City Grant, in which the local authority plays no role; this paralleled the formal exclusion of the TUC from training policy in the same year.

Leveraged subsidy has been allied to *competitive bidding by local economic agencies for central government funds*. Local agencies put forward proposals which are selected for funding from a more-or-less fixed fund on the basis of leveraging and return (the City Grant, TECs), cost effectiveness (TECs), or generalised return (Urban Programme, City Challenge). This aims to bid down costs, to get the maximum economic–social return on government spending, and to organise the competition of localities on quasi-market principles. It combines strong central control with Bootstraps, as localities are compelled to help themselves by low bids and ingenious schemes.

Partly through these means, the Conservatives have aimed to stimulate *a new role for business in urban regeneration* by transferring functions to it from the local authorities. The government-appointed boards of the UDCs and the TECs were predominantly drawn from business. The Conservatives welcomed the corporate financing of local initiatives and community services, gave tax concessions to firms supporting the Enterprise Agencies and TECs, and sought business finance for state-organised services such as the City Technical Colleges. The model evoked is of the nineteenth century 'city father', the local industrialist exercising paternalistic philanthropy and control over his town. The Conservatives also propose that urban regeneration should be 'private sector led'. That the majority of investment and employment should be private sector is hardly radical: what is meant is that local authorities should minimise planning and take their lead from the immediate demands of business.

The Conservatives' vision of declining dependency on the state was also embodied in *an expanded role for the voluntary sector*. 'The voluntary sector' is here pictured as a form of self-help, independent from the state. Some of the organisations aided by the Urban Programme are indeed grass-roots community organisations; but many are qualgos, wholly funded by the state and consisting essentially of professional staff; these include the largest group of 'voluntary' bodies, training agencies funded by the MSC. However, in the late 1980s the Conservatives' emphasis shifted from the voluntary sector to profit making enterprises and agencies.

In view of its effusive verbal support for *small business*, it is at first sight surprising that the Conservatives have not taken more local initiatives in its support. The Department of Trade and Industry (DTI) has run small-business advice agencies, together with many temporary sectoral schemes. The TECs are to incorporate small business development, but this does not appear to involve additional resources. This reticence reflects the Right's view that small business is to be stimulated by the removal of state-imposed burdens rather than positive support, except perhaps advice and information provision.

Paradoxically, the most visible parts of the Right's local economic strategy have been the policies of central rather than local government. This is because its strategy rests so heavily on reducing local authority activities through central control. However, some 'dry' Conservative councils have pioneered forms of privatisation, decentralised wage setting, and spending and tax cutting. The Conservatives drew many Labour local authorities into active collaboration in their policies; many lobbied for an EZ or a UDC because of financial pressures and intense competition for jobs. However, the most distinctive strategy of Conservative authorities has been flagrantly against neo-liberal tenets: most of those in southern England have used land use planning to restrict employment and population growth – a more 'anti-business' stance than any Labour council has recently entertained. The Conservative government opposed this policy, most famously in Nicholas Ridley's 'not in my back yard' campaign, since it not only restricts the market but does so in Britain's most profitable region. But, for electoral reasons, the Conservatives have not sought to dismantle the Green Belt.

We now present some widely voiced criticisms of the Conservatives' local economic strategy; debates around their labour market policies are examined in Chapter 4. This critique will be taken further in Chapter 9.

Evaluation of the Enterprise Zones, Urban Development Corporations and Urban Development Grant

Evaluation of the Conservatives' area and property initiatives is difficult because their aims have not been clearly specified: are they to physically renovate derelict areas, change the supply of property to benefit users, or bring jobs, and if so, jobs for whom? The deregulatory aspects of the programmes have contributed little to their successes. The effectiveness of the EZs in attracting development has been hampered by the fact that the landowners have raised rents on the basis of the financial inducements; most of the latter therefore go to the landowner or developer, a share which tends to rise over time and which in zones in the more depressed northern areas has reached 80–90 per cent (PA Cambridge Economic Consultants, 1987, p. 75). Tax cuts or subsidies specific to small areas are bound to suffer from this problem, unless rents are controlled through public ownership. Nor has relaxation of land use planning played a significant role. Partly this is because local authority land use planning, especially in inner cities, had already been accommodating to business since the mid-1970s at the latest. The small number of Simplified Planning Zones declared suggests that developers do not experience great difficulties with planning restrictions. In a survey of 535 small firms in Glasgow and Belfast, only three said that they had been constrained by land use planning and none favoured simplified planning procedures (Middleton, 1985). Moreover, the development control practised in the EZs and the UDCs has not been a free-for-all. Pressure from developers and the qualgos' interest in profitable development have resulted in control of positioning, layout, access and aesthetics (Hadley, 1984; Buchanan, 1989); most local authority development control does not go beyond these considerations. Similarly, since normal customs duty is not onerous, the Freeports have had little leverage: only two have attracted significant development, and this is in warehousing rather than manufacturing.

The ability of the EZs and UDCs to attract development has thus been overwhelmingly due to their new infrastructures and cleared land, and in the case of the UDCs to grants and subsidised land prices (Griffiths, 1986). On this basis they have been reasonably successful in filling up the empty land. The UDCs, especially that in London Docklands, have attracted high rent uses. There has been no systematic evaluation of whether the property development in the schemes would have taken place within those cities anyway, and if not, what its impact on improving quality and lowering rents has been. Canary Wharf has undoubtedly made a major difference to the supply of Central London offices, both directly and in forcing the City to allow more development, and has contributed to falling rents; but this enormous development may be exceptional.

The take-up of the Urban Development Grant, however, has been poor: in the first five years of the scheme only £87m was dispensed compared with £70m budgeted for the first year alone (Martin, 1990, p. 53). The major financial institutions were not involved as had been intended: the schemes have been dominated by local developers (Pearce, 1988). We present some reasons for these failures in Chapter 9. The grant, like its US model, has been used mainly for developments in central cities and their fringes rather than in poor neighbourhoods and industrial areas.

The physical development of the EZ and UDC areas has not demonstrated a particularly strong leverage. The UDCs were not sited in areas of inner city stress but merely where industry had declined. The economic structure in the EZs is not very different from what would have occured without the programme (PA Cambridge Economic Consultants, 1987, p. 23). Their development was powered by the national property boom of the mid-1980s, and in London Docklands by the special circumstances of 'Big Bang' and Fleet Street's decentralisation. The 'deadweight' of these schemes is therefore probably high (see further p. 22). With the Urban Development Grant, however, evidence on deadweight is conflicting: the proportion of projects that would have gone ahead without a grant was found by Martin (1989, p. 633) to be 27 per cent, but according to PSMRC (1988) was only 8 per cent with a further 36 per cent needing less grant than given.

Urban Development Grant schemes housed 30 000 jobs in 1984–8 (Cabinet Office, 1988), and the EZs 35 000 in 1981–9; in the UDCs – even the first two designated in 1981 – net job growth to 1990 was very small (Colenutt and Tansley, 1990; Turkie, 1991). In all three programmes the majority of new jobs have been national transfers, either moves or jobs which would have been created within Britain. In a sample of Urban Development Grants, only 19 per cent of the associated jobs were new to the British economy (Martin, 1989, p. 637), just 14 jobs per scheme on average; in the LDDC in 1981–7 the proportion was 22 per cent (Docklands Consultative Committee, 1990, p. 25). Since many of these transfers are from short distances (for the EZs, see PA Cambridge Economic Consultants, 1987) the schemes do not even push the problems on to other labour markets. Moreover, the new developments have raised land prices and thus displaced existing users, compounded in the UDCs by their hostility to low-rent manual work uses (though not to manufacturing as such). As a result 11 000 industrial and dock jobs were lost in the LDDC area in 1981–7 compared with around 20 000 jobs in new workplaces (Docklands Consultative Committee, 1990), and similar displacement has taken place in later UDCs such as Bristol; ironically, this displacement is one of the sins of which the Right accused the 'rigid' planning system.

The costs of the schemes are hard to measure. For the EZs, even the direct costs are obscure because capital allowances depend on the marginal tax rate of the ultimate buyer of the property rights. The EZs and UDCs have absorbed many other grants (Colenutt and Tansley, 1990) and additional infrastructure costs have been high. On the other hand, the cost effectiveness of the schemes cannot yet be evaluated since the costs fall heavily in the early years and job gains are yet to come.

For these reasons leverage ratios are of limited significance. Martin (1990) estimates a private: public ratio for Urban Development Grants of 2.5:1 allowing for deadweight. He estimates the cost per job attributable to the policy and new to Britain as £18 300. Other estimates of the programmes' cost per job take no account of deadweight and displacement; however, even these gross figures are high – for the EZs a figure of £30 000 per job has been estimated (National Audit Office, 1990). In all three programmes these costs have been increased by the eligibility of low job-density uses such as retailing and warehousing. The high cost of the EZs, however measured, led the government to end further designations, a clear admission of failure for a policy which was supposed to show the value of decreased state intervention.

Only a small proportion of the jobs associated with these three programmes have been taken by disadvantaged groups and the unemployed. This is similar to the record of property-based regeneration in the USA (Smith, 1988, p. 210); flagship projects such as the Renaissance Centre in Detroit have had no impact on the economy of the surrounding inner city. The displacement of existing users has removed jobs held mostly by local manual workers. In the new developments, retail, warehousing, hotel and leisure have provided the most accessible employment; in large scale tourist projects in city centres local residents take around 45 per cent of new jobs (DoE, 1990, p. 2). Few of the office and media jobs that have been so popular are accessible to working-class inner-city residents; it has been estimated, for example, that only 1800 of the expected 47 000 jobs in Canary Wharf will go to local residents (Peat Marwick and McLintock, 1986, quoted in Parkinson and Evans, 1990), while only 28 per cent of jobs in the Isle of Dogs have been taken by them. The registered unemployed have taken only 18 per cent of the jobs in Urban Development Grant projects (though the take-up by those not previously working may be considerably higher) (Martin, 1989). Very few black people in Liverpool 8 have obtained work from the nearby Garden Festival and UDC. The equity problems of relying so heavily on the market are reflected in the regional distribution of Urban Development Grants: in 1983–8, the West Midlands and the south-east each captured twice as much grant as the Northern region (Martin, 1990, p. 55).

The impact and cost effectiveness of these initiatives on the profitability of the wider city economies is thus unknown. At a high public cost they have spatially redistributed jobs, a large proportion at the expense of other inner city locations. Only a minority of these jobs have been taken by the disadvantaged; policies focused on central area land development are a blunt instrument for helping the poor.

Business drags its feet

In giving business a greater role in local economic initiatives and welfare, the Right hopes to show that there can be a decentralised capitalism in which business cares, where firms' responsibility to the locality can replace the community organised by the state, where international capital cares about the local. The Conservatives' model has been the active role of US business in local affairs: its social responsibility programmes, its business-led growth coalitions, its sponsorship of visionary state leadership and 'entrepreneurial cities'.

But British business has proved very reluctant to take up this role. The Chambers of Commerce were expected to become vehicles for business intervention, but failed to do so. A majority of support for the Enterprise Agencies comes from a handful of firms, and though they were originally intended to be entirely private sector ventures, 60 per cent of their finance now comes from the state through tax relief and grants. *The Economist* (1989) has pointed out that British executives lack the skills, time and commitment to take up their assigned role. Teachers have been much more active than business in developing school–industry links; in the first five years of the City Technology Colleges (to 1990), a mere £14m was raised from business in comparison with the government's commitment of £142m. Business participation in the Conservatives' training schemes has been disappointing; in many inner cities only 5 per cent of Employment Training places were in the private sector. Business support for voluntary welfare organisations taking over from local government has also been below expectations. Property initiatives sponsored by business have been conservative: Inner City Enterprises, set up by financial institutions, has had to act as developer because of lack of interest from its supporters; its few developments have been in relatively easy central-fringe sites. Emblematic of this failure was Heseltine's famous coach trip round Liverpool with leading executives in 1981; seven years after, none of the banks, building societies or industrialists represented had a presence in Liverpool 8 (Roberts, 1988). In Chapter 9 we shall explore some reasons for business's reticence.

Centralism versus local capability: the problem of Sticklebricks

The Conservatives want local authorities to be enterprising and collaborate with the private sector in local regeneration; yet most of them, including Labour ones, have been doing this anyway. Even before 1979, most local authorities with 'problem' economies were giving priority to economic regeneration over their traditional services, and were seeking to accommodate the demands of business. In land use planning, they increasingly looked for any developments which could profitably fill sites and provide jobs; strategic land use planning was effectively abandoned for site-by-site decisions. In their economic initiatives, they generally sought 'to serve business', in the sense of meeting the expressed demands of local firms. This behaviour was the local authorities' spontaneous response to *local* pressures from business and residents. Similarly, most local authorities made strenuous efforts to hold down local taxes, under pressure from *local* business and residents.

In this sense, the Conservatives were pushing at an open door. But worse, they reduced local authorities' *ability* to be 'entrepreneurial' by their financial squeeze of local government and by their increasing centralisation of control. The tradition of British local government has allowed, within the framework of government policy, considerable local discretion in implementation and bargaining and compromise between the two levels of government. This has not entirely disappeared from local economic initiatives: some authorities such as Hammersmith and Fulham have had considerable success in negotiating modifications to Whitehall programmes to meet their own strategy (Allan *et al.*, 1985). However, authorities increasingly have to obtain central approval for each move that they make; the National Audit Commission (1989, p. 26) cited the example of a purchase of £15.64 worth of children's bricks which needed specific Whitehall authorisation. The Commission argued that these 'East European planning laws' (Robinson, 1988, p. 108) and financial restrictions are undermining local authorities' ability to carry out the partnership with business which the Conservatives themselves want. The voluntary sector favoured by the Conservatives is dependent on local government funding. Even their own initiatives may be damaged. The take up of the Urban Development Grant was forecast to be much reduced once local authorities' involvement was removed (Martin, 1990, pp. 55, 63). Encroachment on local authority control conflicts with the overall planning of economic policy within each locality, which the Conservatives ostensibly support (see below), given that the DoE itself cannot have a plan for every area.

The Conservatives' centralism restricts not only local authorities but locally based business, which has been excluded from their appointed qualgos. Neither the UDCs nor the TECs have formal representation of local business since board members sit as individuals; unsurprisingly, then, they are overwhelmingly executives of large firms. This is reflected in policy: the UDCs have generally pursued a post-industrial city model, and have been hostile to local firms which do not conform to this strategy. This exclusion of local business is related to the restriction of local authorities: as the *Financial Times* has argued (Editorial, 13 June

1991), business cannot be involved in local economies through the
intermediary of central government, but only through local democracy.
This enables local business to arrive at common strategies and to win a
popular consensus for them (see further pp. 230–1). In excluding both
local authorities and local business, then, Conservative centralism has
undermined Conservative local economic strategy.

More interventionist and redistributive than it appears

Both the Conservatives and many of their critics have portrayed their
approach as minimising state economic intervention. The reality has
been somewhat different.

The Conservatives retained nearly all the local economic programmes
they inherited, and added many more. As we have seen, their direct
initiatives have involved high public expenditure per job, and the more
successful ones have relied heavily on infrastructure provision. The
UDCs have depended on their draconian and well-financed compulsory
purchase powers. The Conservatives' most spectacular achievement,
the 1 million square metre Canary Wharf office development in the
London Docklands Enterprise Zone was secured by Margaret Thatcher's
promise that a tube line would be built to serve it; its total subsidy has
been estimated as £4bn (Turkie, 1991, chs 5 and 6).

The Conservatives have backed off from many deregulatory measures: in the Enterprise Zones employment legislation and most taxes
were not abolished, as Peter Hall (1977) had urged, nor were firms
deprived of other subsidies, as the minister had originally intended
(Anderson, 1988). The UDCs and EZs have not been a planning free-
for-all but 'a definitive land-use zoning plan with fiscal incentives
attached' (MacLeary and Lloyd, 1980, p. 150). Ironically, some sections
of business have come to regard them with as much hostility as they do
the local authorities for their long planning delays and bureaucracy
(Brownill, 1990, p. 149). The Freeports bear no relation to their Free
Trade Zone models, and their one incentive was curtailed by small print
written by the Customs and Excise.

Moreover, the Conservatives have undertaken interventionist and
'modernising' policies. In secondary and higher education, while they
have introduced greater responsiveness to individual parent and student
demand, they have also attempted to push education towards the
supposed needs of industry (Robins and Webster, 1985). The
Conservative-appointed qualgos have carried out active regulation

of economic development. In Scotland and Wales the Development Agencies have implemented classic Centre policies of sectoral targeting, infrastructure and social development (Moore and Booth, 1986). Following this example, many of the UDCs have targeted sectors, including manufacturing sectors, and gone out to attract them. The LDDC initially adopted a strategy of attracting computer firms, and the Merseyside UDC initially allocated 55 per cent of its land to industrial uses; both switched to service industries only when the market failed to respond. Except in London, the UDCs' strategies have generally not differed substantially from the previous strategies of the (Labour) local authorities for the areas, and the UDCs have worked fairly harmoniously with them.

Nor do the cuts in regional spending mean that the Conservatives have abandoned spatial redistribution; rather, they have changed to redistribution within regions: to cities through EZs, UDCs and City Grant, and to poor areas through the continuing use of the Inner Urban Area Act and Urban Programme. Though these programmes have other aims, spatial redistribution is certainly one.

The Right has been ambivalent about policies directed at poverty and unemployment. On the one hand, it maintains that increasing profitability and growth will automatically trickle down into benefits for the poor; no special policies are needed. This claim has doubtless been disingenuous. But the Right *is* concerned with the political dangers of an underclass and erosion of the work ethic; Banfield (1974) argued that this should be *the* urban question for the Right, and this has been a motive in BP's local involvement (Heal, 1982). Accordingly, the Conservatives' 'training' policy has been almost completely confined to the unemployed; funds are allocated to TECs according to their local rate of unemployment. Regional policy has been altered to address unemployment rather than being a subsidy for firms to increase their capital intensity. This latter shift is part of a more general change made by the Conservatives, from subsidies for fixed capital to labour market intervention, particularly through the enormous growth of the MSC. This reflects the priority given by the Conservatives to class relations, something they are prepared to back with intervention. Nor has the Right been oblivious to the quality and distribution of its jobs. It has sometimes backed manufacturing against service sectors on these grounds: the monetarist economist Patrick Minford resigned from the Merseyside UDC because of its preference for service sectors, and we have noted how other UDCs have given some priority to manufacturing sectors. From the mid-1980s, learning from the ire incurred by the LDDC's ignoring of local feeling, the UDCs (including the LDDC itself) have liaised with and supported community organisations, provided welfare facilities, and set up training schemes intended to enable local people to get some of the jobs.

The Conservatives' willingness to go along with local interventionism and consensus was signalled in 1989 when, for the first time, it enacted a statutory power for local authorities to undertake local economic initiatives. The legislation restricts equity holdings by local authorities and their agencies (such as LEBs); but the legislation places no restrictions on the mainstream activities of local authorities which, as we shall see in the next chapter, are substantially interventionist. Through the Urban Programme, in particular, the government has itself financially supported these mainstream approaches.

From the mid-1980s the government came under increasing criticism for the lack of local strategy in the economic initiatives it presided over, for judging projects in isolation, artificially separating social and economic goals, and failing to coordinate its own programmes (National Audit Commission, 1989; Coopers Lybrand, 1991). The government responded to this criticism. It set up the City Action Teams and Inner City Task Forces to coordinate the initiatives of different central departments and local economic and social initiatives. The TECs are intended to coordinate training and small business support, and possibly other programmes in the future. In 1987 Urban Programme districts were obliged to produce a strategic Inner Area Programme; in 1989 the Transport Supplementary Grant was targeted on the Urban Programme areas; and in 1990 the government stated that it would not supply funding for local economic initiatives unless the local authority drew up a strategic plan – striking demands from a government which crusaded against planning.

The Conservatives' actions, then, have been more interventionist and more concerned with redistribution than is often thought. This inconsistent behaviour shows that there are considerable tensions within the Right's project. These have surfaced in criticisms from sections of industry and the CBI both of the Conservatives' lack of industrial policy and of its failures in distribution and welfare (CBI, 1991). Correspondingly, the local economic initiatives sponsored by business have, on the whole, differed markedly from the Conservatives', taking a more interventionist approach to enterprise and growth, and addressing welfare considerations more directly; accordingly, we discuss these as 'Centre' policies in the next chapter.

In practice, then, the Conservatives' local economic policy has been very far from letting the market rip, and it has moved further towards the Centre over time. The initiatives of big business itself have been largely of the Centre rather than the Right. Explaining these paradoxes will be a major theme of Part IV.

THE LEFT

A Left approach to local economic policy was pioneered by a Labour administration in Wandsworth (1976) in the mid-1970s and reached its heyday in the early 1980s. It had two strands which were always in tension. The first came out of the militant trade union struggles of the late 1960s and early 1970s, and from parts of the women's and black movements, and stood for combative union organisation, self-organisation of oppressed groups, and democracy within the labour movement. It sought public ownership of the economy, but on a more democratic and decentralised model than Morrisonian nationalisation.

The second strand had a long tradition in the British labour movement, most strongly expressed in the Attlee and Wilson governments: a project of 'modernising' British capitalism, of making it more productive and profitable. (We shall use the usual term 'modernisation' though it is obviously a loaded one.) In the 1970s this project took on a new radicalism in response to the depth of the British economic crisis, subsequently accentuated by monetarist policies. This tradition sees British capitalism as encumbered by the City's overseas orientation and speculative habits and its consequent lack of attention to domestic industry; by short termism and lack of strategic planning by both finance and industry; by an individualistic outlook of firms, reliance on pure market mechanisms, and absence of inter-firm cooperation; by lack of long term investment in innovation, training and infrastructure; and by policies of successive governments which connive in these practices and give priority to the interests of the City. State policies are needed to push British capital into more coordinated and ultimately more profitable paths. But since the necessary measures are opposed by most of British capital because of its short-sightedness and individualism, a determined Labour government and pressure from the unions are necessary; statutory industrial democracy, such as was put forward in Labour's 1974 manifesto or in the EC's Vredeling proposals and Social Charter, would push capital into more productive paths. Faster growth would then benefit wages and conditions. Thus it is not merely that better conditions and greater economic democracy have to be based on greater competitiveness; the former are also part of the means to the latter. The combination of benefits for workers and greater productiveness is seen as a step towards socialism.

Left local economic initiatives were informed by both these strategies: on the one hand there were initiatives to support workers' demands and organisation as such; on the other was the productivist strategy, termed 'restructuring for labour' by the GLC, restructuring in the interests of labour and capital simultaneously (Eisenschitz and North, 1986). This combination of strategies resulted in ambiguity and shifts within the Left's initiatives. Individual policies of the Left had varied origin in the two strategies. First, there were productivist policies to increase investment, improve management methods, develop strategic planning, and increase the coherence of local economies; these aims were pursued particularly through the LEBs, provision of sectoral collective services, technology policies, and training initiatives. Second, there were specific initiatives to combat poor wages and conditions and discrimination in the labour market: contract compliance, equal opportunities policies, and information campaigns on employment rights. These policies could be interpreted either as support for the workers (the democratic project) or as a means of forcing capital to abandon sweating and adopt high productivity strategies (the productivist project). Third, there were pro-labour initiatives such as support for union campaigns, industrial democracy, humanisation of the labour process, development of socially useful products, and community control over land. Again, these initiatives were interpreted in different ways: as good in themselves; as prefiguring a socialist society in using resources to meet human needs; or as increasing competitiveness through more cooperative and hence productive industrial relations. The contrast between the two strands of the Left, then, ran through its whole programme. Below we examine in turn each of the three types of policy.

Left local economic initiatives came under intense pressure as soon as they emerged: successive re-elections of the Conservatives; the abolition of the GLC and the Metropolitan County Councils in 1986; the government's attacks on local government; successive defeats of the unions; and the progressive shift to the right in the labour movement. From the mid-1980s the Left Labour councils imposed wage cuts, speed-up and redundancies on their own workforces, in sharp contrast to their professed aims in their economic initiatives. These were the unfavourable circumstances in which the strategy was attempted.

The Local Enterprise Boards

All political currents have supported local initiatives to correct failures of the British financial system (p. 38). The LEBs adopted an approach which is distinctive in a number of ways. First, candidates for funding are more numerous than the Centre and Right allow; it is not only small firms and unconventional entrepreneurs who are thought to be under-funded, but also medium firms, manufacturing as a whole, high risk activities, and investments of long payback period. Second, the Boards have attempted to use the lever of funding to encourage, and even impose, changes in management practices and personnel. Third, British industry is seen as suffering from a lack of planning across sectors, which in France and Japan is organised by the state and in Germany by the banks. The Boards have therefore formed a view of the best strategies open to the local sector in the light of global sectoral developments; this view has not only informed decisions on funding, but has enabled projects to be sought out, firms persuaded to change their strategy, and investment and disinvestment to be coordinated between local firms. Fourth, LEB investment was to be a lever for better wages and condi-tions, industrial democracy, and equal opportunities; these were expected to increase productivity and quality and tap workers' inven-tiveness 'Japanese style'.

In the early 1980s, following considerable industrial investment by Labour authorities in the 1970s, LEBs with this kind of strategy were set up in Greater London, the West Midlands, West Yorkshire, Merseyside and Lancashire; these later spawned District Council level Boards. They were largely dependent on property powers and section 137 money. Most of the Boards were composed solely of councillors from the funding authorities. Autonomous boards may have been necessary to avoid legal restrictions; but they also facilitated maintenance of commercial confidentiality, recycling of profits, and an image acceptable to business.

The core activity of the Boards has been equity and loan funding to medium-sized firms (50–500 employees) in manufacturing, non-financial producer services and – sometimes – consumer services. They have invested only in firms which have been unable to raise funding privately, but they nonetheless sought relatively safe returns on their investments, both to recycle their own funds and to show the financial institutions the profitable investment opportunities they are missing. This has generally meant a 2–3 year payback period on loans at near-market rates of interest, a target of few failures, and a 1:3 to 1:5

leverage of private investment (CLES, 1987a). However, a large part of the Boards' activity has been in providing an infrastructure to business: funding for small firms and cooperatives, speculative industrial property development, consultancy, publication of regional economic data, technology transfer, and training. Up to 1986 they received a total of £92m from their sponsoring authorities, £44m of which was invested in enterprises employing a total of 14 000 people (ibid.).

The Boards have promoted strategic planning, using legally binding agreements to adhere to the business plan, or non-executive directors who may have overriding votes if the agreement is broken. Investments are made according to sectoral strategies, which have been promoted through discussion forums involving management and unions. In a few cases, such as the London furniture sector and the West Midlands foundries, the Boards attempted a reorganisation of the local sector as a whole, reallocating and cutting product areas and capacity between firms.

The benefits for labour sought by the Boards have varied widely. In all cases funded firms have had to agree to certain basic conditions: the right to join a union, compliance with employment legislation, wages and conditions not inferior to those prevalent in the local sector, and sometimes equal opportunities practices. The London and Merseyside Boards required enterprises to commit themselves to 'Enterprise Planning', that is, to reach agreement with the workforce on their business plans, including investment, products and marketing. The Boards have encouraged workers' share ownership; the Greater London Enterprise Board sponsored Workers' Trusts – collective ownership of a block of shares by the workforce, while Yorkshire Enterprise encourages individual share ownership.

Since the mid-1980s the Boards have become more commercial. The immediate reasons were the costs of supporting loss making firms through their restructuring and the loss of local authority funding. This forced the Boards to act as venture capital agents, using funds from the clearing banks and pension funds managed by committees of financial sector executives, and operating on a regional rather than county level.

The success of the Boards in attracting institutional funds would seem to indicate that they have indeed located a funding gap. Moreover, according to Brunskill and Minns (1989), the growth of private-sector regional venture capital funds has been led by the LEBs. The Boards have shown, not so much that there are *ready made* investments which the private sector has previously missed, but rather that these investment opportunities can be *created* if the funding body plays an active role with new forms of finance, support and strategy. The argument of the Right and Centre against industrial intervention, that the state cannot guess the market better than investors, misses the point that, with its resources and coordination, it can construct new market opportunities.

Nevertheless, one should not exaggerate what has so far been demonstrated. Total LEB investment is still minute compared with overall manufacturing investment in their regions. Much of the Boards' investment has been in the conventional areas of property, small firms and, as with private venture capital funds, in buyouts. It is only the equity element of enterprise funding which breaks the mould of traditional British financing. Thus, contrary to what is sometimes claimed (Brunskill and Minns, 1989), the implications of the LEBs' experience for the practice of British finance are not clear.

Strategic planning, while it has exceeded that done by conventional British financial institutions, has been uneven and limited. This is partly because the funds have been too small to restructure whole local sectors: just one could absorb the whole annual funding. Funding according to strategic and holistic considerations often means more involvement with weaker firms than in a reactive approach, and the Boards seek to avoid such high risk investment. From the perspective of the Boards, a crucial barrier to strategic planning is the quality and habits of managers, who are reluctant to undertake long term planning and to coordinate their investments across local sectors (Best, 1986). But, as we shall argue in Chapter 10, the quality of British management and its conservatism are embedded in a wider matrix of processes which are beyond the reach of the LEBs' present policies and powers.

Sectoral collective services and coordination

In local sectors containing many small firms, the Left has pursued an alternative to LEB investment: modernisation through providing services and stimulating synergy within the sector. These services can include stages of production whose minimum efficient scale is large, information on final and input markets, technical research, marketing facilities, serviced property tailored to the sector, and training. The approach has been most fully developed in the Fashion Centres set up in Hackney, Birmingham, Coventry and Nottingham to serve the clothing and textile industries. It has also been used to develop a local sector more or less from scratch, as with the Glasgow Food Park and the cultural industries quarter in Sheffield. In contrast to modernisation through large integrated firms proposed in the manifestos of the 1964 and 1974 Labour governments, modernisation is here to take place through local integration of small firms.

The underlying strategy has been the revival of the 'industrial district', a fragmented local sector within which there are strong linkages, including subcontracting, a pool of appropriate skilled labour, means for workers to set up as entrepreneurs, local banks with a commitment to the industry, and circulation of sectoral knowledge (Marshall, 1961). It has been argued that an industrial district offers greatest benefits when it follows a strategy of 'flexible specialisation', often-cited examples being in the Third Italy and Baden-Württemberg. Firms specialise in a particular product niche, thus avoiding pure price competition; they also specialise in stages of production, resulting in dense links between local firms. Production is flexible with respect to product design through using task-flexible skilled labour and, recently, computer-aided production equipment, allowing rapid response to changes in demand. This strategy is strengthened if there is a business culture of quality competition which prevents destructive cost-cutting, encourages firms to train, and creates productive industrial relations.

This version of the industrial district is an appealing realisation of the Bootstraps strategy. The strong linkages and business culture tie the sector to the locality, compensate for the weaknesses of small firms, and provide a cohesion which balances, yet stimulates, enterprise. In fragmented sectors producing consumer goods such as clothing and furniture sold to large retailers, a strong industrial district can prevent the retailers from shifting their purchases from one firm and area to another and pushing the sector into destructive cost competition; in Bootstraps fashion, it strengthens the small and local against the large and national. Moreover, it is to the benefit of labour as well as capital: the strategy promises high skill, high wage jobs funded by the profits of technological and design innovation.

This approach is seen as offering a way out of the poor traditions of British manufacturing, which the undirected subsidies of the Centre may merely perpetuate. In fragmented industries it is also seen as a better strategy than direct strategic investment in individual firms by LEBs since the benefits are spread across the whole sector. Collective services can promote a collaborative business culture in the local industry, and thus prevent the better firms being dragged down by the worse. Moreover, the supervision practised by LEBs inhibits the entrepreneurial style of small firms; collective services are an enabling but non-bureaucratic policy.

A central question is the extent to which contemporary trends lend themselves to the formation of industrial districts and to the flexible specialisation strategy: we examine this in Chapter 5. A second question concerns how to create such a district. If, as is so often the case in Britain, the starting point is a local sector dominated by uncollaborative, non-innovative, cost cutting firms, then unselective provision of services may actually sustain them in these habits. It may therefore be necessary to provide services only to the better-run firms as, for example was, the policy of the Hackney Fashion Centre; but this is politically difficult, and can leave the facility with too few clients. Alternatively, firms may not take up the services, or may be unwilling to contribute to their cost: the 'hands-off' strategy may be insufficient to shift them towards a new set of interdependent practices. The Hackney Fashion Centre was closed in 1986 largely because of these problems; the other Fashion Centres have tended to become unselective and reactive.

Using the law to combat discrimination and sweating

The Left sought to clamp down on low productivity firms, low wages and discrimination, as both a modernising policy and a way to support the worst exploited workers. This was pursued through training initiatives and voluntary agreements with employers on positive action, and through support to workers' organisation (see below). It was also pursued through attempting to enforce employment legislation, an approach we examine here.

One method is contract compliance, in which the local authority makes its suppliers and commercial tenants comply with certain minimum standards in employment. This uses a traditional activity of local government for economic ends, and the size of the 'stick' that can be wielded is large: in 1989/90 local authorities in England purchased around £18bn of goods and services from the private sector. Contract compliance has a long history: 'good employer' clauses in central government contracts were introduced in the 1900s. Local authorities are however statutorily required to trade according to market criteria and are therefore only able to insist that firms meet legal requirements. This has ruled out favouring unionised firms, or using purchasing to back up

LEBs' initiatives. The main use of contract compliance has been to promote equal opportunities. The Sex Discrimination Act and the Race Relations Act allow local authorities to refuse to trade with discriminatory firms; this includes *de facto* discrimination arising from social disadvantage, enabling insistence on positive action programmes. Contract compliance has also been used to attempt to enforce the Health and Safety Act and to oppose 'the lump' in the building industry. A few authorities have attempted to use it to ensure payment of 'fair wages', but this has been possible only in the few surviving Wages Council industries. The policy can have considerable effect: the GLC, which carried out the most ambitious policy to date over a three year period, investigated 274 of its suppliers, of which 50 per cent were persuaded to change their employment procedures and 8 per cent had their contracts terminated (Smith and Carr, 1986). The difficulties are indicated by the fact that 12 per cent of non-building suppliers investigated refused to comply but were not cut off; weaknesses of the policy are discussed in Chapter 8.

Left authorities have supported campaigns to inform workers (including homeworkers) in sweated industries of their legal rights and have helped to enforce them. A central problem has been the immigration laws, under which many sweated workers are illegal residents and are therefore powerless against their employer. Another difficulty has been the low threshold for income tax: many low paid workers collude with employers in working off the cards in order to avoid tax, preventing them from using any of their legal rights. Moreover, there is a danger that the firm will go out of business if it operates legally. Thus a union campaign in the early 1980s to get the regulatory authorities, including the Inland Revenue, to clamp down on the London clothing industry incurred the opposition not only of the employers but also of most of the workforce. Without changes in income tax, immigration law, and in some cases sectoral profitability, employment law is a weak instrument in the sweated industries.

Socially responsible production

The Left has promoted different types of production from those chosen by the private sector, notably community-based use of land, 'socially useful products', and human-centred production processes. It supported campaigns against the encroachment of high rent uses, particularly offices and high income housing, into inner city areas previously dominated by manual workplaces and working class housing. These were in the tradition of the campaigns of the 1960s and early 1970s except that they put greater emphasis on manual employment. The GLC declared 'Community Areas' adjacent to the central business district, attempted to use its land use planning and land acquisition powers to protect low rent uses from displacement by offices, and assisted in campaigns. This policy had few successes. The Conservative government overruled development control decisions on appeal, and transferred local authorities' powers and land to UDCs. The price of land often prevented its purchase by the local authority, and when thwarted, developers used the lever of blight. From the mid-1980s, community campaigns in these areas have taken developers' and UDCs' choices of land use as unstoppable, and have sought to negotiate jobs for local people in the new industries.

The Left took initiatives to promote the design and/or production of goods which meet human needs and to oppose harmful ones. First, it gave support to campaigns directed at large producers: conversion from arms production, against nuclear power, and for the building of combined heat and power stations. This was inspired by the campaign of the shop stewards at Lucas Aerospace in the 1970s for the company to produce technically advanced, socially useful products in place of armaments. Second, the Left authorities provided resources for R&D and production of new products. A national 'bank' of such products was set up. The GLC set up Technology Networks, based on serviced premises, which aimed to network progressive technologists, local workers and consumers. Third, the LEBs supported production of useful low tech goods and services which were inadequately supplied because of blockages in production: services to lighten women's domestic work including nurseries, laundries and corner shops (GLC, 1985a, pp. 19–24), minority ethnic products, wholefoods, alternative culture, and community printers.

One of the remits of the Technology Networks was to promote machinery which makes greater use of workers' skills and discretion, such as a human-centred lathe and the Utopia project of the Swedish printing unions to develop newspaper typesetting equipment to combat deskilling. The hope was to promote work which was of high productivity *and* within which workers could have high skill and a corresponding degree of control. In the late 1980s the development of alternative products and processes continued only when they promised to be profitable in the short term or were commissioned by a public sector buyer; the anti-capitalist aspiration had disappeared.

Supporting workers' organisation locally

The Left authorities gave considerable support to workers' organisation. Assistance was given to international organisation in multinationals
and to workers faced with closures. But the major form of support was
to area-based organisations which had emerged in the 1970s to give
support to weakly organised workers, particularly in fragmented sectors:
the local ambit is essential here. Resources were given for information
on employment rights and to encourage unionisation; for homeworking
projects, where organisation has to be area rather than firm-based;
for women's employment projects concerned with childcare, training,
sexual harassment and entry into traditionally male trades; for organisations of black, migrant, lesbian and gay workers; and for local Trade
Union Resource Units (Mackintosh and Wainwright, 1987, chs 5, 10,
14).

These resources were welcome at a time when workers and unions
were under severe pressure. They played a major role in some innovative forms of organisation such as the multinational meetings and homeworker organisations. Nevertheless, this support was not unproblematic.
First, oppressed groups are not politically homogeneous, and choices
have to be made about which organisations to support. In the unions the
leaderships tend to be happier with aid to weakly organised workers
than to stewards with a strong base with whom they are often in conflict
(ibid, pp. 265–9, 270–1). There have also been policy differences with
the funded organisation; the GLC had dilemmas in funding some organisations whose practices it saw as discriminatory (ibid, pp. 129, 273–5,
319). Aid was thus not merely 'enabling' but directive. The Left's aim of
diffusing power to the people is limited by the pressures on an elected
authority to take responsibility for the uses to which its money is put.

A second problem is that publicly funded organisations can become
an alternative to collective activity. Public funding has in fact shifted in
this direction, to centres for information on employment rights and to
neighbourhood groups which play a lobbying role; there is neglible
support for collective organisation against employers.

The heritage of the Left

One of the two elements of the Left strategy, to strengthen the power of
labour irrespective of the impact on capital, had all but disappeared by
the late 1980s. This was partly due to attacks by the government, partly

to the general shift to the right in the labour movement; national unions and the TUC (1988) gave no support to the Left strategy. But it was also due to the internal problems of the policies, some of which we have mentioned and which are discussed further in Chapter 8. At the end of the 1980s the Left strategy was found only in isolated cases such as Swindon (Basset *et al.*, 1989) – significantly, a prosperous town.

Given these problems, Left initiatives in radical localities like Sheffield had the effect of legitimating local authority support for business, and laying the basis for explicitly pro-business policies (Cochrane, 1991). Some of the institutions pioneered by the Left, such as the LEBs, Fashion Centres and Technology Networks, survived; these now pursue, unadulterated, the modernisation strand of the Left's strategy. As we shall see, this can be compatible with the strategy of the Centre, and these institutions have now been integrated into the consensus.

Further reading

For guides to policy formation see Johnstone *et al.* (1988) and the CLES Information Briefings. The DoE publishes a series of best-practice guides, and the Local Government Training Board produces distance-training packages. There are numerous studies of economic policy in particular localities; book collections are Hausner (1987b), Harloe *et al.* (1990) and Judd and Parkinson (1990). The Right's approach to urban policy is set out in Banfield (1974), and its local economic policy in Cabinet Office (1988), Mobbs (1987), and successive addresses of Conservative Environment Ministers to the summer school of the Royal Town Planning Institute (reported in *The Planner*). Reviews of Conservative policies, with critiques from the Centre and Left, are Haughton and Roberts (1990) on centralisation, Hegarty (1988) on inner city funding, Barnekov *et al.* (1989) on privatisation, Thornley (1991) on land use planning, Boyle (1985) on leveraged subsidies, Green (1991) on EZs, and Colenutt and Tansley (1990) on the UDCs (for training see Chapter 4). The DoE has published evaluations of its main economic programmes.

The Left strategy is set out in GLC (1985a, Introduction), Ward (n.d.), Mawson and Miller (1986), and Keith and Rogers (1991); on the US Left see Davis *et al.* (1989). The productivist left critique of the Centre-Right is set out in Fine and Harris (1985) and, in urban context, Miller and Tomaskovic-Devey (1983). Arguments for locally rooted worker democracy within a productivist approach are Bye and Beattie (1982) and Hodgson (1984). The 1970s Alternative Economic Strategy which was the starting-point for the productivist Left was set out in London Conference of Socialist Economists Group (1980), and recently developed in Costello *et al.* (1989); the class struggle approach is argued for in Coventry *et al.* Trades Councils (1980). Wainwright and Elliot (1982) argue for workers' plans, and these are developed as a local/regional policy in Cooke (1984). Elkin *et al.* (1991) give a Green Left local strategy.

GLC (1985a) contains sectoral strategies from both strands of the Left; for the productivist view see Blackburn and Sharpe (1988), Hirst and Zeitlin (1989) and Best (1990), and for the class-struggle approach see Furniture, Timber and Allied Trade Union (1986) and Gough (1986b). For the debate between these approaches see Best (1986) and Gough (1986a), with reference to clothing, GLC (1985b), and with reference to cable and telecoms Hughes and McCarthy (1983) and Robins (1983). On the promise of the revived industrial district see Piore and Sabel (1984) and Scott (1988); on flexibly specialised districts see Brusco (1980) and Totterdill (1990a). For the local productivist strategy towards finance, see GLC (1986b) and Brunskill and Minns (1989), criticised from the left by Murray (1983a). GLC (1986a) is a Left strategy for labour markets and working conditions; on black employment see also Centre for Local Economic Studies Black Employment Group (1987) and on women's employment Stubbs and Wheelock (1990). Mole and Elliot (1987) give a local strategy for socially useful production.

4 The Centrist Mainstream

The mainstream approach to local economic initiatives seeks to combine policies for increased growth and competitiveness with policies for redistributing their benefits. Like the Right, the Centre sees markets, profit and individual enterprise as the basis of a dynamic economy; but unlike the Right, it sees them as sometimes in need of steering, direction or support in order to deliver high growth. The Centre shares parts of the critique of British capitalism's short termism put forward by the modernising Left (p. 75), but does not envisage a wholesale, comprehensive reform of its structures. The market is also seen as inadequate in distributing income and jobs, and intervention is needed to combat poverty and marginalisation providing this does not conflict with competitiveness.

Unlike the Right, the Centre seeks to enhance the cohesion of localities, in the sense of cooperative relations between different social groups, productive linkages, and the interdependence of production and consumption. This approach requires pragmatic, undoctrinaire policymaking, which can balance the claims of different groups. Increasing competitiveness will help the disadvantaged, but only if measures are taken to ensure a 'trickle down' of jobs to the most needy. Conversely, the unemployed are a wasted resource which, if mobilised, can help to revive the local economy. The balance between these aims has evolved from providing aid to business, to helping the victims of the early 1980s recession, to the current emphasis on training, infrastructure and balanced development.

Again in contrast to the Right, local authorities have a central, though not exclusive, role in this strategy, and the Centre supports greater powers, funding and autonomy for their economic initiatives. The Centre's conception of 'partnership', as balanced collaboration of public, private and voluntary sectors, evokes a softer alternative to the military language of the Right – 'Task Forces', 'Flagships', 'Missions', 'Targeting', 'Challenge' (Turkie, 1991, p. 42).

This is the mainstream of local economic policy, and has been pursued by most Labour local authorities, by the centre parties, by some

87

Conservative councils, by most of the private-sector-backed organisations such as the Enterprise Agencies and Business in the Community,
and by the voluntary sector. Even councils on both right and left of the
political spectrum have carried out some of these policies. Emblematic
is the support for the Centre strategy of the Church of England
(Archbishop of Canterbury, 1985) and Prince Charles, patron of Business in the Community, who take the national unity symbolised in the
Church and the monarchy down to the local level.

The combination of aims in Centre strategy produces dilemmas.
Should support be given to sectors with the greatest competitive potential or those providing jobs to the disadvantaged? Is it enough to
improve the access of the unemployed to jobs through training or
information, or do firms need to change their practices too? If so, what
degree of leverage over firms is possible without antagonising them?
Under what circumstances can market forces benefit the disadvantaged?
As we shall now see in examining the main policies of the Centre, these
sorts of questions have produced much variation and experimentation.

Small firm support

The Centre argues that the Right's verbal support for small firms is
contradicted by its broad economic policies, and that it gives insufficient
aid. The Centre's strategy, shared by most local authorities and private
sector initiatives like the Enterprise Agencies, is to provide non-
directive support in fields where small firms are thought to be weak, and
to improve the supply of inputs. In the mid-1980s, the most popular
policy of the local authorities was provision of software – advice,
information and management training, followed by help with land and
premises, finance, and marketing (Sellgren, 1987).

Local policies are constructed around the unselective national
schemes such as the Loan Guarantee Scheme, the Business Expansion
Scheme, the Enterprise Allowance, the Enterprise Initiative and Business Growth Training. Local agencies help firms to take up these
schemes and combine them with other forms of support, and sometimes
strengthen the central government schemes.

Policies for software address lack of management skills, a 'management gap' which may be as significant a barrier to growth of small firms
as the more celebrated 'funding gap' (Caves, 1980); certainly one important reason for failures to secure funding is the lack of a long term firm
strategy (Advisory Council on Science and Technology, 1990, p. 31).

Some local agencies have found that approaches to them for finance or premises were really for management consultancy (Allan *et al.*, 1985). Small firm support centres provide advice on finance, grants, premises, markets and suppliers, and training in the preparation of business plans, risk assessment, market research, and legal and tax matters; some provide fully fledged consultancy. The Enterprise Agencies channel the managerial expertise of large firms to local small firms via secondments.

Local policy has seen finance as one of the major problems of small firms. They are more dependent on bank loans than large firms are; the clearing banks are said to be excessively cautious in funding them, requiring fixed assets as collateral and a low-risk business plan, and only making short term loans. The collateral requirements particularly disadvantage working class and women entrepreneurs. Contrary to this view, a series of reports have exonerated the banks of short-termism, and have placed the blame for the low investment rate in Britain on the poor profitability of industrial firms and/or their aversion to investment (Wilson Committee, 1980). Critics of British banking have also focused on its national, indeed international, centralisation as compared, for example, with the US banking system where banks have to invest in the State in which deposits are taken; this centralisation is seen as discriminating against areas with weak economies, as preventing an intimate relationship developing between banks and local sectors, and as inhibiting local discretion in lending (Brunskill and Minns, 1989, p. 297). Thus Collinge (1983, p. 13) has argued that 'a region's economic problems probably begin when it loses control of its local financial institutions'.

Lending to small firms certainly eased during the 1980s. The clearing banks, after getting their fingers burnt with Third World debt, turned to domestic small firms as an outlet for funds for which there were too few other profitable investment avenues. This was reinforced by the government's Loan Guarantee Scheme and by varied local-authority funding policies. These have included loan guarantees, unsecured loans, top-up loans in which the authority has second charge and often a major share of the risk, rent and rate rebates, wage subsidies, and start-up grants. Local authorities have provided rescue funding, sometimes making loans conditional on other parties increasing their lending. Some funding schemes concentrate on functions that small firms have particular difficulty with, such as marketing, new technology, training, management consultancy, and property. In depressed economies, local authorities have organised financial networks to support local firms unable to get bank support through coupling public finance with other sources, such as a fund set up by S.G. Warburg in Hackney.

During the mid-1980s expansion, these developments made it considerably easier for entrepreneurs, including ones from disadvantaged groups and ones with little collateral, to obtain loan funding (Mason and Harrison, 1991, p. 2). However, the banks had not been persuaded to make a fundamental change in their approach. They did not move into equity funding, as in Germany; loans remained short term; the banks continued to charge a substantial premium on interest rates to small firms, exacerbating the high interest rates obtaining in Britain; and they did not develop active strategies for local sectors or a greater engagement with firms' business planning.

There has been a growth of sources of equity funding as venture capital funds and a wider financial infrastructure have emerged in some regional centres. However, many of these are subsidiaries of City firms with very limited autonomy, and the regions are still losing key decision making functions; decision making may also be becoming concentrated in the regional centres at the expense of other cities and towns (Gibbs *et al.*, 1989). Moreover, the venture capital funds concentrate on medium sized firms, high tech high flyers and management buyouts; they usually require a large proportion of the firm's equity in relation to the capital injected and expect high, immediate returns. Thus there still remains a gap in equity funding for start-ups and young firms. The Centre wishes further to develop small firm funding with new markets and institutional arrangements. Informal capital markets have been mooted in imitation of the 'business angels' in the USA who provide the bulk of equity for start-ups (Mason and Harrison, 1991). Small firms are encouraged to enter relationships with larger ones, for instance through 'corporate venturing' (p. 105), which can provide them with technological support and markets as well as finance.

Funding policy illustrates the evolution of Centre strategy during the 1980s towards creating a local business infrastructure which can sustain small firms rather than giving them individual help, and which would supply the services that large firms internalise. Information networks have been fostered, particularly for technical information, and many local agencies have introduced services to strengthen marketing which has been argued to be a central failing of British industry (Williams *et al*, 1983, pp. 47–58). Provision of small units has been a major part of the package. Reform of education to encourage the acquisition of skills and attitudes 'appropriate for employment' is seen as particularly significant for small firms given their difficulties in retaining skilled labour; it is also intended to change attitudes to small firm formation. The various services to small firms are being increasingly coordinated: One Stop Shops bring together all the advice services from different sources, while the Chambers of Commerce are currently planning to provide a comprehensive nationwide coverage of standard services.

Policies to increase local linkages have been introduced, partly to increase small firms' efficiency, partly to increase local demand and employment. Services to encourage local purchasing have evolved from directories to active 'marriage bureaux' linking large and small local firms, using data bases of large firms' requirements coupled with permanent exhibitions. Some local authorities have attempted, within a restrictive legal framework, to channel their purchasing to local firms and encourage large firms to do likewise.

Problems emerge

In its early stages, small firm policy was unselective: not only advice but funding was either given as of right, or was conditional on an acceptable business plan. Demand for assistance has been strong, and some studies have credited it with increasing start-ups and preventing failures (Robinson *et al.*, 1987). However, by the mid-1980s it was widely accepted that this approach had serious problems.

First, some unselective forms of financial aid such as rate relief appeared to have little effect (Townroe and Brenton, 1987). Second, many firms applying for aid did so as a last resort, and had multiple problems. Turok's study of small firm aid in Southwark (Turok, 1989, p. 605) found that financial aid was often rendered useless by poor management; in consequence, a third failed within seven years. Moreover, the help given to them was resented by their local competitors. Third, small firm formation did not provide the solution to the loss of industrial jobs; entrepreneurs remained predominantly middle class, white and male. The BSC Industry workshops in Scunthorpe, for instance, attracted very few ex-steel workers, and only one was involved in the eighty-five projects supported by the Business Advice Centre (Groom, 1985).

Fourth, few jobs were transferred into the area by small-firm support, and they could be dwarfed by one large closure; the 92 per cent of firms which have fewer than twenty employees account for under 20 per cent of employment. The growth record of small firms has been disappointing; even in the Cambridge high-tech sector, Saxenian (1989) found that three-quarters of the firms had fewer than thirty employees. Most owners are not motivated by economic aims, and very few are growth oriented (Gray, 1991). Finally, it was hard for agencies to gauge the effects of aid on their client firms, given the multiple influences on them and the dominant effect of demand and sectoral conditions; there have been many processes unconnected with any policy which could explain the small firm expansion of the 1980s (pp. 173–4). As the problems began to emerge this made it hard to justify small firm policies, particularly unselective support.

Behind these problems lie some fundamental features of small firms. The promise of small firms is that they are dynamic, innovative and flexible by virtue of being small. Yet their limited capital and lack of managerial resources tends to make them weaker in these respects than larger firms (GLC, 1983b). It limits their expenditure on training: 30 per cent of firms with fewer than ten employees carry out no training whatever, whereas this is true of only 3 per cent of firms with more than 200 employees. Although small firms play an important role in innovation in some sectors, their innovative capacity tends to be weakened by lack of capital and contact with key information networks (Oakey, 1984). In developing basic inventions into marketable innovations small firms' performance is greatly inferior to that of large firms (Freeman, 1971). Many copy their competitors' product and compete solely on the basis of cost or location; others are subcontractors who use designs supplied by the contractor with little or no input of their own; others are franchised or licensed by larger firms. Many small firms, then, are as lacking in 'higher level' functions as the worst branch plants; they cannot reap technical or design rents, tend to have a low rate of profit, and are consequently unstable.

Problems also often arise from the dynamics of sectors dominated by small firms. Most have low barriers to entry, exceptions being principally sectors with rapid innovation. Many firms operate with minimal capital, using suppliers' credit and renting premises and machines, producing a chronic tendency to sectoral overcapacity. This is especially so in times of stagnation when more people attempt to set up small businesses. A large part of the 'flexibility' of small firms consists in restless shifts between such low-barrier sectors. Unselective small firm promotion exacerbates this problem. It is not merely that each entrant encouraged displaces an existing firm: by increasing the tendency to overcapacity, prices and profits are lowered, reducing investment in fixed capital, training and innovation, and thus inhibiting the qualitative development of the sector as a whole; this in turn keeps the sector the domain of small, undercapitalised firms. Sectors like contract clothing and building have long suffered from this vicious circle.

Stagnation has increased the number of people setting up small businesses for lack of other employment opportunities. Mason (1990, quoted in Storey and Strange, 1991, p. 4) has found that 'positive considerations, notably market opportunities and technical innovation, have been much less prevalent amongst new firm founders in the 1980s [compared with the 1970s], whereas redundancy, insecure employment and the failure of previous business ventures have been much more prevalent'. The result was that start-ups in the 1980s were smaller and of lower quality, concentrated in low growth, locally marketed sectors with low barriers to entry – in Cleveland a quarter were in hairdressing and motor repair (Storey and Strange, 1991). Black small business in the USA also experienced an increase in quantity and deterioration in quality between the two decades (Oxford, 1987, p. 26). Increasing numbers of start-ups were offset by an increasing number of failures.

Jobs in small firms are of lower quality than those in large in terms of wages, conditions of work and terms of employment (Rainnie, 1989). This is partly due to their lower average productivity, as well as the cost competition in many fragmented sectors, to which management reacts by holding down wages and intensifying work. Ease of entry into these sectors and lack of distinctions between firms can lead to a high degree of instability in each firm's output and thus employment. Length of job tenure in small firms was half that of the large in 1983 (Leadbeater and Lloyd, 1987, p. 171). These problems are exacerbated by the patterns of industrial relations in small firms. Some owner-managers build up commitment from the workforce using the personal contact absent in larger firms. But this personal mode of management can make workers subject to managers' whims without the mediation of formal rules, a problem compounded by the difficulty of organising unions in small enterprises (Rainnie, 1989). Unselective support for them thus conflicts with improving working conditions and combating poverty.

These industrial relations in turn affect small firms' productivity. Poor jobs and a dictatorial management style can weaken workers' commitment; high labour turnover produces a failure to accumulate experience. (As we see below, *these* problems of small business are substantially overcome in Third Sector small businesses.) Contrary to what is often said, the non-bureaucratic style of small firm industrial relations does not necessarily make them more productive.

The diversity of small firms makes the category a misleading one for policy making. While their size produces systematic problems, many are innovative, efficient and profitable. Policy makers should focus on the characteristics of the sector such as the barriers to entry, forms of competition, the nature of the innovation process, and the relations of power between firms. This indicates the need for targeting, and for small firm policies tailored to local conditions (Storey *et al.*, 1987).

Policy becomes more selective and strategic

In response to these problems, support for small firms has become more selective and strategic. First, attempts have been made to make financial assistance conditional on improvements in the firm's business strategy and on the setting of job targets. Second, aid has been more focused on firms thought to have higher chances of survival and growth, on established firms, on firms with better management, or on firms with proprietary products. There is an attempt to pick winners – the 4 per cent of start-ups that produce a third of the jobs (Storey *et al.*, 1987, p. 170). Third, there has been increasing targeting by sector using a variety of criteria: improving growth, job quality or local agglomeration economies; reducing volatility; or matching jobs with local skills, particularly those of the unemployed. Fourth, strategies have been set for specific classes of small firms, for example, the attempts of some Enterprise Agencies to move Afro-Carribean-owned firms out of ethnic products. Finally, special policies have been introduced to encourage small enterprise formation by manual workers and oppressed groups.

These changes have been accompanied by moves to reform the small firm aid agencies themselves. The early, unselective strategy produced a boom in these agencies, resulting in duplication. For the same reason, the quality of the aid given has in many cases been poor (Segal, Quince, Wicksteed, 1988). Lack of selection meant ever-increasing demand and expenditure. The corporate sponsors of the Enterprise Agencies did not expect to be subsidising them indefinitely, nor by so much, particularly with decreasing funding by local authorities. The institutional framework is consequently beginning to be rationalised: Mentor, for instance, has been set up to coordinate the nine Enterprise Agencies on Merseyside!

These shifts in strategy and implementation have created new dilemmas:

• The degree of intervention becomes problematic. The provision of workspace, for example, has been found to be inadequate by itself: management training and information have often been added, and other services can usefully be supplied.

• The attempt to address the multiple weaknesses of many small firms, especially those in crisis, has pushed policy into deep water. To improve management, shape a new business plan, ensure job quality, and monitor loans requires a hands-on approach, and a degree of control by the support agency that verges on the approach of the LEBs – far more interventionist than the Centre had intended.

● The delivery of aid to small firms remains structured by function: funding, property, new technology, and so on. But the effects of enhancing these functions may miss or even contradict the agency's strategic goals; new process technology, for example, may either widen the product range or shed jobs. The delivery of aid to each function therefore needs to be skewed towards the agency's aims (Turok and Wannop, 1989); again, a major strategic shift.

● Though support for start-ups remains popular, a recognition that they are not a solution to unemployment and a desire to lower the failure rate have shifted the emphasis towards established firms (Advisory Council on Science and Technology, 1990, p. 25). This produces dilemmas about the stage at which to intervene – expansion, diversification, launch into international markets, and so on.

● Targeting policy at particular sectors raises new problems. There are multiple criteria for choosing sectors; some of these have been touched upon in Chapter 2, others are discussed in Chapter 5. Having decided the sector, aid may be delivered firm-by-firm or as services to the sector as a whole. The latter approach avoids the difficulties of choosing good management and influencing individual business strategies; but as we have seen (p. 81), it has its own problems.

These dilemmas point to a strategic problem. To make choices local agencies need to acquire more knowledge of the local economy, of competitive strategies, the labour market and local multipliers. They are compelled to specify the goals which govern their selection; bland goals are no longer enough. They have to find ways of influencing firm's strategies. This represents a significant shift for the Centre. Early policy had centred on the removal of restrictions on small firms and mild measures to stimulate them. But the more interventionist policy implies that enterprise does not simply flower when obstacles are removed; on the contrary, it needs extensive support. This questions the previous ideology of 'enterprise' as an absence of restraint and as individual; it now appears as dependent on social support and political choice. Rather than grasp this nettle, the Centre may weaken its commitment to the small-firm strategy and hope that the recent changes in private sector funding will sustain it. This strategic dilemma is examined further in Chapter 10.

A second strategic problem is that the evolution of small firm policy creates a bifurcation between support for mainstream, commercial firms and support for enterprises of the disadvantaged. The earlier integrated strategy in which small firm support would not only be commercial but also solve welfare problems has unravelled. (Other problems of small firm policy are discussed in Chapters 5 and 7.)

The new entrepreneurs

The Centre has attempted to widen participation in enterprise in three ways: through helping members of oppressed groups to set up conventional small businesses; by supporting non-commercial enterprises; and through promoting enterprise, particularly among young people. We examine these in turn.

Small business for disadvantaged groups

Specific facilities have been set up to promote small business formation by black people, by women, and by the long term unemployed. They attempt to circumvent the barriers caused by lack of capital, confidence, technical and business expertise, by discrimination, and by domestic responsibilities. Some mainstream small firm agencies have been active, sometimes using special funding from the Home Office for black business development, or specific programmes of local authorities or the EC. There are also centres for particular consituencies, including alternative enterprise agencies, innovation centres and property based community projects. Over time these centres have built up services such as managed workspaces, incubator units, business services, crèches, and technical, business and personal skills training.

Training schemes, too, can provide experience useful for enterprise formation. The Conservatives, however, prevented the use of MSC funding for starting commercial enterprises because of competition with the private sector. Trainees on the Community Programme, for instance, were able to run businesses but could not retain earnings or move on to the Enterprise Allowance. Numerous local schemes were set up to remedy this, sometimes managing to tap smaller MSC programmes such as the Information Technology Centres or the Training Workshops, but also using other sources such as the European Social Fund (McArthur and McGregor, 1987, pp. 147ff).

The Third Sector

Cooperatives and community businesses (p. 33) promise to spread enterprise to the most deprived areas. They can be seen as part of a wider

Third Sector, alongside consumption initiatives like credit unions and housing associations, which attempts a more balanced form of development than the market, reconciling economic viability with social goals. There is a wide range of organisational forms, reflecting a divergence between enterprises motivated by the sector's liberatory potential and those supported as a means of job creation. Thus community businesses recycle profits within the locality and have representatives of the community on the management committee, while cooperatives retain their surpluses within the business. Similarly, while the whole sector tends to concentrate on socially useful production, the cooperatives operate more strongly in the market. The sector as a whole, however, is a cushioned path to entrepreneurship, heavily reliant on external support.

The Third Sector grew rapidly in the inner cities of the USA following the black uprisings of the late 1960s. In Berlin the sector has grown as a political project of non-exploitation of people and the environment, and now comprises hundreds of enterprises and projects with strong mutual links. In Southern Europe cooperatives are part of mainstream business.

In Britain there has been strong growth of the movement following legislation in the late 1970s. It nonetheless remains small, developing principally in the cities where it has been supported by local authority funded Cooperative Development Agencies. The Scottish Development Agency has played an important role in funding community businesses, which by 1987 had grown to 126 firms and 3700 jobs and which have coalesced politically to become a movement for empowerment (Herrmann and Ward, 1989, p. 159). Reflecting the consensus around the sector, the initiators and backers of community enterprise are diverse, including voluntary agencies, unions, tenants' associations, community resource centres, the MSC, the banks and private sector, as well as the Development Agencies and local authorities.

The Third Sector is more stable than conventional small firms (pp. 33–4), and its record outside Britain, particularly in the rescue cooperatives, compares favourably with other forms of job creation (Paton, 1989, p. 156). However, even more than conventional small business, Third Sector enterprises tend to be confined to labour intensive, low innovation and overcrowded sectors, due to undercapitalisation and lack of technical and managerial expertise. The pressures for self-exploitation are therefore intense. Moreover, their ownership form leads to inflexibility: they cannot be taken over or take over, they cannot easily diversify by setting up new plants, nor can they relocate outside the travel-to-work area of the participants. In these respects they are constrained compared with both the private sector and publicly owned enterprises. These rigidities are experienced most sharply by the more commercially successful cooperatives, and often result in their conversion into conventional businesses. Similarly, the more commercial community businesses experience conflict between their need for growth investment and the recycling of their profits to the community (Jacobs, 1986).

While interest in cooperatives has recently been sustained by privatisation of council services and continuing subcontracting by large firms (Edwards, 1991), the sector does not appear to be as popular as it was a decade ago. It has not become large enough to benefit from internal trading, and has been weakened by the financial squeeze on support agencies.

Youth enterprise

As the Jesuits might have advised, the social group which has been most subjected to stimulation of enterprise is youth. This policy was pioneered in Britain, reflecting the high rate of youth unemployment and the failure of government training programmes to deal with it. Some initiatives have been directed at academically successful youth in order to divert them from the professions into business. The main target group, however, has been youth from manual working class backgrounds in depressed localities; in Cleveland in the late-1980s there were a hundred organisations devoted to youth enterprise (MacDonald, 1991). Enterprise training is given a broad interpretation, to include management of personal and social, as well as economic, life. It aims to instill self-reliance as much as skills, in order to deal with uncertainty, rapid change, and a situation where having a job is no longer the norm; it is as much about living with unemployment and survival as with getting a job or setting up a business. Once again, local economic initiatives combine economic and social goals.

Youth enterprise initiatives are run by diverse organisations with a network of overlapping projects, including the DTI, a range of voluntary organisations both national and local, the universities, local government, schools, most of the training organisations, and a handful of multinational firms; the MSC in the 1980s introduced a strong enterprise and self-employment component into youth training. The network extends to many local economic agencies such as job creation initiatives and workspace providers. Some national youth enterprise organisations are the result of longstanding youth organisations taking up enterprise;

others are funded by business. The young entrepreneur can obtain a grant from the Prince's Fund or the Shell Enterprise Fund, enter a competition organised by Livewire, and exhibit their product at BiC's 'Work For Yourself' fair. Such has been the growth of youth enterprise that local and regional bodies are emerging to coordinate and initiate schemes, as well as acting as local agents for national schemes. Projects often started in particularly acute local conditions and then spread nationally; Project Enterprise, for example, was started by BSC's closure programme. The political consensus around youth enterprise is striking.

Within many secondary schools, training for self-employment has been incorporated into the curriculum, with businesses run in the schools under schemes such as the central government Schools Council Industry project. In Young Enterprise teenagers run their own businesses producing and selling goods in the premises of sponsoring firms. Outside school, projects are tailored to particular groups: Project Fullemploy, for example, is aimed at those with a poor educational record. There is considerable overlap with the rapidly increasing work experience programmes; the balance between enterprise and waged employment is varied with the state of the local labour market. The skill content varies from work with unskilled youth in community enterprises to support for young craft workers in design workshops. The level of support also varies: some schemes such as BAT's Into Business Project on Merseyside and the burgeoning Youth Enterprise Centres provide premises with flexible tenancies, finance, marketing, and technical assistance.

Policies for enterprise, then, show a strange convergence: while small firm policy has become increasingly directive, a sort of social work on firms, social work with disadvantaged clients directs them to form new enterprises. The competitiveness of the enterprises of the disadvantaged is a problem. Some support agencies acknowledge that their job is to help them to survive in the informal economy (Neary, 1989, p. 26). For most, business means 'a twilight world of hard work, low pay, casual labour and insecurity' (MacDonald, 1991, p. 2).

Property, physical infrastructure and area renovation

The Centre has developed an approach to property quite different from that of the Right. The built environment, by nature of its costliness, longevity, spatial interconnections and uniqueness, gives rise to innumerable market imperfections for both developers and users. The Centre attempts to address these in ways which facilitate development, enhance the competitiveness of users, improve the environment, and reduce disadvantage; these multiple aims have produced a high degree of consensus.

The first phase of local economic initiatives saw property and environment as the crucial constraints, particularly for small firms in inner cities. Policy centred on small industrial units, some serviced, and often conversions of large derelict industrial premises; there was strong demand for these, particularly for easy-in, easy-out tenancies aimed at start-ups. Over time a great variety emerged including really tiny units, different support services, such as secretarial, accounts, or showrooms, and premises for particular sectors or activities such as technology workshops. Property strategies thus became linked to other Centre policies for small firms, community business, technology, sectors and training, fostering small firm competitiveness while helping the disadvantaged. In characteristic Centre fashion, they aimed both to facilitate individual enterprise and to build agglomeration economies.

Small unit conversions were undertaken by the local authorities and the voluntary sector using grants, because developers were not interested in non-prime sites and non-prime tenants. However, when they were shown how profitable these activities were, developers entered the market, often through partnerships in which the local authority gives a favourable lease on prepared land or guarantees the return by taking a fixed rent lease; in exchange the local authority usually retains some control over lettings policy. During the 1980s the private sector became more innovative, particularly in niche sectors such as technology centres and serviced office villages. Large firms converted their redundant premises to small units, often with local authority support, thus showing their social conscience 'at 4 per cent'. This, then, has been a classic example of Centre policy, where the public and voluntary sectors, using subsidy, show the private sector the way, and then collaborate closely with it.

The Centre has also evolved particular approaches to the development of areas, from an acre to a whole neighbourhood. Private investment in difficult areas often requires collective action. While an area may have development potential, landowners are unwilling to invest individually because of dereliction, lack of infrastructure, and absence of agglomeration economies. The Centre approach, distinct from both Right and Left, is for a coordinating group, usually including the local authority, to take an active role through subsidy, cross-subsidy, overall planning and infrastructural investment, while leaving landownership and building to the private sector.

In Germany this approach has been used since the turn of the century in the Building and Renewal Exhibitions, in which central and local government work over a limited period with the private sector in areas which it would not tackle alone. The state concentrates its infrastructure spending and controls externalities, thus protecting the private sector's investment. This strategy has recently been adopted for a 40 mile stretch of the Ruhr, with the state working towards a high quality environment, cross-subsidised by the subsequent private investment inflow (Couch, 1991).

In Britain an early policy of this type was the Industrial Improvement Area, which since 1978 has been supported in designated areas by Inner Urban Area Act funds. They concentrate grants and loans for property improvements and environmental work in run-down industrial areas. Their aim is to maintain job numbers and bring private investment back by pump priming; while they often succeed in these aims, they are expensive, success typically requiring the addition of Urban Programme and small business initiatives within the area (Etherington, 1987). The idea has since been applied to commercial and retail areas.

The same principle is used in more complex and higher value developments in fringe central areas, where deindustrialisation has left dereliction but where new external economies can be gained. The characteristic Centre approach has been to coordinate development over as wide an area as possible so that the costs of infrastructure can be spread and cross-subsidies realised. These developments usually include a mix of industry, commerce, consumer services and housing, and often require extensive new transport infrastructure. In the 100 acre Nottingham Lace Market, a public–private development company is carrying out selective high rent developments which subsidise the council owned area and thus conserve the historic fabric for tourism and protect low rent manufacturing uses. This type of development helped to fuel the commercial property boom of the 1980s, as well as renewed interest in urban transport: in 1990 fifty local authorities were planning rapid transit systems.

Some of these developments have been carried out by utilities with large prime landholdings. Most have required local authority involvement, because of fragmented landownership and the need for infrastructure. Moreover, private investors have needed the confidence given by that involvement, while local authorities, with memories of the 1970s property boom, want greater control. Within this framework, there is room for variation in the balance between public and private interests. At Salford Quays, for example, the local authority both raised funds for the developer and bought the land. In contrast, some developers, with local authority cooperation, are willing to carry out the whole of a large area development because they use internal cross-subsidy and have the political leverage to buy land at its value in its existing use.

These developments are politically complex because of the large areas and long time-scale involved, the land assembly problems, the balance of uses, and the consequent local authority and resident pressure for planning gain. They have attracted a new type of developer: specialists such as Lovell and Regalian; non-profit developers like Urbed, often acting for the community; and privately-supported agencies such as Phoenix and British Urban Developments which are sponsored by building and property companies. These agencies provide the enterprise lacking in the property majors, while priding themselves on their sensitivity to communities. Indeed, the voluntary organisations have achieved a kind of legitimacy which both local government and the private sector have lost. As the head of Phoenix said, 'we can drive around the city with our "CD plates" because we do not represent any vested interest' (Duffy, 1987).

The 1980s saw inner area developments of unprecedented scale. These were a response to the destruction of manufacturing and utilities which cleared large tracts of land, a rapid shift of urban economies into business and consumer services, and the increasing spatial concentration of many services. The UDCs are organising some of these developments; but others are being run by local authority–private sector partnerships. These are in many ways similar to the post-war partnerships for city centre redevelopment (Marriot, 1967); as in those, the local authority sometimes provides a short term subsidy by taking an equity stake. But now the developer is usually a consortium of banks, financial institutions, construction and development companies, in order to raise the enormous capital required and, given the sometimes non-central locations, to reduce individual risk. Development takes place in stages and parcels over a long period; a contract and outline plan are agreed at the beginning and the developer then effectively acts as the planning authority. This model is another Centre alternative to the UDCs and EZs. Leeds is undertaking a programme of this kind in a partnership with Bovis and others, comprising multiple sites with a rolling five year plan, and including job creation, housing, public developments, social amenities and environmental improvement; the DoE seconded a civil servant to build the political bridges. Birmingham Heartlands, covering over 2000 acres and a population of 13 000, was seen as a model partnership, carried out through a company owned jointly by the council and five construction groups; however, insufficient central government support and declining private sector interest in the early 1990s' recession led to its being taken over as a UDC.

While property initiatives are attractive in letting local economic agencies avoid difficult decisions about which activities and firms to support, this is also their fundamental weakness (Wannop, 1986). For example, the retail giant BAT redeveloped its Bon Marché store in Brixton into small workshops, offices and shop units, ostensibly to benefit the local community; but the rent levels mean that it has been largely occupied by middle class entrepreneurs providing upmarket goods and services. Because of the high costs involved, 'success' in property policies tends to consist in filling buildings or areas; but to achieve the Centre's goals of increased competitiveness and welfare often requires a policy which goes beyond property.

Technology policy

Technological innovation and adoption have been central to competition throughout the history of capitalism, and the pace of technical change has tended to increase over time. The Centre and the Left put greater emphasis on technical change than the Right: whereas the Right sees competitiveness as proceeding through more perfect markets, the Centre emphasises the importance of the quasi-monopoly rents bestowed by technical lead – that is, market imperfections. Here again, there is the disagreement on cost versus quality competition (pp. 35–6). Moreover, in the Centre's view, technological dynamism is not merely an attribute of individual firms but of a web of economic, social and political institutions and practices. In the strongest version of this thesis, periods of world economic stagnation such as the past twenty years are due to a failure to construct the institutions and practices appropriate for the dominant new technologies (Freeman *et al.*, 1982).

Accordingly, the Centre identifies technological weakness as the central aspect of the British disease. Industry is weak in exploiting the results of basic scientific research, in producing and selling innovative products, and in adopting the best process technology. The continuing decline of R&D relative to GDP in the 1980s and its continued concentration on armaments are symptomatic.

This technological weakness is also seen as central to local economic problems. In its most simplistic form, the injection of any part of the electronics industry into the area is thought to give it technological dynamism (for a critique, see pp. 42, 131–2; Morgan, 1987). A more sophisticated view sees technological innovation and adoption in many regions to be limited by the internalisation of R&D and technical and managerial expertise in large firms, even where these are located within the region; by lack of ties between large firms, research establishments and universities on the one hand and local small firms on the other; by the increasing centralisation of higher technical work in the South, and by the consequent absence of an informational infrastructure and culture within other regions (Oakey, 1984; Malecki and Nijkamp, 1988). A characteristically Bootstraps strategy follows: to support innovation in smaller, locally controlled firms, to build up the internal knowledge interconnections within the locality, and, in so doing, to help disadvantaged groups to find a place in 'tomorrow's economy'.

In another of its inconsistencies, the Conservative government retained an essentially Centrist approach to technology policy (Freeman, 1987, p. 122). It continued support for innovation in advanced technologies, alongside European programmes. It operated a plethora of short term, small budget, sectoral schemes for technology diffusion, using grants for investment and consultancy. For the Centre, however, these policies are insufficient in scope and duration, and are unrelated to local conditions and networks.

Innovation Centres

Central to local technology initiatives have been the innovation centres (Leigh and North, 1986). These range from 3 to 100 employees, and are funded by national and local government and corporations. They undertake three types of activity:

- *Technological innovation* With the exception of the GLC's Technology Networks, local initiatives have not sponsored development of particular products due to the expense and risk. But the innovation centres have provided an infrastructure for product development: technical advice, workshop facilities, and information on grants and consultancy. Large firms too have started to support such infrastructure: ICI at Billingham has developed its own science park and gives firms access to its research facilities and personnel.

- *Technology transfer* The innovation centres help the transfer of product ideas to local small firms for them to manufacture and sometimes develop further. Some keep product banks and information on licensable technologies; others like ENTRUST in Tyne and Wear identify local firms which could exploit these innovations (Johnstone *et al.*, 1988, p. 54). Links between firms and local higher education institutions are strengthened by innovation centres acting as brokers; they also encourage large firms to license or jointly develop with small firms ideas which they do not wish to exploit. This parallels corporate venturing programmes, in which the corporation gives financial and technical support to innovation in small firms in exchange for equity or first refusal on innovations. This is mutually beneficial: the large firm can lever more research than it pays for, while avoiding the problems of managing knowledge producing workers.

• *Technology diffusion* Local initiatives also encourage adoption of the most advanced product and process technology. The centres act as network organisers, introducing clients to sources of finance, arranging technology audits, as well as acting as local agents for central government schemes; this support is generally sectorally specific. Another form of sectoral support is the provision of advanced machinery for use on a bureau basis where local firms are too small or backward to buy it themselves (p. 80).

Technology training

Many local agencies have seen training in technological skills as the key policy. Venture capitalists complain of the shortage of managers with the skills to handle potential projects, and innovation centres, science parks and Enterprise Agencies have set up training courses. Britain also suffers from a lack of technologists with intermediate level qualifications. While this training is largely supplied by local authority colleges, new initiatives have been taken to increase it, notably the Information Technology Centres which grew to 170 in number in the early 1980s. The ease with which their trainees obtained jobs in the 1980s indicated that there were indeed shortages. They are concentrated in inner cities, and the Centre hopes that they can thereby provide both a stimulus to national growth and high quality opportunities for disadvantaged groups. There are also schemes in prosperous areas; these are mostly run by central government with a low political profile because of their spatially regressive distribution (Davies and Mason, 1984). A third type of scheme provides basic IT skills such as electronic assembly.

Science parks

The science park has been a favourite method of fostering technological innovation and transfer; as with so many policies, its popularity has hidden vital differences in implementation (Massey *et al*, 1992). The original ones were for small firms to carry out the intermediate stages between research and production – testing of prototypes and experimentation with manufacturing techniques, and were built close to major higher education research facilities. Offspring like Hewlett Packard, Wang and Polaroid gave them promise as incubators of the giants of tomorrow. By the end of the 1970s there were only two dozen worldwide, but a decade later this had grown to several hundred.

A true science park is seldom profitable, since the building standard is high, rents need to be low, tenants are hard to find, and by definition they have a high turnover. They have therefore typically been developed through partnerships between local authorities, Development Agencies, higher education institutions and the private sector. The private sector has, however, successfully used the science park name to market business parks which cater for established firms. The dilution of the concept is indicated by the fact that in 1989 only 38 of the 53 self-styled science parks in Britain were recognised by their official body. The difficulty of obtaining public funding and financial pressures on higher education have led to hybrid developments on the model of the French Technopolises, in which the developers of business parks subsidise a science park and use it as advertising and as a sweetener for planning permission.

Even with adequate funding, real science parks are limited by their emphasis on property and proximity to institutions of higher education. There is typically little interaction between these institutions and firms in the science park (Oakey, 1991, p. 141). The fostering of innovation in new firms is a more complex process than the policy suggests. Indeed, science parks have increasingly added support services such as managerial training and venture capital funds, making them more like innovation centres. The usefulness of science parks to localities is limited since much technology transfer from them is non-local. For information-poor regions, innovation centres are a better model.

There are problems with the Centre's technology policy which go to the heart of its strategy; here we indicate the major issues, taking the discussion further in Parts III and IV.

First, the stage in an innovation's life at which a firm adopts it can be crucial. Often the first users experience problems and the second wave do better. Local agencies face the dilemma of whether to attempt to acquire sufficient knowledge to target sectors, technologies and even firms, on the LEB model, or to give unselective support with the danger of a large waste of resources and of being left behind.

Second, even for small firms much technology transfer and cooperation is not local but national and international, something that the EC is now encouraging. There is variation by sector; according to White (1988), medium technology, mature sectors are weakly integrated at the local level. Local agencies therefore need to assess which sectors or technologies have the greatest potential for local linkages (Chapter 5).

Third, the assets which technology policies create are spatially mobile. Newly trained labour, new innovative firms and technologically fast-changing firms are liable to migrate to technologically-rich regions. This points to another question: can every region be informationally rich (see pp. 132–7)?

Fourth, firms' difficulties with technological change go beyond the acquisition of knowledge and the availability of skills: they involve the organisation of the work process and its industrial relations. Yet the Centre's policy, in contrast to that of the Left, does not address this, but focuses narrowly on technology (see pp. 75–6, 252–4). Fifth, local technology policies generally do not directly create many new firms and jobs; their promise is, rather, that the innovative activity stimulated will snowball. But this requires the integrated development of technological capability across the whole local or regional economy: each aspect of technology policy – education, training, research, development, finance, links between institutions, production facilities, industrial relations, risk-taking – is related to the others within the area (Sabel *et al*, 1989). By this measure the Centre's technology programmes address an excessively narrow range of issues in each locality, in contrast, for example, to the Japanese new technology towns, the Technopolises (Fujita, 1988). The science park, in particular, falls far short, and consequently gives benefits only in the most information-rich localities like Cambridge. In contrast to France, local authorities have been excluded by the Conservative government from participating in the development of a key infrastructure, telecommunications (Hughes and McCarthey, 1983). Moreover, vital aspects of Britain's technological problems are national in scope. The local, regional, and national integration of technology policy is therefore a major problem (pp. 186–9).

Finally, following from the previous point, there are enormous problems in building a technological capacity in regions where it is weak. Malecki and Nijkamp (1988, p.385) have suggested that below a fairly high density of appropriate networks, no amount of enterprise policies will stimulate innovative small firms; yet without these the networks will not grow – a Catch 22 (p. 136).

Training, labour-market policy and equal opportunities

Local training and labour market policy has been dominated by the MSC and its successors with their neo-liberal strategy. The local authorities have been, more than in any other field, agents for central government schemes, with few powers to do more than implement national policy despite being the major providers of further and adult education. Even with the leaway they have, they generally respond passively to employers' and trainees' demands rather than develop a local training strategy. But local training agencies to a limited extent have been able to bend central government schemes towards their own aims, and have developed a significantly different approach to labour market policy.

Britain has the lowest rate of training of any OECD country, particularly in manual and technical skills. Both the causes and the effects of this remain controversial. For the Right, a low level of training may be appropriate for firms and workers. The best competitive strategies may be low skill, cost competitive ones, or skills may be learnt on the job. Even in the midst of skills shortages in 1990, employers ranked honesty and motivation top among the qualities they sought in workers, and training and education tenth and eleventh (Symonds, 1991). This raises the question, to which we return in Parts III and IV, of the role in productivity of managerial discipline and worker initiative rather than skill (pp. 152–3, 166, 253). At any rate, for the Right the choices over training should be made by individual firms and workers. Collective choices smear over differences in labour process strategies, tend to become inflexible in the face of technical and organisational change, and give workers undue power over definitions of skill.

The Centre contests this view. The stock of skilled labour in Britain is thought to present a major constraint on the economy. Employers report severe skills shortages throughout most of the business cycle, and cite these as affecting both quality and quantity of output. Some Centre commentators also criticise employers' strategies for their bias towards low skill cost-competition, explaining why employers sometimes give a low importance to skill. But for the Centre these backward strategies themselves are to a large extent a result of skilled labour shortages. More training is therefore needed, and this has to be collective given that employers tend to rely on poaching, particularly in short-termist

Britain. Employers should be compelled to train, as was the case with the Industrial Training Boards; but since local agencies do not have the powers to impose this, the Centre uses subsidies and persuasion.

For the Centre, a local level of action has been forced on it; but training ought anyway to be local, because skills are locally variable, because the competitiveness of a local economy depends crucially on its skills pool (Lovering, 1988), and because training is the central policy for helping the local disadvantaged. Failures in supply also vary by place; the inner cities, in particular, have suffered from the closures of large factories which perform most training.

Local agencies have adapted central government programmes to the local labour force and local production. They have also implemented more independent policies, involving collaboration between the MSC, the local authorities, the EC, the voluntary sector, and firms individually and collectively. In some instances they have managed to wring concessions out of the MSC, in others they have escaped its constraints by finding alternative finance.

The Centre has undertaken four broad types of initiative. First, it has attempted to make markets for disadvantaged workers operate more effectively, benefiting both them and employers (Davies and Mason, 1986). This is done partly through provision of information and exhortation to employers and workers, an attractively cheap policy, exemplified by the Training Access Points programme. Job Clubs help the unemployed to 'keep trying', and the disadvantaged to apply for jobs in fields where they are under-represented. Using techniques from social work and psychotherapy, solidarity with people in a similar situation is used to support individual advancement; as in the promotion of enterprise, welfare and employment policy merge both in content and method. On the other side, employers are given information about the unemployed on their doorstep and arguments to overcome their various prejudices. Freeing labour markets has also been pursued through costlier policies which attempt to diminish barriers to employment: provision of crèches, facilities for disabled people, and social housing for key workers; in Nottingham and Sheffield investment in rapid transit has been partly aimed at facilitating access from high unemployment areas to jobs.

A second policy has been the provision of training. Some schemes provide high-level, sectorally specific skills. This is sometimes done by implementing national schemes in a way that provides better quality training, often within the local authority, and some councils top up the basic allowances. However, many schemes provide training in basic manual skills: electronics assembly, retail work, clerical skills, and so on. Others provide low level skills such as the 3Rs to enable entry into training or further education.

Provision of basic skills thus plays a surprisingly large role in view of the Centre's commitment to 'real training'. This is partly because existing training is so poor that workers with even those skills are lacking. But it is also because the Centre's training is targeted on the disadvantaged. Some schemes for those groups aim to get them into skilled jobs, and there are training schemes for women to enable them to enter male dominated trades. But many schemes aim simply to lever the disadvantaged into a job, and basic skills make this more likely. Some large employers in inner city areas using low skill labour are funding basic training schemes to enable more local residents to be hired. Through being spatially and socially targeted, these policies again demonstrate how welfare can be achieved through production

A third policy aims to ease the passage of working class youth into local employment. These schemes have learnt much from the USA, where corporate initiatives are strongly concerned with education. The Centre does not disagree with the orientation of the Conservatives' education reforms towards employment, but has supplemented it. Compacts have been set up between secondary schools and major local employers, in which the latter guarantee a job to school leavers if they fulfil a basic programme and behave acceptably. Work-experience has been built in to the school curriculum, combining education in work and life skills with technical training. Firms take teachers on placement and help in curriculum development. For school leavers there is a multiplicity of basic training and work experience schemes located in the private sector and community projects.

Finally, cities have attempted to attract skilled and professional workers by changing their image and providing consumption facilities. The assumption is that shortages of these skills in the cities and in peripheral regions is due to residential preferences rather than declining demand from employers. Unlike training initiatives, this is a beggar-my-neighbour policy.

The Centre's alternative local strategy appealed to employers seeking real training, and has influenced central government strategy. A paradox of the Right's abstention from training and industry's short termism is that they have produced intense pressure for state action. The MSC made a number of attempts to build local corporatist structures which could organise real training to meet employers' demands, but these were frustrated by government pressure to concentrate on managing the long term unemployed. Its Area Manpower Boards had representation from local authorities, industry, the voluntary sector and unions. The Local Collaborative Projects of 1984 brought together employers and training providers; although there were more than 500 of them, they were short term. The Local Employer Networks, initiated three years later with employers' associations, aimed to support and coordinate employers' training. There have also been a number of similar locally-initiated bodies such as the Coventry Consortium.

The TECs developed out of these underfunded initiatives, responding to pressure from employers and the local consensus. Though most of their funding is still earmarked for unemployment schemes, they can raise private sector funds which are tax deductible and are matched pound for pound by the government, which may enable some high level training. They are thus another tentative attempt at collective control by employers for real training. Their formation is an example of a move from national to local control in response to acute tensions in policy (pp. 10–11, 23).

These tensions, however, have been given new form rather than resolved. The potential of the TECs to develop local labour market strategies and to integrate these with small business support is in conflict with the continuing imposition of central government strategy. Moreover, because the TECs are area based, in contrast to the sectoral organisation of the Industrial Training Boards, they are suitable for providing basic skills which are common between sectors and which encourage local mobility, corresponding to the Right's local economic strategy. The efficacy of the TECs as a political lobby for real training provision is reduced by their local fragmentation and by the fact that executives sit on the boards only as individuals and not as representatives of business. Under the employers' influence, the TECs are likely to oppose the MSC's schemes for the unemployed and youth, as these are directed more at maintaining a work ethic than at providing skilled labour. But many Centrist training agencies, although they think these schemes are inadequate, are opposed to dropping training of the disadvantaged (Peck, 1991). The formation and policy of the TECs thus reflect the tensions between the Right and the Centre and between the Centre's competitive and welfare aims; they will be a continuing battleground.

Direct job creation and production of public goods

The Centre acknowledges that, in the short term at least, reducing local unemployment may require creating jobs directly through employment subsidy (Botham, 1983). This can often be done at zero or negative cost, through the savings on social security payments and social service costs and increased tax revenue. Nor does this policy tend to increase wage pressure: many, perhaps most, of the unemployed concerned are not competing effectively with workers in employment, because of their location and skills and the slow turnover of many firms' labour (Glyn, 1988; Robinson, 1988, p.14). Moreover, employment subsidies, most commonly a wage subsidy paid to the firm, can more effectively be targeted on particular groups of workers than can subsidies to improve competitiveness.

Central government wage subsidies in the past 25 years have been targeted on regions, youth, small firms, and crisis-hit manufacturing. In 1984 thirty local authorities had wage subsidy schemes, most using EC funds, targeted on the long term unemployed, and typically providing a 30 per cent grant for six months. However, schemes can run up against employers' unwillingness to employ the target group. Moreover, the jobs created displace jobs elsewhere, even of people within the target group. Thus Robinson (1988, pp. 123–6) estimated that youth employment schemes increased employment of that group in the local labour market by only 10 per cent of the jobs subsidised because of the displacement effect, while local authority schemes typically have only a 20 per cent effectiveness.

The large displacement effect can be avoided if the enterprise subsidised is not competing with others, as is the case in public work schemes. The extra production may also be more socially useful than in wage subsidies. The benefits are especially large if they replace less efficient subsidies; for example, the sum spent on mortgage tax relief would make a far greater improvement in the housing stock if spent on employing people to do repairs (Layard *et al*, 1986, p. 184). This is the rationale behind the Local Jobs Plans produced in 1987 by fifty Labour councils (Campbell *et al.*, 1987), which proposed an expansion of direct local authority employment to work on local infrastructure and social services at little net cost to the state. However, the savings would accrue mostly to central government, and the programmes would not be self-financing for local authorities. Because of their wish to reduce local government spending and employment the Conservatives rejected this approach.

The Conservatives nevertheless had their own public work schemes operated by the MSC, which were used by local authorities and voluntary agencies for work such as environmental and housing improvements and education projects. But they have been constrained by government, local authorities and unions from competing with either the private or the public sector; in consequence, although some Centre commentators have seen potential in the Conservatives' schemes (Howl, 1985), they have not met the kind of aims set in the Jobs Plans.

Another way in which employment creation and public works have been combined is in community businesses. To some extent these sneak through the problems of displacement and subsidy: the jobs usually do not require a full subsidy, often because they sell to the local authority, and do not compete with the private sector since they operate in markets where it dare not tread, although they do sometimes displace public sector jobs. But this niche does limit their growth. For the Centre, however, community businesses have the advantage over local authority employment and Community Programme-type schemes that they foster enterprise.

Having examined individual policies, we now make some general remarks on the consensus strategy.

Methods in policy-making and the construction of local consensus

The methods of policy-making in local economic initiatives tend to obscure the diversity of choices available and the complexities and conflicts of interest at stake. This weakness is found across the political spectrum. But it is particularly pronounced in Centre policy: in obscuring the conflicts involved, it helps to construct collaboration between different groups, depoliticise local economic policy, and thus build a local consensus.

First, policy-makers have been reluctant clearly to define their aims. Where aims are stated at all, they are often anodyne, such as 'regenerating the local economy' or 'tackling unemployment'. These kinds of aims sidestep the fact that there are different interests involved in the local economy: 'regeneration' may mean quite different things for different social groups. Even for a particular group, aims may conflict: we have noted the conflicts between increasing the number of local jobs, their quality, distribution and stability (pp. 52–3). These kinds of conflict are often left unacknowledged by leaving aims unspecified or vague.

In the absence of clear aims, *strategies* such as 'increasing local control' or 'stimulating enterprise' come to assume the status of goals. But these are not social aims in themselves, since they do not refer to the needs of either people or firms. Even *policy instruments*, such as filling empty buildings, helping start-ups, or stimulating technology transfer, may be regarded as aims. The apparent concreteness of such policies gives them wide appeal (Chapter 2), sidestepping the difficult and politically sensitive question of whom these policies will benefit. It also covers over real choices about *how* the policy is to be carried out. 'Helping small firms', for example, can be done in a great variety of ways, within different political–economic strategies, and benefiting different social groups (pp. 94–6); these differences are not mere details, but are the real content of the policies.

Vagueness in aims is connected to a vagueness about the effects of policies. The likely knock-on effects are typically not examined in advance; yet the consequences of policies are usually complex, going far beyond the variables and the unit, sector or locality on to which they are targeted. Monitoring policy effects is also weak (Coulson, 1990); that which does take place usually considers a narrow range of variables, most often jobs 'created' or 'sustained', even though other variables affected may be just as socially important. Both prediction and monitoring of the effects of policy are dependent on the economic theory used, yet within local economic policy the difference made by economic theory is seldom acknowledged (see further, pp. 265–6; Massey and Meegan, 1985; Massey and Allen, 1988, Introduction). In these ways politically contentious outcomes such as displacement effects are ignored.

Local economic agencies avoid the difficulties of defining aims and thinking through policies by a number of characteristic short-cuts:

● *Assuming that the facts give an immediate guide to policy* Problems are assumed to reveal themselves through observation; and policy then directly addresses the 'problem variables'. Thus data collection is often undertaken without theoretical or policy guidance. It usually focuses on variables which are the most easily measured, which then come to define both the aims and means of the policy (Ozbekhan, 1969, p. 70). For example, sectoral studies measure the number of local jobs but seldom carry out the difficult investigation of the location of employment in competing firms; this then sets an agenda of local job creation ignoring displacement effects. Similarly, training is a favourite labour market policy because it has (or promises to have) a quantifiable output; yet problems in the labour market and in industrial relations may be untouched by training or subvert its effect.

● *Falsely claiming consensus goals for policies* Training, for example, is often presented as meeting skills shortages or reducing unemployment; yet it often fails in these aims but succeeds in others, such as keeping the unemployed within the labour force or building collaborative industrial relations. These latter achievements, however, are not presented as aims since they are politically contentious (Raffe, 1983, p. 20); this lack of clarity and explicitness inevitably reduces the efficiency of implementation.

● *Adopting policies which have been successful elsewhere, without analysing the specific local conditions which produced that success* We have seen, for example, the vogue for science parks following their success in very special locations; yet the innovation centre is more appropriate for most locations in Britain. Environmental improvement of old industrial areas is used irrespective of the type of industry located there; it may be useful for industries using scarce labour, but may be irrelevant for semi-skilled manufacturing. The EZs were modelled on economies such as Hong Kong and the Free Trade Zones of the Third World, some of which have had rapid growth on the basis of low wages, absence of union rights, low taxes and lack of planning. But in Britain it is socially and politically impossible to create small areas with dramatically different conditions of employment; and here the cutting edge of competition does not lie in wage reduction. The promise of cooperatives is often read off from their success in Mondragon; but these developed under the Franco regime where they provide an avenue for collective activity in the economic sphere which was blocked at the political and cultural level. The level of industrial competition in Spain at that time was also far lower than in Britain now. Garden Festivals were borrowed from Germany; but there, because growth was strong, they were used to improve environment, not to catalyse the revival of a depressed area. In the early 1980s, the GLC attempted to introduce workers' participation in business planning into aided firms, following the experiences of strongly unionised workforces in large firms in the 1970s. This attempt floundered because the GLC's firms were smaller and more weakly unionised, and because in the changed political situation unions were preoccupied with simple defence. The specifics of time as well as of place are important. (For further examples see pp. 260–5).

● *Assuming that the key to success is optimism* A widespread view is that the key to local economic growth is the expectation of success. The hype produced by local agencies becomes more than the usual exaggerations of advertising: it becomes a key policy, and it must be believed not only by potential inward investors but by local actors too (Guild, 1988). It is true that developers are more likely to invest if they think that others will, and the same can be true for businesses with local agglomeration advantages; but it is doubtful that many firms are impressed by local agencies' predictions of growth. At any rate, a stress on 'optimism' has a corrosive effect on policy-making. Almost any initiative becomes valid, especially if it is visible in the built environment, since it shows that 'things are moving'. The approach *obliges* local agencies to make extravagant claims for the success of their policies in order to inspire confidence; sober public discussion of effectiveness is thereby ruled out. In the lead-up to the World Student Games in Sheffield, for example, public debate about the wisdom of the event was effectively branded as treachery to the local economy. Localities become like nearly bankrupt firms, where no one must speak of the problems lest the creditors hear.

These methods of policy-making lead to policy fads. A succession of policy instruments – property, small firms, high tech, training, and so on – have been regarded as the key to local economic policy through ignoring the diverse aims which they might serve and their different effects in particular places and times.

Part of the promise of local economic initiatives was to demystify social policy. Land use planning, housing policy, social work and so on all had hidden economic effects; now these would be made explicit. In the 1960s these services were increasingly used as surrogates for local economic policy; now economic policy would be direct (p. 7–9, 11). Yet local economic planning has reproduced the lack of clarity of aims and effects of earlier social policy. The aims professed by most agencies have a strikingly similarity to the neutral goals which British land use planning has traditionally set itself – 'a good environment', 'orderly development' and so on, which helped to create the post-war consensus.

At one level, this discussion suggests some simple recommendations for policy-making. Local economic policy-makers should define their aims explicitly and in terms of social actors and their needs. They should acknowledge conflicts between aims, and should evaluate policies in terms of them. They should think through the multiple effects of policies in an imaginative and theoretically informed way, taking account of the specifics of time and place (Storey and Johnson, 1987; Turok, 1989).

This is simple to say; but a rational method of policy-making conflicts with the construction of local unity around and through economic policy. Ambiguity about aims, lack of analysis of effects, adoption of promising fads, and a suppression of debate in order to talk up investment expectations, all serve to minimise local conflict. And it is not just that ambiguous formulations hide potential divisions of interest; slogans like 'enterprise' and 'community' have positive, albeit different, meanings for different social groups, and thus actively construct their collaboration (Chapter 6). Making policy-making more rational may therefore jeopardise the coalitions on which it depends and which it constructs.

The consensus in local economic policy

There is a consensus surrounding local economic policy in three distinct, though linked, senses. First, there is a consensus that a local level of economic policy is valuable. Second, the distinctive policies of the Right and Left have for the most part either been abandoned or have evolved towards a Centre mode of implementation; the mainstream of local economic policy is consensus in the sense of resting in the middle of the political spectrum. Third, the predominant mode of local economic initiatives is consensual in attempting to win the support of business, workers and residents, to unite the locality in improving its competitiveness and welfare.

This conclusion is controversial: many people think that current local economic policy in Britain must be of the Right, both because of the domination of national over local government, and because being pro-business is now commonly thought of as being Right. But this chapter has shown that the mainstream of local economic initiatives is pursuing a pro-business policy through a strategy which is not neo-liberal, involving a considerable degree of support and even direction by the state and other agencies. Certainly, this 'Centre' strategy has incorporated themes most strongly articulated by the Right: it is concerned to maintain individualism even through collective support, to link welfare to economic competitiveness, to make local government responsive to business's demands, and to weaken combative trade unionism. But it has also incorporated themes of the Left: the need for substantial change in the financial system, for sectoral strategy, for collective services to industry, for forms of workers' participation, and for community self-activity against poverty.

The rather meagre funds, powers and autonomy of local economic agencies have not prevented them from developing a corporatist strategy distinct from that of central government (King, 1985). Indeed, while central government maintains tight formal control over most local economic agencies, in practice it tolerates centrist policies at the local level. This paradox will be explored in Part IV; for the moment we would say that it is the powerful economic and social logic of the consensus approach, and the promise of the Bootstraps strategy, which have enabled this politics to flourish under a neo-liberal government.

Local economic agencies thus still have considerable ability to determine their own strategies.

The consensus, however, is not a monolithic and stable one; quite the contrary. It has changed over time, and we have encountered many tensions within it: how comprehensive should support for entrepreneurialism be?; what elements need to be included in sectoral planning?; how much intervention is needed to steer the banks, multinationals and property companies into local commitment?; what balance is there to be between traditional universal services and new *ad hoc* ones?; should training be for 'real skills', for what individuals want, or for what businesses demand?; and so on. The consensus on 'partnership' between local government and the private sector is compatible with quite different degrees of state direction and coercion, and quite different industrial, labour market and social strategies. In the remainder of the book we shall delve more deeply into the tensions within the contemporary consensus.

Further reading

The overall Centre approach is given in OECD (1985 and 1987), Association of District Councils (1987), Association of County Councils *et al.* (1988), CBI (1988), Trades Union Congress (1988), Coopers Lybrand (1991), and, in a version which learns from international experience, Martinos and Humphreys (1990). Statements from different strands of the Centre with a strongly Bootstraps flavour are Donnison and Soto (1980) and Fanning (1986).

On Enterprise Agencies see Moore and Richardson (1989). Storey and Johnson (1986) and Storey *et al.* (1987) review small firm performance, and Giaoutzi *et al.* (1988) their role in local economic policy; GLC (1983b) is a critique from the left. On Centre policies for the Third Sector see Crowther-Hunt and Billinghurst (1990) and publications by Councils for Voluntary Service (London: NCVO) as well as the references in Chapter 2. On the enterprise of the oppressed, see MacDonald and Coffield (1991) on youth, OECD (1986) on women, Waldinger *et al.* (1990) on ethnic minorities, and Nabarro *et al.* (1986) on the unemployed. Mattera (1985) gives a critical view of the informal economy. Fothergill *et al.* (1987) review property policies. Writing on local and regional technology policy is a sunrise industry of explosive growth; Amin and Goddard (1986) is useful. Finn (1987) criticises the Conservatives' training policy from the left, while McArthur and McGregor (1987) discuss local training policy, OECD (1984b) education, Haughton and Peck (1988) skills audits, and Hayton (1989) training to overcome disadvantage.

Part III

The Localness of
Local Economic Policy

Introduction

We have seen that the spatial level of local economic policy gives it both specific strengths and specific problems; these are the subject of this part of the book. In Chapter 5 we examine the changing organisation of production: does internationalisation leave any place for local economies? In Chapter 6 we look at how local economic initiatives have addressed the locality as a whole by linking policies for production with the social sphere and with notions of community. In Chapter 7 we discuss how, and in what senses, local economic policy can enhance local control of the economy. The emphasis in this part of the book is on consensus strategy; we return to the diverse political alternatives in Part IV.

5 Are There Local Economies?

There are three popular views of current trends in 'localness'. In the first, national economies, and large parts of the international economy, are becoming increasingly homogeneous. Production is dominated by the transnationals and consumption by mass-produced world products. Ever-improving communications are rendering production footloose. Skills, culture, technologies and methods of work are becoming equalised – a McDonalds' world.

A contrary view is that distinctive local economies are forming, or can potentially be formed, through flexible specialisation (p. 80). Markets are fragmenting and products becoming more differentiated, and these favour small production units and firms. Such production has strong local agglomeration economies. The grain of economic change is towards local specialisation and local control.

A third view is that the economy is becoming geographically polarised. Skilled and variable work and higher control activities, involving well-paid secure jobs, are becoming concentrated into certain privileged localities, the 'core'. Other places, the 'periphery', have to compete for routine, non-skilled, low wage, insecure work, controlled from outside. At both the national and international level, there is a widening gap between core and periphery (Reich, 1991).

These views tend to lead to particular local strategies. Within the first view, localities have to compete by holding down costs and increasing productivity. Within the second view, qualitative features of the local economy and its internal integration are crucial. The third view suggests pursuit of cost competition in the periphery and qualitative forms of competition in the core, but also the desirability of peripheral areas pulling themselves up into the core. We shall see that, while there is some truth in all three views, they are one-sided and static: there are definite processes which are shaping local economies, but these are not resulting in any simple *pattern* of localism.

Is internationalisation destroying local economies?

Internationalisation often undermines the coherence and autonomy of local economies; but it can also reinforce their specialisation and uniqueness. This contradictory relationship means that local economic policy cannot simply oppose international mobilities; it also has to harness them.

The history of capitalism is one of ever-increasing internationalisation, first of trade, then of finance, and then of the organisation of production. In each of these senses, the world economy is now strongly integrated and becoming more so (Thrift, 1988). During the 1980s world trade continued to increase much faster than output, particularly in business services, technical information, and tourism. In finance, the major institutions now operate internationally, facilitated by liberalisation of the financial markets; even nominally national and regional financial institutions are linked into international networks. In the organisation of production, transnational companies are spreading from their traditional activities into business and consumer services. Many types of production shift their locations restlessly, their mobility made possible because facilities are quickly written off through technological change.

But these forms of internationalisation do not necessarily mean greater homogeneity. Increasing internationalisation has not merely left vast differences between countries but has intensified them (Amin, 1974). At the local level, economic differences are reproduced by the internal interconnections of local economies: the relations between employers and workers, their local organisations, the circulation of knowledge, services and goods between local firms, institutions and government, and communications and physical infrastructures. These linkages perpetuate the specialisms of local economies and tie capital and labour to them. They involve parts of the economy which are both long lasting and spatially immobile. This is true not only of buildings, plant and physical infrastructures: workers and their skills are also largely immobile in the short to medium term, and particular local business practices and industrial relations can be resilient. The inertia of local economies is strengthened by the private nature of capitalist investment decisions: each decision tends to reflect and use the existing specialisation of the local economy and thus reinforce it.

We shall refer to this web of interdependencies as the 'local socialisation of production'. The word 'socialisation' signals that profitable production is not a purely private affair but depends, 'socially', on the local economy as a whole. In the next chapter we shall see that it depends even more widely on local *society* as a whole.

The local socialisation of production and the international mobilities of commodities, finance and production are both mutually dependent and mutually destructive. On the one hand, internationalisation can reinforce local socialisation and specialisation. Widening trade and markets, and increasing flows of information, facilitate (as well as reflect) greater local specialisation. The spatial mobility of capital enables it more easily to flow into localities with a strong and profitable local socialisation. Transnational firms are best able to take advantage of, and develop, local specialisations. On the other hand, internationalisation also breaks up local socialisation. Widening trade and information flows bring new competitors and competitive strategies to bear on localities. International financial markets encourage capital to flow out of low profit localities, and transnational companies ease such shifts and transfers.

International mobilities can therefore promote local specialisation and coherence, but they can also disrupt them. The broadcasting industry in London, with a long-developed workforce and tapping into particular cultural traditions and milieux, produces a differentiated product which it can sell worldwide using concentrated and internationalised distribution channels; yet the latter are putting increasing pressure on the London industry to cut costs, deskill and casualise the workforce, and produce a cheaper and more standardised product. The differentiation of local economies is thus quite compatible with internationalisation, but the pattern of specialisation is under constant threat.

This contradiction is of central importance for local economic policy. The key means through which mainstream local policies try to create stable local economies is through reinforcing local interdependencies, strengthening the local socialisation of production, and sharpening the specialisation of the local economy. To do this it makes use of open trade, finance and ownership; yet these constantly threaten to turn against the local economy. This tension will be a central theme of the rest of the book.

Spatial hierarchies and types of local coherence

We can use this framework to understand the processes shaping the contemporary local economies. How footloose are different types of production? What are the barriers to constructing coherent and specialised local economies? What are the new divisions of labour between regions and localities? How do profitability and stability differ between different types of local economy?

The socialisation of production which local policy attempts to reinforce varies strongly in both form and intensity between different sectors and stages of production. In manufacturing and in producer services, we can distinguish:

● The production of *control information* – headquarters, specialist producer services, software production, R&D and design – has very strong local socialisation. Within each activity of this type there are dense webs of information exchange between workplaces, much of it by face-to-face contact. Each activity both produces, and is dependent on, a local pool of skilled labour; and since much information is borne by individuals, local poaching of labour is important. Some of the branches are strongly linked to each other: for example, industrial and banking headquarters to each other and to government ; or the linked milieux of fashion, design and the media. All these control activities involve the design of social relations, and hence are themselves strongly socialised. All are locally linked to up-market consumption – housing, hotels, restaurants, and so on. We have, then, the 'world city' and the informational city with a multiplicity of informational branches. However, some informational branches are fairly spatially autonomous, so that some cities and subregions specialise in particular branches of design, technology or software.

● Within some sectors, there are dense local exchanges of goods, services and information, and use of sectorally specific managerial, technical and skilled manual labour. The mutual proximity of design, marketing and production can be important. This is the *'industrial district'*, found not only in manufacturing but also in cultural production and producer services. The complex of R&D, software design and batch production of electronic goods in the Sun Belt is an example. The strength of this kind of local cooperation between firms varies strongly between different European localities (McArthur, 1989).

● For some sectors there is a weaker form of local socialisation, *local exchange of goods and services*: general business services and service-type manufacturing supplying the local economy, or subcontractors clustered round a major plant. This form of local socialisation is addressed in policies for local subcontracting and for key sectors.

● In other cases, local socialisation lies solely in *the use of labour power*. Some otherwise footloose skilled manual and white-collar work is tied to localities with a pool of the appropriate skills. Footloose non-skilled work, the classic branch plant, tends to be located in areas with low wages and high unemployment; since such areas are numerous, this work is weakly rooted in the locality. In these cases, socialisation is addressed through labour market policies.

These varied forms of local socialisation and specialisation are being both produced and undermined by advances in telecoms and goods transport (Castells, 1989, ch. 3). On the one hand, improved communications are making possible the fragmentation and decentralisation of certain tasks. If the essential information and negotiation needed to coordinate a stage of production can be easily handled in digital form, its informational linkages are loosened. Production of light goods and that using lower level skills are becoming more footloose. On the other hand, improved communications allow command functions and design and monitoring linked to production to be increasingly centralised in the informational centres.

The development of these new forms of centralisation and decentralisation is part of a more general process of increased vertical coordination (sometimes misleadingly called 'flexible integration') between each stage in producing and selling a good or service. The design of products and processes, the various stages of production, quality control, distribution and sales are increasingly jointly planned and the flow of information between them increased. This makes possible reduction of capital tied up in stocks, faster response to market changes, better quality control, and better match between process and product design. This coordination is taking place both within firms and between them. The impetus towards this change has been the increased competitive pressure and greater unpredictability of markets arising from economic stagnation. The essential means towards it is not technology but organisation – such integration has been practised in Japanese manufacturing for decades. But new electronic technologies are facilitating it, through the linking of computerised equipment in design, production, stock control and sales.

Thanks to telecommunications, this intensified vertical coordination can be compatible with increasing geographical dispersal of vertically linked stages of production and distribution. But it is also leading to the opposite, spatial concentration. Many information flows are facilitated by face-to-face meetings, despite telecoms. Shortening of supply lines makes it possible to reduce stocks of goods in transit, a more speedy reaction to demand, and rapid correction of faults. Manufacturers and retailers are therefore increasingly using a 'just-in-time' system of nearby suppliers, shifting from international to national sources, and from national to local ones. These strengthened local links can be exploited by local policy.

The separation of activities between different localities has been facilitated by large firms. Their activities are more likely to be of a size where a spatially separate unit is worthwhile; the transactions between the activities are facilitated by their taking place within a single firm; and they have greater resources for planning such separations. The continuing concentration of ownership (p. 173–4) thus tends to promote increasing specialisation of localities.

In spatial economic policy, consumer services have traditionally been considered unproblematic because of being tied to population and their location thus dictated by that of 'basic industry'. Consumer services are still for the most part produced and supplied face-to-face to local residents; however, these ties are weakening. First, the consumption of services by non-local consumers is growing because of improvements in passenger transport: increasing trips outside the local area for shopping and leisure, increasing international tourism. While this has caused some decentralisation and fragmentation of service sites, its main effect has been to facilitate spatial agglomeration, either within a single firm (e.g. theme parks), or across firms (shopping centres and tourist towns). While some locations are dictated by existing beauty or interest, increasingly they are created from scratch or expand through economies of scale and scope. Second, just as in manufacturing and business services, improved communications are increasing the spatial separation of stages of production. Kitchens and sandwich factories are separated from restaurants; the banks are centralising many functions away from their branches. Third, consumer services which are produced and consumed in different places using post and telephone are now joined by burgeoning electronic informational services. Increasing parts of the production of consumer services, especially informational parts, are thus being removed from the site of consumption, enabling them to be sited in localities with appropriate labour pools.

The dynamics of consumer services are therefore converging with those of manufacturing and business services. They are becoming increasingly footloose and poachable (Davies, 1988), a part of 'basic industry', explaining why current local economic policy, unlike previous spatial economic policy, has addressed them. They are becoming less differentiated by local spending power, and the local multiplier effect of 'basic' job creation is declining (Coulson, 1990, pp. 185–6).

There are, then, strong forms of the local socialisation of production which can potentially be used to enhance the coherence of local economies. Note that changing communications between localities – including goods and passenger transport as well as telecommunications – are playing an important role in altering their specialisations, an issue generally neglected in local economic policy because of its spatial focus (see further p. 186). But neither communications nor production technologies determine the spatial division of labour; central roles are played by local economic pressures and industrial relations, to which we now turn.

The internal tensions of local economies

The coherence of a local economy is, then, dependent on its external relations with the national and world economy. But local policy also has to confront internal disruptions.

One lies in the use of land. Technical and organisational change in production tends to increase the amount of floor space per worker; with the partial exception of office work, this means fewer workers per area of land (Fothergill and Gudgin, 1982). Similarly, the amount of housing land used per resident is increasing in the long term. Ever-increasing goods transport and car use demand more land. Mature local economies thus tend to experience chronic pressures of land availability and land price rises; local property initiatives have attempted to address these problems.

During the 1980s, despite overcapacity and unemployment at the national level, some local economies experienced high inflation of land prices and wages and congestion of infrastructures; these were particularly marked in the prosperous 'Sun Belt' of central-Southern England and in some cities. Inflation was a result of the local disparity between strong investment and profitability in leading sectors and underinvestment in infrastructures. The long period of stagnation has led to firms being unwilling to invest in training, and to central government being unwilling to invest in transport, housing and higher education. The roots of local inflation and congestion therefore run deep: geographically uneven growth combined with capitalist patterns of infrastructure investment.

The relations between capital and labour also can disrupt local economies 'from the inside', particularly in times of low profitability. Since the late 1960s, employers have increasingly attempted to raise profits at labour's expense by intensifying the pace of work, increasing the flexibility of task allocation, holding down real wages, extending payment by results, and reducing security of employment. To push through these measures, management has used the threat that inadequate competitiveness would lead to job loss. Effective opposition to these measures has declined since the early 1970s as the unions have been weakened through successive defeats and by legislation. However, management's offensive continues to face both organised and informal opposition, which varies between localities. Union organisation is generally strongest in long-established industrial areas and in cities (Massey and Meegan, 1979). In tight labour markets, and also in some cities where management regards labour as 'indisciplined', there is covert resistance such as working at lower speed or quality and high voluntary turnover of labour. Thus both long industrial traditions and fast growth in a locality strengthen the formal and informal resistance of labour. Capital has responded by shifting from these labour markets. It is not only that other areas are thought to have a more compliant labour force: a workforce new to the firm and possibly to the industry facilitates the introduction of new working methods. Industrial relations, then, are central to local economic policy.

New forms of the local organisation of production have contradictory implications for industrial relations. On the one hand computer-based processes and increased vertical coordination of production are being used by management to tighten work supervision as well as to shed labour. But on the other hand, the learning required for continuous change in technologies and their potential versatility require active collaboration from workers to maximise their potential. The high capital intensity of many of the new production processes, and the increasingly tight coordination of stages of production, render the new systems more vulnerable to worker discontent and industrial action (Oliver and Wilkinson, 1988, chs 2, 3; Gough, 1992a). Again, intensification of local coordination increases the efficiency of production but renders it more vulnerable to disruption.

The stronger the local socialisation of production, then, the more it tends to be disrupted by inflation, congestion and problems of labour control. In the subsequent shake-out, it is the sectors with the weakest local interdependencies which tend to be preferentially expelled, reinforcing the specialisation of the local economy. But the shake-out is inevitably crude and chaotic: it expels some firms and workers which are integral to the local economy, resulting in further inflation and bottlenecks; the expulsion of building workers from southern England during the 1980s through high living costs led to inflation in their wages and further rises in building prices. Local policy cannot simply rely on the market to restore equilibrium.

Internal disruptions of local economies arise, then, precisely because of the interdependencies that make up local socialisation, which enable social groups to shift balances of power in their favour, and which make the local economy vulnerable to imbalances. The local socialisation of production is inherently contradictory: it provides a distinctive competitive edge for the locality, but it also produces internal disruptions and instability. The promotion of the socialisation of production by local economic policy is therefore more than a technical and organisational matter: it concerns transfers of resources between different interests, and the relations of power between them; it is inextricably political.

Spatial shifts in employment and patterns of local specialisation

Mainstream local economic initiatives depend on, and try to reshape, the specialisation of the local economy. We have seen that local specialisation is shaped by both the external relations of the local economy and its internal make-up. These result in complex and ever-shifting divisions of labour between areas; however, three broad patterns can be discerned.

First, *regional specialisations by sector*, resulting from regional socialisation of production, are still important. The traditional industrial specialisations of the Development Areas and the Midlands continue, though reduced in importance. But there are also new regional specialisations, such as electronics and software in the Sun Belt, south Wales and central Scotland, and intensifying ones, such as the tourism and retirement industries in southern England.

Second, there are area specialisations constructed by the *hierarchical spatial divisions of labour*. In administration and business services the higher functions are becoming increasingly centralised in London and the regional centres, while routine clerical work is decentralised to lower wage locations. R&D is becoming increasingly concentrated in the Sun Belt, while design of culture and fashion products remains strongly anchored in London.

Third, and partly connected to these hierarchies, there is an increasing *differentiation within regions*. Manufacturing is shifting from cities and large towns to smaller towns and rural areas (Fothergill and Gudgin, 1982), pushed by the various internal disruptions in the older areas, and in some sectors made possible by a weakening of local dependencies. A hierarchy of business services operates within each region, between cities and towns of decreasing size. In consumer services, there is outward movement to the fringes of the conurbations, reflecting decentralisation of housing and increasing car use, but also a reinforcement of city centres as internally connected consumption districts. The economies of cities and large towns are thus becoming increasingly dominated by business and consumer services.

These local and regional divisions of labour combine in complex ways. For example, in some cases manufacturing is moving to small towns and rural areas in order to use cheap, non-skilled labour, sometimes following deskilling. But in other cases, especially in southern England, almost the opposite process is involved: manufacturing has followed the move of skilled manual workers, technicians and entrepreneurs to rural suburbia. The urban–rural shift and the consequent pressures faced by local economic agencies are different in different regions.

The new differentiations between cities, towns and rural areas have been one of the reasons for adding subregional, 'local' economic policy to regional policy. However, local specialisation is not replacing regional specialisation. Nor is local differentiation and specialisation simply becoming stronger, contrary to some commentators (Duncan and Goodwin, 1988; Dickens, 1988; cf Warde, 1985). The division of labour within regions is sharpening, and economic crisis is producing greater differentiations in profitability and growth between localities; but the loosened ties of some types of production, better communications, and in some sectors multiplication of competing centres are also tending to homogenise localities in the same and, particularly, in different regions.

Some authors have argued that the hierarchical divisions of labour mean that localities are arranged in a single hierarchy, a new 'core and periphery', from international control centres down to branch plant economies (Lipietz, 1987). We have seen that this sort of picture has been a motivation for greater regional and local autonomy (pp. 10–11); it would certainly mean that there were distinct possibilities and strategies for localities corresponding to their place in the hierarchy. But this view underestimates the complexity and rapid change of current hierarchical organisations of production. First, while the hierarchies make use of differentiations within labour power, these differentiations are not on one axis but several: spatial distinctions of skill, of wages, of union strength, of 'discipline', and of ease of hiring are not coincident. Second, as we saw above, the form of the hierarchy varies from sector to sector. Third, even within one sector, the locations and the geography of the hierarchy may be very variable. Keyboarding serving offices in central London may be put out to homeworkers in London, *or* to white collar factories in the north of England *or* to the Caribbean. Fourth, within some sectors most stages of production remain, or are becoming, locally linked, so that localities are specialised by sector not hierarchical stage of production. Fifth, particular types of labour power are not confined to particular locations. For example, non-skilled labour is reproduced not only in branch plant economies but also in consumer services in every locality, and in many sectors located in high level centres because of market ties: the 'periphery' is also located in the 'core'. Sixth, the contingencies of history in each locality produce very varied inherited combinations of sectors and of labour power. The various sectoral hierarchies use these differentiated local economies, but they do not totally recreate them in their own image. Seventh, as we have seen, the formation of the hierarchies themselves is not a smooth, functional process, but is subject to constant disruptions.

For these reasons, there is no *single* 'core–periphery' hierarchy on which localities are arranged. Each locality is continuously reshaped by multiple spatial logics in unique combinations. There is no simple typology of local economies, and therefore no formulae for local economic strategy. However, the division of labour between localities reflects a systematic tension between the attractions of local socialisation of production and of low cost and virgin locations, a tension which we explore further below.

Capturing employment shifts

This picture of employment shifts has implications for the attempts of local agencies to capture jobs. As we saw in Chapter 2, these attempts are often focused on sunrise sectors. In the recent past differences in growth rates between sectors have certainly been spectacular: between 1978 and 1990 employment in finance and insurance grew by 82 per cent, in distribution by 10 per cent, while in manufacturing it declined by 30 per cent.

It is however misleading to base local strategies on these trends. First, in many sectors geographical shifts make the local trend quite different from the national one. Second, both growth rates and geographical distribution vary between different stages of production *within* a sector; in these senses clerical work and higher control in the financial sector, say, should be treated as different sectors. Third, economic stagnation means that in many sectors geographical shifts are occurring more through contractions of employment and outright closures than through any form of growth. Local agencies concerned about 'mobile investment' should pay as much attention to declining sectors as to growing ones.

Most importantly, the relevant consideration is not the existing trend but the difference that local policy can make. We have seen that spatial shifts are often associated with technical, organisational or industrial relations change; it may be possible for the local economic agency to address these. But there is no reason to think that policy can make a bigger difference to growing or declining sectors as such: the key issues are the qualitative features of the sector and its potential local interdependencies.

How many localities can be 'special'?

A common strategic aim is to shift the local economy 'upwards' into more specialised, more informational, or more skilled activities. In the next section we look at local barriers to achieving this aim. But we first argue that there is an external constraint: since the national and international economy is hierarchically structured, there are only so many localities that can develop a higher economy, and many will necessarily be consigned to lower activities.

In sectors with a division of labour within the country, this constraint is particularly clear: centres which concentrate into themselves the higher activities of the sector thereby necessarily deprive other localities in the country or the region of those activities. For example, the market in waterfront developments is already oversubscribed (Hall, 1991). In sectors with an international division of labour, it has been argued that localities in Britain could perform the higher activities, with the lower activities located in other countries, particularly the Third World. This is morally questionable. Practically, present patterns are not promising. For example, many areas would like to specialise in the higher activities of the electronics and software industry. But *worldwide* there are only a few such subregions. In Britain there is only one, the Sun Belt; the two other centres of the industry, central Scotland and south Wales, operate, despite their efforts, at lower levels of the industry's division of labour (Morgan and Sayer, 1988). It appears, then, that some localities in Britain will be consigned to lower activities.

There are two possible objections to this conclusion. The first is that a national policy for low unemployment, national systems of pay determination and an effectively policed minimum wage can expel some low wage sectors and eliminate low pay in the rest of the economy; Sweden has been an approximation to this. We examine this strategy in Chapter 10. A second optimistic scenario, the Third Italy model, is that flexible specialisation is becoming the dominant paradigm, and is changing what are at present lower activities into higher ones (p. 80). It is argued that, in both manufacturing and services:

(i) the use of IT for production and coordination allows greater pro-
    duct variety, leading to quality rather than price competition, and
    hence ability to pay good wages;
(ii) these technologies are most productive when used by skilled
    workers, with good conditions and secure employment to ensure
    their active cooperation.

Thus, with appropriate strategy, most activities could become skilled and high paid. Moreover, it is argued that flexible specialisation involves strong local socialisation, giving an important role to local policy. In fact, not only flexible specialisation but all strategies for 'becoming special' centre on product specialisation and variety linked to skilled work; it is therefore worth examining current trends in product variety and skills.

Product variety

The idea of ever-increasing variety and differentiation in goods and services does not stand up to scrutiny. Mass production has always included a substantial degree of product variety (Clarke, 1990). This is not changed qualitatively by IT-based processes, which lend themselves to minor but not major variations within a product (Williams *et al.*, 1987). Flexible manufacturing systems are extremely expensive; to be amortised they have to be used continuously, and thus for the pro-duction of long runs (ibid). Moreover, demand for components and machines is not simply moving towards greater variety. Modular pro-duction is increasing the demand for standardised components. To the extent that machines are becoming more product-flexible, they them-selves become more standardised since producers of different products can use the same machinery. In manufacturing, then, the standardised product is far from dead: consumer electronics and microcomputers are obvious cases in point.

In consumer and business services, improved electronic communications make possible production for ever larger mass markets. As we noted above, many consumer services are becoming increasingly spatially concentrated and thus standardised. Others, such as car repairs and fast food, are being standardised through their increasing domination by large chains guaranteeing a standardised product. Thus mass production is spreading in services.

Where product variety *has* increased, this is often due, not to permanent changes in production paradigm, but to temporary changes in the market arising from economic stagnation (Gough, 1992a). Consumer products have tended to shift up-market, and therefore to become more varied, as a response to the increase in income differentials produced by the economic crisis. In the sectors where increased product variety has been most marked, clothing and building, it has been achieved essentially through the use of traditional, not IT-based, craft work: a shift in demand, not an epochal change in production organisation.

In some products, then, there is increased variety within a limited range of variation. But there continue to be powerful dynamics towards standardisation and mass markets. Stimulation of product design and product-flexible production as strategies for making the locality special are therefore limited; nor is IT necessarily the key to such strategies. Many localities will remain dominated by production of standardised goods and services.

Skills

The upgrading of skills through training initiatives is widely regarded as the royal road to a higher local economy. Yet current developments in skilling are more complex than this strategy assumes. First, many tasks are being subdivided in order to employ less skilled and therefore cheaper labour, or to split work between different labour pools, or to increase management control of the work process (Braverman, 1974). The march of this 'detailed division of labour' can be seen in administrative and clerical work, and also in more glamorous areas such as software writing (GLC, 1985a, ch.13). Second, management's control over the work process is being extended through the use of IT-based processes. The ability of IT to carry out complex and exact processing of information means that mechanisation now often replaces skilled as well as non-skilled labour. But as always, extended mechanisation creates new skilled jobs in designing, coordinating and servicing the plant.

The extension of the detailed division of labour has been partially contradicted by one of the means which employers have used to intensify work, namely to increase the number of different tasks undertaken by each employee. This enables workers to be used with greater continuity in the face of fluctuations in task requirements. It can reduce hold-ups through production workers being made responsible for quality checks and for minor machine repairs (themselves deskilled using IT). Increased functional flexibility, however, does not usually involve qualitatively increased skilling since the constituent tasks are already so deskilled. In some sectors, management is devolving a certain responsibility for work organisation to workers or work groups. However, this does not involve workers acquiring technical or managerial skills; decentralisation is intended to encourage workers to intensify their own work, and to dispense with supervisors, while the important and complex decisions are still taken higher up. Functional flexibility and work group autonomy should therefore not be identified with reskilling (Garrahan and Stewart, 1992).

IT-based production *as technical processes* may be more productive if carried out by skilled workers with a high degree of autonomy (Best, 1990). But the high wages, rigidities in use of labour markets, and levers against management that this gives labour mean that employers often prefer deskilling and disciplinarian strategies. Local agencies, then, cannot rely on any general tendency towards up-skilling such as is proposed in the flexible specialisation thesis.

Local initiatives have a greater role in creating general, sector-wide skills than workplace-specific ones. Here again, there are contradictory tendencies. Product-flexible technology tends to produce greater homogenisation of operator's skills: keyboarding is a striking example. On the other hand, the use by firms of these processes in *de facto* dedicated fashion, the variability produced by experiments in work organisation, and the use of 'learning-by-doing', tend to make skills more workplace-specific. Again, there is no clear pattern.

The contradictory processes at work here explain why the debate between the Right and Centre-Left concerning skills remains inconclusive (p. 108–11). It cannot be assumed that upgrading of a locality's skills base is an essential or cost-effective strategy: in each case a concrete analysis is needed (see further pp. 252–4).

To return to our initial question: there is no general tendency toward increased product variety or upgrading of skills as proposed by the flexible specialisation thesis. The possibilities of local economies in these respects is strongly unequal; there is no *general* potential to become special.

Becoming special: problems of implementation

Attempts to create 'special' local economies also face severe problems of implementation. The high internal interdependencies of such economies make them hard to construct. Each piece of the system exists only because of the others; yet in a capitalist economy most of these pieces have to be created through private initiative: a Catch 22. This is why such local economies have typically been created over long periods, and often by quite fortuitous circumstances (Piore and Sabel, 1984, ch. 2; Lipietz, 1987). Local initiatives can put some of the pieces into play, such as collective services or supply of skilled labour, though these will not be sustained unless firms make use of them and thus reproduce them. More difficult is for local agencies to influence firms' strategies towards stronger local linkages and quality competition. Moreover, the sector needs to reach a minimum critical mass before it becomes self-reinforcing. At best, then, building a new, locally interconnected sector is a long term project – the order of perhaps 15–20 years.

The problem is also one of industrial relations. We have seen that production which has tight vertical integration, high skill, product variability or high quality depends on both compliance and initiative from workers. The Third Italy is a much-cited model; but the creation of its industrial relations involved a long history of conflict. The collapse of large firms in the 1940s and 1950s created an atomised workforce, which was the basis for the subsequent 'collaborative' industrial relations climate; this has been perpetuated partly by using a secondary workforce of immigrants from southern Italy for the unstable and low paid jobs (Solinas, 1988). Again, the conversion of a local economy to higher activities is more than a technical slotting in of appropriate factors and services: it depends on the existence or development of appropriate social relations.

Another dilemma is deciding in how many sectors to attempt to specialise. The difficulties we have discussed suggest that developing just one high level sector stretches the capacities of local economic agencies to their limits. On the other hand, these difficulties also indicate the riskiness of putting all the eggs into one sectoral basket; and a narrow range of industries is obviously more unstable in the long term. Moreover, the development of different sectors is often linked: Sheffield, for example, has seen as mutually dependent the attraction of offices, the development of cultural industries, and becoming the nation's sporting capital, all three initiatives starting from a very low base. The degree of diversity to aim for is thus problematic.

Becoming special: problems of results

There are important limits to the benefits of a high level local economy. They tend to be more stable than low level ones since, as we have just seen, it is difficult for other localities to imitate them; but they are still subject to many forms of instability. We have already examined some of the internal sources of disruption. Highly integrated local sectors are vulnerable to shocks because a small dislocation, the closure of a major firm for example, can be amplified as the webs of dependency unravel; again, the problem lies in the tension between the strong local socialisation of production and private decision making. There are also external disruptions. Most obvious are changes in final markets; the collapse of the 'Massachusetts miracle' in the late 1980s due to cuts in arms purchasing is a case in point. Radical worldwide innovation may make the skills of the local economy redundant, particularly if competition comes from what was formerly a different industry, as in the undermining of the Swiss watch industry by Japanese electronic watches; the very specialisation of local economy may prevent it from meeting such competition. Some localities with higher functions – for example chemical industry towns – are dependent on a few innovatory products which may be imitated or superseded. Diffusion of technical expertise, and cost competition, can undermine an advanced specialised local sector, as in the overwhelming of the British craft shipbuilding industry by the Taylorised Far Eastern industry. In sectors of fast growth, world economic stagnation both limits demand and encourages an inflow of capital with few other options; the result is a chronic tendency to overcapacity and sharp cycles, in which local sectors can be devastated; microprocessor production is a notable example. In short, high level specialisation cannot perform 'miracles'.

Moreover, even a stable high level local economy does not create *only* secure and well-remunerated jobs. Informational centres, for example, contain consumer services, leisure industries and hotels in which employment conditions are poor. This is part of the reason why cities which have been successful in becoming information centres continue to experience widespread poverty. Even within the high level sectors themselves there can be enormous inequalities; in the model industrial districts of the Third Italy, for example, there are many firms doing overflow subcontract work on a sweated basis (Solinas, 1988). This kind of unevenness arises partly from the quantitative instability of final markets, partly from the inevitable inequalities of firm profitability. It also results from the tensions we noted in our critique of the flexible specialisation model: quality competition does not eliminate the drive to reduce costs, to deskill and cheapen labour, and to divide work between different labour forces. A high level local economy, then, should not be equated with high level jobs.

If the opportunities and means for high level specialisation are limited, some localities will have to go for standardised production or production which gains little from local socialisation – what Morgan and Sayer (1988) call development *in* a locality rather than development *of* the locality; this requires cost reduction strategies, with all their undesirable implications. The tension we have explored between the local socialisation of production and price competition, and the consequent differentiation of local economies, mean that quality- and price-competition are alternative local strategies. This alternative is investigated further in Chapters 9 and 10.

The importance and tensions of local socialisation

The local socialisation of production, then, is central to the contemporary economy and to local economic policy. This differs from the view of some influential commentaries. Castells (1977) and Saunders (1984) have argued that intervention into production is the province of national government whereas the province of local government is welfare services. But if socialisation of production exists at the local level then there is potential for local policy for production – either to strengthen *or* to break up this socialisation (p. 212). Duncan and Goodwin (1988) argue that local policy, in whatever field, rests essentially on the spatial unevenness of society. Economic differences between localities have certainly been one motive for local economic initiatives; but our analysis suggests that they also aim to address the internal interdependencies of localities. These go far beyond the property and physical infrastructure stressed by Logan and Molotch (1987): they include services to production, marketing, sub-contracting, labour power and industrial relations (Cox and Mair, 1989a).

Mainstream local economic strategy centres on strengthening the local socialisation of production. But we have seen that it is subject to internal disruptions by markets and social conflicts; it is always in tension with the mobilities of capital, labour and trade; and it is threatened by firms' private decision making and the fragmentary nature of mainstream local initiatives. The problems of local economic strategy do not lie merely in inadequacies of technological capacity or economic organisation, as is argued by enthusiasts of flexible specialisation and post-Fordism, but involve a contradiction between the profitability of individual firms and sectors and that of the local economy as a whole, and conflicts between capital and labour. We have seen that these contradictions often make the effects of local initiatives quite different from their aims. In Part IV we shall examine how different political projects attempt to deal with these tensions of local socialisation.

Further reading

The concept of the local socialisation of production is developed in Harvey (1982, pp. 415–19; and 1985) who calls it 'local coherence', Cox and Mair (1989b) who call it 'local dependence', and Gough (1991a). The mobilities of capital, labour and commodities are discussed in Harvey (1982, ch. 12), and the tendencies to both equalisation and differentiation of the spatial economy in Walker (1978) and Smith (1984, chs 4 and 5).

On contemporary patterns of local agglomeration and dispersal of different economic activities see Massey (1984) and Storper and Walker (1989), and Amin and Smith (1986) on its relation to the internationalisation of production. Harvey (1982, pp. 426–38) discusses the disruption within localities arising from the overaccumulation of capital, and Roweis and Scott (1981) discuss the land aspect; the eruption of these problems within the 'strongest' local economies is depicted in Saxenian (1983) and Smith (1988, pp. 102–9). Analytical accounts of crises of local economies are given in Sheppard and Barnes (1990, Parts III and IV) and Gough (1991a).

For the debate on trends in – and meaning of – skills see Braverman (1974) and Wood (1989). The stability, consistency and benefits of flexibly specialised industrial districts are questioned in Murray (1987), Lovering (1988) and Amin (1989). The idea that 'post-Fordism' or 'flexible accumulation' is emerging as a dominant successful paradigm of production and is fundamental to local economies is argued in the special issue of *Society and Space*, vol. 6, no 3, 1988; this view is criticised along the lines of our argument here in the special issue of *Science as Culture*, no 8, 1989, Clarke (1990), and Burrows *et al.* (1992). Ramtin (1990) discusses the way in which new elements in the organisation of production are subject to long-standing capitalist contradictions. The negative effects of task and employment flexibility for labour are discussed in Bluestone and Harrison (1987) and, in a regional setting, Sadler (1992, Part II).

6 Community, Locality and the Erosion of Place

New solutions [are being found:] the concept of state, market and community partnership working to common agendas; the transition from a dependency culture with 'providers' to an enterprise culture with 'enablers'; and the idea that local communities can hold the key to their own destiny through personal and community enterprise. A new spirit of optimism prevails and, to some degree, civic pride is being restored (Knevitt, 1986, p. 6).

The community aspect of local economic policy is commonly thought to be aimed at 'social' problems rather than increased competitiveness. It is seen as concerning consumption, as helping those who are unable to benefit from renewal, as picking up the pieces of deindustrialisation. All parts of the political spectrum profess to use community initiatives in this way: the Right prompted by its worries about the social order; the Centre to ensure adequate safety nets during restructuring; the Left to redistribute jobs towards the disadvantaged.

Community economic initiatives, however, do not concern only social life, but link the reproduction of the workforce and residents with production and competition. They benefit not merely non-profit and small enterprises but the largest firms. Moreover, they not only provide resources and services for production but are changing the social relations through which these are organised. The Bootstraps approach seeks to address the connections between the social relations of local production and those of local reproduction of population, to blur the boundaries between production and social life; the potential and problems of doing so are the subject of this chapter.

The role of community in local economic initiatives is highly contradictory. Both capital and labour have ambivalent attitudes to community ties, using them here, undermining them there. Sometimes capital accumulation breaks up community and is opposed in its name; sometimes it benefits from the collaborative social relations and good quality labour

140

power produced by community. Red Glasgow and the Scottish community businesses both arise out of a strong sense of community, yet have opposite political content: a collective resistance to capital versus populist self-help. This ambivalence is exacerbated by economic crisis, which increases the importance of local ties to both capital and labour yet renders them increasingly fragile.

Local economic policy thus faces profound difficulties in using and strengthening community. We examine below different aspects of local dependency: welfare and the reproduction of labour power, local industrial relations, local attitudes to work and enterprise, and the ties of local culture. We examine whether local initiatives are successful in integrating localities or whether they create new forms of division, and the problems for firms, residents and local agencies in using community ties within different types of locality. We shall find that community is both central to local economic policy and deeply problematic for it.

Ambivalence to locality

To what extent arc capital and labour dependent upon, and committed to, particular localities? In the last chapter we saw the tension for capital between spatial mobility and the importance of local dependencies of production. But this ambivalence extends beyond the technical organisation of production to all the social relations of the locality. Consider industrial relations. On the one hand, mobility enables capital to shape social relations to its benefit. It intensifies competition between workers, puts pressure on them to accept managerial discipline, and pushes wages downwards. It breaks up the organisations within and outside production through which labour can exert controls over capital. On the other hand, mobility can have severe penalties for capital. If workers are treated as interchangeable and replaceable, they tend to become equally fickle. They have no commitment to their employer who treats them so instrumentally and who may be gone tomorrow. Since skills are so likely to become redundant they have little incentive for self-improvement. Productive collaboration is undermined. In Teesside over the past twenty years, for example, ICI's internationalisation, the cutting of linkages within the region and disruption of its coherence have weakened the area's fabled solidarity of labour and capital (Beynon *et al.*, 1989, pp. 282–5).

Capital, then, may need to attend to locality (ICI has been doing just that: ibid, p. 278). The availability, commitment and abilities of labour depend on local social life. The local supply and price of housing, consumer commodities and transport affect wages and labour supply. Social life and welfare services affect participation in the workforce. Employers have an interest in influencing local attitudes to work, authority and initiative developed within the family and other social institutions. Absenteeism, for instance, which at £6bn p.a. costs employers more than industrial action, may be addressed through its roots in social life. Capital can also be vulnerable to pressure from local residents over welfare facilities, increasing the costs borne by capital in wages or taxes and threatening greater local politicisation. Capital may be forced to address these local pressures because of technical or market ties to the locality; but it may also positively choose to do so in order to benefit from collaborative industrial relations. This may be a more profitable option than seeking discipline and low wages through mobility. Many local economic initiatives reflect a recognition by capital that intervention in local culture and social life is an alternative to mobility.

But this local engagement is problematic for capital. To influence local social life typically requires a collective response by employers; yet this is disrupted by competition, diverse requirements, and free loaders. In consequence capital may relocate, often at great cost, rather than attempt this local collective action.

Labour, too, experiences tensions between mobility and fixity. Mobility makes possible pursuit of higher wages and career. But family and social ties may prevent mobility; and often local ties offer better, or the only, economic prospects. Jobs and work in the informal economy are obtained through family and social connections. Strong union organisation takes a long time to develop in localities, and is often embedded in local social life as well as in production. Lazonick (1991) argues that the local rootedness of nineteenth-century British trade unionism prevented management from taking control over the division of labour on the shopfloor, in contrast to the USA where labour was more mobile. However local collective action by labour, like that of capital, is beset by social divisions, diverse needs, and free riders. Moreover, what are useful local social ties and collective organisation for some sections of labour can be exclusionary for others; what roots some in the locality may marginalise or expel others. Community solidarity and hostility to the state are unusually strong in Liverpool (Meegan, 1989); so is the exclusion of black people from employment (Gifford, 1989).

One side of the picture, then, shows strong pressures on both capital and labour towards local commitment and collaboration between employers and workers, between firms, and between workers. This is why both capital and labour are inclined to ignore the fact that localistic competition is a negative sum game (Sayer and Morgan, 1985, pp. 157–67). Since capital accumulation can be furthered by such collaborative social relations, our notion of the local socialisation of production should be extended to include them. The essence of the Bootstraps approach is to attempt to strengthen these local commitments in both their social and spatial sense, and combat their being undermined by mobility, individualism and conflict.

Community and crisis

The notion of community tends to reappear in just those periods when it is most under pressure, especially times of economic crisis (Open University, 1980; Cesarini, 1988). This is not because it is a political smoke-screen, as is often thought, but because, for capital and for labour, austerity both intensifies and disrupts ties to locality. The concern for community in the face of crisis expresses both its importance and its fragility.

Economic stagnation weakens local socialisation; yet its problems encourage attempts to use local economic, political and social ties, dubbed 'community'. These ties become more important for firms as means of competing, yet they also become more likely to disrupt them. They look outside the locality in search of investment opportunities; wage restraint, intensification and redundancies jeopardise collaborative relations with labour; the local reproduction of labour power is undermined by wage cuts and by firms becoming less willing to fund local services; firms economise by withdrawing from local collaborative ventures; local supply networks may falter as workplaces close. Thus short term pressures cause firms to destroy local collaborative structures whereas their long term interests suggest the need to preserve them. Firms may have an interest in collectively preserving local society, yet in pursuit of their individual interests they undermine it. The tensions also increase for labour. High local unemployment increases pressure to collaborate with employers; it makes workers more dependent upon local social networks to get work, and on the family for support. Yet it also compels people to leave the locality to find work.

These contradictory pressures produce enormous variation in local class relations. Employers may seek greater collaboration with local labour or may use the opportunity to subordinate it further. High unemployment and local ties may lead workers to collaborate with local employers in order to increase their profitability and thus secure their employment. Or they may encourage collective action against employers and the state through unions or community organisation. In crises some collective organisations grow spectacularly while others disintegrate. Community economic initiatives can involve any of these diverse class relations.

The onset of economic crisis in the late 1960s led to a renewed interest by sections of British capital in community. Deteriorating profitability, a wave of major strikes, fiscal crisis, ever-growing demands on and disillusionment with the welfare state, demands for equality from blacks and women, and the failure of interventionist and repressive measures by the Wilson and Heath governments marked the end of the effectiveness and legitimacy of the form of class rule established after the Second World War. The financial panic of 1974 compounded the feeling of crisis. Capital turned to neo-liberalism to reimpose discipline; but it also turned to the grass roots and to community. Community employment initiatives developed because they had the potential to combine a move away from statist welfare with collective provision; individualism and enterprise could be revived with community support; collaboration between the classes, even corporatism, could be rebuilt at a community level where it would be tempered by fragmentation and localism. This, it was hoped, could help to restabilise class relations as a basis for economic revival.

The turn to community was not, however, simply imposed by capital: it appealed to workers and residents as a way of dealing with acute problems of employment, welfare and equality, and with antagonisms and fragmentation in family and social life engendered both by the previous long boom and the onset of crisis. Community economic initiatives have in part been a stupendous exercise in top–down social engineering, attempting to change identities, aspirations and culture; but the impulse towards them has also come from below.

Reproduction of the workforce and social life

The reproduction of labour is the site of bitter conflicts both within capital and between it and labour, conflicts that embody an ambiguity towards locality and community by all parties. Local socialisation demands attention to reproduction by labour and capital, yet both have short term reasons for neglecting it.

The expansion of capital involves the destruction of many of the non-market aspects of the reproduction of labour. In this sense, the community often appears to be the victim of economic development. The values of social life – stability, predictability, mutual support, cosiness – are the opposites of capitalist values – the impersonal rule of money, constant change. Social life is seen as a compensation for and a defence against the brutality of the economy, as 'the heart in a heartless world'. One of the roots of local economic initiatives has been the defence of community against its destruction by capitalist development.

Capital expansion tends to erode the local particularity of social life. The family and neighbourhood cooperation are weakened by the demand for female labour and by the growth of uniform consumer goods and services which replace domestic labour and community support. Commodified reproduction enables workers to detach themselves from support networks and follow mobile production. Capital accumulation thus undermines family and neighbourhood in a double sense: it erodes non-market relations within localities, and it weakens the differences of social life between localities (Gough and Macnair, 1985, pp. 45–54).

But there is no guarantee that either a labour force appropriate for employers or acceptable living conditions for workers will emerge from market dominated reproduction. The inefficiencies of market provision of subsistence may impose huge costs on employers. Health care in the USA accounts for 12 per cent of GDP, a cost generally acknowledged to be inflated by its private production; health insurance costs Chrysler $700 per car and $6000 per worker p.a., and employers are now calling for social provision (Kaletsky, 1989). Market based reproduction of labour is vulnerable to the gyrations of international finance; that housing costs can double for a sizable section of the population as they did between 1987 and 1990 for British mortgage-holders is a striking instance of this instability. How these costs are allocated is the subject of political struggle: in Britain much of the pressure for higher wages in the 1980s was fuelled by the house price boom, while in the USA health care has overtaken wages as the most common cause of industrial disputes. There is a spatial element too: when production shifts and local unemployment rises, commoditised reproduction of labour means that people are left with weakened institutions of family and neighbourhood for their survival; the negative effect on labour causes further problems for firms in the area.

The welfare state was a response to these kinds of problems, meeting reproduction needs not met by wages. But it has many tensions. Because the welfare state has internalised aspects of the market and family which it ostensibly replaced, the delivery and consumption of its services has been differentiated by class, gender, race and place. This has invited constant pressures from users, and the expectations which the welfare state has generated have become increasingly out of line with what it can deliver. For capital the welfare state has done both too much and too little to provide an appropriate workforce. For political reasons it has been unable explicitly and systematically to concentrate its services on key groups of workers. Its investments lag behind the spatial movements of production, and behind the private sector's rapidly changing labour requirements. The productivity of its output, though in most cases higher than private sector provision, is neither measured nor disciplined directly by markets; one consequence is the relatively strong level of unionisation within the welfare state. In addition welfare can be a powerful symbol of a collectivist alternative to a chaotic private sector. Capital's commitment to the welfare state therefore has always had reservations.

These problems of the welfare state have contributed to, and been exacerbated by, the present period of economic stagnation. One response has been community economic initiatives, which provide for reproduction needs in a new way. For capital, these initiatives promise to resolve problems of the welfare state through providing services on a local and discretionary basis. This has a fiscal advantage: provision of services is limited to what local capital can afford. The UDCs' social programmes are dependent on the proceeds of land sales; in some US cities developers pay a levy related to the size of their buildings that is spent on low-income housing and training. The *ad hoc*, non-statutory form of provision deflects pressure on services from residents. Community service providers can choose their clients, in the same way as opted-out schools can; and by abandoning the promise of universality, the state may be more adventurous. Services can be tailored more closely to particular local demands of labour and capital, and can be more explicitly linked to the demands of production. There are, for instance, a number of schemes to link housing, training and jobs, with employers, the voluntary sector, central and local government forming new networks. The local nature of provision allows services to be expanded without being generalised in other areas. The Community Programme took the state further into the process of reproduction of labour than welfare programmes ever did – for example, with talking newspapers in minority languages and socialised baby sitting. The housing associations and the City Technology Colleges also demonstrate the possibility of greater local variation once statutory constraints are over-come. These forms of service delivery can have the advantage for clients of responding to differentiated needs and helping in access to the labour market.

This form of provision weakens the bargaining power of welfare workers because of its fragmented organisation and the politics of Third Sector enterprises. Strongly anti-union corporations have been promi-nent in sponsoring these initiatives: Citibank has been involved in hous-ing initiatives in both Flatbush and Brixton; United Biscuits, a key member of BiC, refused to support a union plan to take over its redun-dant Merseyside factory in 1983, and in 1988 announced the closure of its Halifax plant shortly after its chief executive was involved in setting up BiC's One Town initiative there. Community economic initiatives thus promise to address local reproduction needs while mitigating some of the tensions which have built up in the welfare state.

Community economic initiatives in abandoned areas

Localised deindustrialisation is often followed by a decline of the local welfare state, reflecting the failure of welfare provision to become independent of the market. As well as the obvious problems for local residents, this double decline can jeopardise productive class relations for capital: it hinders the integration of the local labour force into the labour market of the future, and poses political dangers articulated in the recently renewed discourses on the 'underclass'.

These pressures have resulted in the growth of community economic initiatives in these areas. They are providing services which the market and the state are failing to provide, while eroding the politics of uni-versal provision. Services like crèches, housing management, domestic insulation and graffiti removal which were previously carried out by the local authority, or even, in the case of domestic appliance repairs, by the private sector, are taken up by community businesses. By using small subsidies from the state and business and council contracts, they provide services in a commercial form and with the ethos of a small firm. They thus embody the disciplines of the market in areas where the market cannot function. Through these means the areas are put on a care-and-maintenance basis.

The combination of market and community in these initiatives has created a powerful consensus. Because they are not commercial small firms, and because of their local rootedness and usefulness, they com-mand the loyalty of workers and consumers, increasing their viability and allowing activities to be commercialised that would otherwise not be profitable. It is this ability to bring market conditions into non-market activities that so excites their supporters. Community economic initiatives show that community support and welfare, rather than depending upon the state, can be achieved through small enterprise and individual initiative; they construct a caring capitalism.

The introduction of an infrastructure of enterprise in poor areas and the blurring of work and unemployment in community enterprises have also stimulated the informal economy. This has reduced the price of certain services, in particular to the poor. There is a continuum between jobs done without payment for family and friends through to local services on a 'self employed' basis, which were once the domain of the private sector or the local authorities.

High localised unemployment has generated fears that, at the worst, lack of exposure to managerial authority could lead to a local culture of opposition to work discipline, even to capitalism; at the least there could be a failure to socialise youth into work (Raffe, 1983). Since some of the policies tried in the 1930s such as the 'slave camps' or the large scale 'transference' of young people from the distressed areas to the South East are currently not politically possible, other approaches have emerged: quasi-workfare, making social security benefits dependent on work, and enforced self-employment as in the Enterprise Allowance. But an alternative approach is through community-based socially useful work, as in the Community Enterprise Programme and the more locally rooted community businesses. Workfare can then be seen, even by the left, as a positive merging of work and voluntary activity (p. 47–9). These programmes again recreate market disciplines under conditions where the market cannot operate, by dropping the separation between job-creation and welfare and between economic and social goals.

The tensions reappear

Community economic initiatives then, appear to have created a model of welfare which combines the best of the state and market; but there are severe problems. The schemes are squeezed between the state and the private sector; this is reflected in the large subsidy to many community services, making them vulnerable to cost saving exercises. Yet a shift towards more market forms is opposed by private-sector competitors. Business interest has been sporadic, and selective by area and populations; if its sponsorship is a guide, the majority of services will remain with the state (p. 70). Moreover, subjecting welfare services to local market conditions does not necessarily tune them to the needs of local employers; even more than in the old welfare state, services will tend to be focused upon the better-off social groups and localities, whereas for many employers it is the poorest workers whose subsistence most needs support. In these respects the new forms of welfare combine the worst of state and market.

These forms of provision are still far from changing popular expectations concerning work and welfare delivery. Unpaid labour and cooperation with neighbours to provide services are hard to elicit since they cut across the individualism of the dominant post-war forms of consumption and conflict with women's expectations of paid work. Although community businesses and self-employment may have contributed to softening workers' demands, they have not legitimated social-security-level wages. The British Social Attitudes survey shows that support for free, universal services is still strong; expectations embedded in previous phases of development are not easily reversed.

While community economic initiatives have so far embodied a shift to the right (Mowbray, 1983), they have the potential to be a site of resistance to it, particularly, though not only, in the context of a national shift to the left. As has happened to some extent in Berlin (Katz and Mayer, 1985), community initiatives can suggest how publicly funded welfare could come under the direct control of its users, and thus become more innovative and integrated. The political dynamic of community enterprise is not necessarily stable.

The quality and composition of the labour force

It has become a cliché of local economic policy that the quality of the local labour force is the key to local prosperity. But improving this 'factor of production' is uniquely difficult. Policies have to address both production and social life; they face profound dilemmas over how deeply to intervene into social life, and the extent to which social life can be integrated with production. The apparently innocuous aim of improving the labour supply is embroiled in all the tensions of community.

First, policy faces something of a Catch 22: changing production depends on changing the labour force; yet the labour force is generated and sustained to a large extent by production. When large employers move out of a locality, training declines and the skills base shrinks. Workers with skills in national deficit, as is commonly the case in Britain, move out of the area if jobs are temporarily unavailable (though the housing market is a barrier). The skills of unemployed workers are not updated; and employers generally prefer to retrain existing workers rather than the unemployed. Programmes like the TECs tie training to the immediate requirement of employers, so that low quality production reproduces low quality labour power. For a locality to step out of these vicious circles requires strategies which simultaneously upgrade both skills and production (see further pp. 254–8).

Policies for education, housing, health and transport can affect the labour force and its capacities. To do so effectively these policies, like those for training, have to be integrated with strategies for changing production and employment (Haughton *et al.*, 1987). But this raises delicate political problems. It involves explicit targeting of services onto clients on the basis of their role in production. The post-war welfare state achieved this by spatial targeting, notably in the concentration of public services in the new production complexes of the New Towns; this was politically acceptable because it appeared as an environmental policy. The political difficulties of economic selectivity in services are illustrated by the broad opposition aroused by the City Technology Colleges, which has scared off corporate sponsorship.

Moreover, such strategies run up against the separation in capitalist society of social life from production. Social life and the production of labour power are formally under the control of workers; for financial and political reasons capital seeks to limit its responsibilities in this field, and preserve for the population this area of real and illusory personal freedom (Barrett and McIntosh, 1982). Capital is therefore tentative in linking policies for production and reproduction. We have seen that community enterprise initiatives have attempted such a fusion. But their limited success in doing so has depended on the extreme pressures of poverty and unemployment in deprived areas; in more buoyant areas such a strategy could invite strong political reactions from both labour and capital (see further pp. 246–8).

Local initiatives have also sought to change the composition of the labour force, through attracting white-collar labour to the area and by reducing the barriers to the participation of oppressed groups. The former has relied on providing new consumption facilities, which may elicit local opposition on grounds of equity. But it is much more difficult to change the social relations which marginalise oppressed groups. Racist and sexist prejudice, and their internalisation by those groups themselves, have been addressed in schools, training and enterprise initiatives, while a degree of material support such as nurseries have been provided. But overcoming oppression requires broad political movements, and local economic agencies have been unwilling to embroil themselves in these: their initiatives have seldom been based on the self-organisation of blacks or women, nor have they challenged the legal underpinnings of oppression. The Centre, and even the Left, have feared to link their initiatives to the self-activity of these groups (pp. 200, 246); *that* meaning of community action has been avoided.

Indeed, community economic initiatives often actively perpetuate these divisions. Measures for 'the locals' can be a code for distributing jobs to whites, as has been noted by Brownill (1990, p. 115) in London Docklands. Community initiatives here continue the long tradition of racism in the allocation of jobs and services by local authorities and in the collaboration between employers and white workers carried on by many trade unions – pertinent to the example of Liverpool mentioned earlier. The community of capital and labour is here based on exclusion. Just as national citizenship is defined by those it excludes (Taylor, 1989), so a project of local citizenship (Cooke, 1989a) lends itself to divisions.

Changing the local labour force can thus be far more politically charged than at first appears.

Community, industrial relations and attitudes to work

The 'quality of the labour force' also includes the ways in which workers are prepared to be managed. By reputation, localities vary sharply in their industrial relations climate: London and Liverpool are seen as indisciplined, the coalfields militant, rural areas compliant, and southern England socially mobile and cooperative. Although industrial relations are generally too political to appear explicitly in local economic strategies, they are central to them. On this basis commentators have favourably compared Glasgow to Liverpool: Glasgow is said to show the virtue of labour and the Labour Party collaborating with, rather than opposing, capital (Donnison and Middleton, 1987, pp. 286 ff). Can local economic initiatives really influence local industrial cultures?

Mainstream strategy seeks to foster collaboration between capital and labour, using varied policies. First, symbolic means have been important. Advertising typically claims that the workforce is hardworking and the climate of industrial relations excellent. Cultural monuments and up-market consumption announce that the city has left its proletarian and conflictual history behind; Glasgow exemplifies this strategy of self-fulfilling optimism. Second, industrial harmony has been promoted by organisational means, by including both sides of industry on the boards of local economic agencies and of LEB-aided firms, and by including community groups in the local economic networks. Third, training schemes, in benefiting both capital and labour, can cement their collaboration. As a Jaguar manager said of his firm's programme, 'it has helped to engender a culture of participation, involvement and openness to change' (Leadbeater, 1987).

Fourth, local economic initiatives have encouraged Third Sector enterprises in which there is only one side of industry; paradoxically this makes them particularly effective in instilling industrial discipline because the workforce experiences the market unmediated by management. Fifth, local initiatives have tried to integrate the unemployed into the disciplines of waged work; in seeking to preserve workers as workers, this addresses capital–labour relations at the most basic level (Berndt, 1977). As the Holland Report (MSC, 1977, p. 7) put it, 'unless some constructive alternative can be found [to youth unemployment], the motivation and abilities of a substantial proportion of the working population may be prejudiced for years to come'.

Finally, the gentrification of the inner cities, often encouraged by major redevelopments, may have some impact on the work attitudes of manual workers. This has been the aim of a long tradition of intervention stretching from the model towns of nineteenth century industrialists to the New Towns. An 'improved' social mix in the inner city has been seen by many commentators as crucial for changing its social relations: on the Right *The Economist* (1988) urged council house sales for this reason, while in the Centre Ermisch and MacLennan (1987) urged housing improvements. The effectiveness of this policy in changing attitudes is limited by the separation of the social life of the two classes. Nevertheless, it may change the self-identity implied by being a resident of Stepney or Salford from a proletarian one.

These attempts to foster local collaborative industrial relations face complex problems. We noted at the beginning of the chapter the tension between collaboration and market discipline involved in localistic competition. This is reinforced by tensions within the work process itself: eliciting the active cooperation and initiative of workers has to be balanced with maintaining the discipline required for effective management (Friedman, 1986). There are many possible combinations of discipline and initiative in the management of the labour process. The disciplinary side of management is particularly pronounced in Britain, with its bias towards low-skill labour processes and formal, exclusionary industrial relations. But both pressures are always present and local economic initiatives therefore have to negotiate a tension at the heart of the production process; this is a central theme in the rest of the book.

Local initiatives have also to negotiate a fine dialectic between profitability and fostering cooperative attitudes. Pressure of final markets may be necessary to compel collaboration, but it can also create conflict. The active collaboration sought by the LEBs, for example, was often derailed by market pressures (pp. 193–9). Without a tradition of collaboration management has little option but to use market discipline. But there are also problems for the many local initiatives which do not operate in the market. For instance, schemes to (re-)accustom the unemployed to work discipline are weakened in this aim because they operate with large or total subsidies and because there are no jobs at the end. These schemes can impose discipline, but this then cuts across the cultivation of initiative. The creation of new industrial relations cannot be done as a separate, ideological policy but, as with skills, it has to be realised in profitable production.

Discourses on spatial variation in industrial relations imply that there are locality-wide industrial cultures, and that this local homogeneity gives them stability: all Liverpudlians, and not just dockers, are said to be indisciplined (Meegan, 1989). But, except in small one-industry towns, industrial relations tend to be diverse, partly arising from the contradictory pressures towards collaboration and conflict. Industrial relations vary by labour process, labour market segment and workplace size: clothing workers in coal mining areas are usually unable to be very militant. Management makes tactical switches between discipline and cooperation according to the economic cycle and the strength of labour. In one locality there can be some employers seeking a casualised, unskilled labour force, while others want a low skilled, but stable and disciplined workforce; others still may wish for workers' active involvement, some through the trade union and some on an individual basis. This diversity is offset by ways in which attitudes to work can spread through a locality: through family and friendships, through local union organisation, and through movement by workers between sectors. These homogenising influences are, however, rather weak compared with people's experience in their own workplace.

These tensions make it difficult for local economic agencies to promote a new locality-wide model of industrial relations; this is likely to require a very strong local politics. The creation of remarkably homogeneous industrial relations in the Third Italy since the Second World War, for instance, depended on the dominance of the Communist Party in local government, labour organisations and those of small employers (Murray, 1987). Such political dominance is obviously hard to achieve.

Local culture: commodities and social relations

Local culture is at the centre of community. It spans production and social life. It expresses the distinct history of the locality, a sense of continuity and stability against the internationalism of the economy and the destruction and uncertainty of crisis (Hewison, 1987); it is central to the sense of belonging to a particular locality and thus to constructing its unity. The labour power which people bring to work is marked by local culture; its reproduction is itself cultural production. These are aspects of the local socialisation of production, and the concern with local culture in the last two decades reflects the increasing importance of local socialisation.

The contradictions of community are writ large in this field. Capital tends to obliterate local cultural differences – but also uses them to give product distinctiveness. The class traditions embodied in each local culture can typically be interpreted and deployed to reinforce a variety of political projects; and the sense of belonging to a place can construct unity between, and exclusion of, quite different combinations of classes and social groups.

The production of cultural products, both goods and software, seeks to tap local distinctiveness; but this is problematic. Social life within Britain is still somewhat locally differentiated, and within that sphere there are areas of non-commercial cultural production: the skills and knowledge of domestic work, of home-made entertainment, of DIY, of music making. But these activities are themselves increasingly shaped by goods and images which are national and international. Moreover, to become cultural commodities they must meet non-local tastes since cultural products are overwhelmingly traded on a national and international basis. This homogenisation is reinforced by the dominance of media distribution by the transnationals. Local policies for cultural products have attempted to set up alternative distribution channels with more diverse and risk-taking policies than the majors, exploiting the plurality of channels of communication opened by the new technologies (McKellar, 1988). But these do not sidestep the pressures to homogenisation involved in non-local distribution.

The cultural industries have strong local interdependencies due to the importance of face-to-face contacts and professional services. But while *production* may be locally tied, the *products* are not necessarily rooted in a wider local culture. The distinctiveness of the Manchester pop music scene of the late 1980s, for example, appeared to be internally generated rather than based on Manchester culture. Similarly, local economic agencies have supported minority ethnic cultures partly because of their local form. But these cultures are specific as *national* ones, and local only by virtue of the spatial concentration of minority ethnic communities.

One cultural product that *is* locally constructed is the built environment, a result of the social relations of past production and reproduction. It has particular importance in local culture because of its historical longevity and public visibility. It is central to tourism, leisure and retailing, as well as to place advertising, all of which increasingly use not merely beautiful buildings but industrial and social archaeology. This heritage can be read in a multiplicity of ways: as the glories of British industrial enterprise and imperial dominance, as the dignity of craft work, or as hell-holes of exploitation; as the settled good old days, or the devastation of change; and so on (Wright, 1985, ch. 2).

But all these meanings tend to be obliterated by the bland marketing of these artifacts aimed at mass markets. They are rendered arbitrary by the radical invention of history and atmosphere typified by the conversion of a Manchester tyre depot to a Roman fort with Urban Programme money. Nor is post-modern architecture locally differentiated, though it is hailed as diverse. While it uses a wider repertoire of significations than classical modernism, these are popular – and populist – styles which are marketable internationally (Harvey, 1989, pp. 77–92): the look of the new city centres and waterside developments is much the same in Salford as in London. There is, then, not merely homogenisation; the need for capital to expand beyond anything given by local history turns that history into gobbledygook.

Local culture is thus replete with contradiction for both labour and capital. In its very use and cultivation it tends to be subverted. The results of this are unpredictable. Capital's expansion using cultural signifiers may damage collaborative industrial relations where these are built on a sense of shared history. But labour may trade the anihilation of its past and its identity for jobs. Local cultural initiatives walk these tightropes.

Large firms and community

It is often thought that large firms are less concerned than small ones with the society and economy of the localities in which they operate, because of their greater spatial mobility and geographically wider ties. Increasing external control has certainly been accompanied by a weakening of local involvement by major employers (for south Birmingham, see Smith, 1989). But transnationals are just as concerned as small firms with the local socialisation of production. Indeed it can have a particular importance for them: the often high capital intensity of large firms makes harmonious, uninterupted production particularly crucial; their typically stronger union organisation makes them vulnerable to industrial action; and they often organise their own local networks (p. 173). Many large firms therefore seek to restructure not through relocation but through changing the local forms of socialisation of production and reproduction; to do so they attempt to influence local political culture, the local delivery of welfare, and enterprise and small firm formation.

Large firms' interest in local politics has been intensified by the increasing importance of plant level rather than national bargaining, tying wages either to the profitability of the workplace or to local labour market conditions. This requires them to show how each plant, and indeed each worker, contributes to profits, through better communications with the workforce at the plant level. The growth of employee share ownership schemes – involving 2 million workers in 1990 – similarly reflects large firms' attempts at more collaborative and locally responsive industrial relations; significantly, cooperatives and the LEBs were early, locally based proponents of employee share ownership, which was subsequently taken up by the Conservative government. A local atmosphere of collaboration for revival is a useful backdrop to these changes in industrial relations. Local labour market policies help to remove rigidities in wage bargaining such as customary differentials and exclusion of disadvantaged groups. Transnationals, then, can be intensely concerned with local work attitudes, and in a wider way with local culture; their aspirations have been described as 'a hazy composite glow of Birmingham libraries, Manchester orchestras and Glasgow institutes' (Lloyd, 1988).

In the 1980s large firms' influence over local political culture was particularly important in localities where cumulative closures have led to severe social dislocation. Some of this involvement, particularly by the enterprise arms of the old nationalised industries, has been associated with closures. It has been aimed partly at heading off union opposition; but it has also aimed to lay the basis for renewed accumulation by other firms – in Britain a rare example of collective action by capital. Other corporate initiatives have been associated with contraction rather than closure, with the difficult task of maintaining collaborative industrial relations during continuous restructuring. Pilkingtons, for instance, set up the St Helens Trust, an early Enterprise Agency, in 1978, with memories of a bitter strike still reverberating; a venture capital arm fosters diversification of the previously one-company town. This helped to repair their industrial relations while at the same time shifting production abroad.

As well as attending to the localities in which they operate, many large firms also contribute to nationwide initiatives. In part, this is intended to provide political cover for corporations in sectors which are sensitive at a national level (oil, banking, tobacco) or a local level (retailing); these sectors dominate the sponsorship of BiC and the Enterprise Agencies. The retailers, clearing banks and food and drink manufacturers have been particularly active because of their dependence on a strong domestic market. But large firms are also concerned with national political stability. In the early 1970s, and again in the early 1980s recession with the inner city riots, there has been concern that Britain's decline could create serious instability. Though more than half the assets of British corporations are overseas, the country's political stability remains of real concern to them since the domestic economy determines the value of sterling in the long term, and the British state defends its value in the short term and protects firms' interests abroad. The social responsibility movement in business is an expression of these concerns. What these corporations seek above all in local economic initiatives is to establish harmonious social relations in potentially unstable localities.

Large firms face dilemmas over the means by which to intervene locally. While the local authorities are open to pressure from business, their reduced legitimacy and resources limit their effectiveness. But large firms are not returning to the direct paternalistic service provision of the one-company towns. Public companies' duties to their shareholders legally restrict them. The rapid pace of organisational and technological change increases uncertainty about their future needs. The political visibility of corporations makes them cautious lest local commitment in the future become a brake on spatial mobility. The links between the firm and residential areas have been weakened by the diversification of local economies.

Large firms are therefore looking for 'hands off' forms of intervention. They support independent agencies such as Enterprise Agencies and Development Corporations, where the participation of many firms reduces the commitment and exposure of each. They prefer *ad hoc* arrangements, such as compacts, to institutionalised ones. These forms of intervention fall short of the direct and formal involvement and the funding of local welfare and infrastructure sought from business by the Conservatives (see further pp. 224–30).

Community around residence or community around production?

The potential for community initiatives is conditioned by the diversity of local employers and of the labour force, which affect the heterogeneity of political interests, the strength of links between production and social life, and the range of local options open to workers and employers. The spatial arrangement of these divisions within the locality – the composition of residential areas and their relation to production sites – is also important. All this contributes to local variation in the ambiguities of community politics.

The self-contained town has been attractive to all parts of the political spectrum, indicating the political ambiguity of strong community: it has been supported by anarchists, utopian socialists, liberals (Donnison and Soto, 1980, ch. 12) and fascists. Leon Krier, enthusiast of integrated communities and advisor to Prince Charles on his self-contained town in Dorset, has been influenced by Nazi urban design and anti-industrialism (Davey, 1980). Of enclosed towns, those dominated by a single employer or industry tend to have particularly strong community organisation; but this may take diverse political forms. Employers not only have a captive labour force, but can use their control over welfare facilities to elicit workers' cooperation (for Lancaster see Bagguley *et al.*, 1990; for rural areas see Newby, 1977). The social ties forged at work can also strengthen self-help projects. In yet another variant, community may take the form of militant collective action by workers and residents, facilitated by shared economic experience, as in mining areas. Enclosure can produce very different kinds of 'community'.

Minority ethnic communities in which most residence and employment are spatially coincident have similarities to the one-industry towns, and similarly ambiguous community politics. The closeness of home and work can facilitate workers' collective organisation against employers, as in the case of Turkish clothing workers in North London. It facilitates policies linking production and labour power, as in the clothing training schemes tailored to the social life of women from the community. However, it also lends itself to domination of labour by employers through a lack of alternative employment options and paternalist and 'godfather'-based employment relations. The existence of many sweat-shop sectors depends on these relations: in New York's Chinatown wages in the garment trade are lower than in the Dominican Republic. The solidarity of the community is important in dealing with racism and exclusion. But this solidarity can be a basis for suppressing conflict of class and gender. Local economic initiatives in these areas therefore usually have a strong community dimension, but this can take opposing political forms.

The socio-geographical containment of one-industry towns and minority ethnic communities is being reproduced in new forms. Local interdependencies in many sectors are leading to production and residential areas that are specialised by type of labour power. This new form of homogenisation – areas with a preponderance of technical workers or office workers – provides a potential both for domination by the employers and for collective action by labour. Just as in the 1950s outer London engineering became strongly unionised two decades after its take-off, so may the software–electronics complex of the Sun Belt.

Nonetheless the links between work and home are generally becoming increasingly blurred, because of longer journeys to work and the diversification of local economies arising from increased spatial mobility of most sectors (Chapter 5). Prince Charles's dream of a return to self-contained communities is just that. This presents major barriers to creating a distinctive local industrial relations culture and to corporate interventions. The diversity of capital in each labour market with respect to its degree of internationalisation, attachment to the locality and labour requirements inhibits a common capitalist view of local economic policy, just as the heterogeneity of British capital has blocked the development of a coherent capitalist approach to national economic policy (Leys, 1985).

It is for these political reasons, and not merely a wish to dominate the labour market, that major employers often try to keep others out of the locality (see e.g. Beynon *et al.*, 1989, p. 269). They may also have contributed to the shift of manufacturing from cities to small and medium towns, where firms can exercise greater local control. Nevertheless, in localities with heterogeneous economies, large firms can have some purchase through Enterprise Agencies to develop a collective capitalist view, and through networking to leverage favourable responses from local and central government and the voluntary sector.

Increasing separation between home and work has meant that working class residential areas have tended to become larger and more homogeneous, and to contain less local work for residents. The outer

city estate is the best known example (there is now a national association, Radical Initiatives for Peripheral Estates), but it is also true of
much of the inner cities whose residents are excluded from central area
jobs. The shared poverty of these residential areas has lent itself to
community economic initiatives. But their isolation both from the resources of firms and from established union organisation limits these
initiatives and tends to channel them into self-help. For example, campaigns to improve homeworker's conditions have been most successful
when organised by residential neighbourhood; but this creates a problem since the campaigns are detached from the firms which put out the
work, and which may simply find their labour in another locality (Allen
and Wolkowitz, 1987).

The geographical and social separation of home and work can create
dilemmas over *whose* community is being constructed. The GLC's Community Areas policy (p. 83) suffered from a tension between supporting
the community of workers in local businesses and the community of
local residents: many of the workers were skilled men living in outer
London, while most local jobs were not accessible to local residents.
The GLC faced a similar problem in setting up the Technology Networks: whether to base them on residential areas, social groups, or
communities of sectoral skills; in the event it did all three, the first being
the most ambitious and the least successful (GLC, 1985c). The separation between production and residence again weakens community
initiatives.

Pressures for socialisation, then, lead to policies which link home and
work and tend to create more homogeneous communities. But these are
weakened by diversification of local economies, the development of
communications and weak coordination of employment and housing
markets. As with local culture and industrial relations, widening market
linkages and the mobility of production have made community both
more important and more difficult to achieve.

Do community policies divide the community?

It is tempting to see local economic initiatives reinforcing a division
between mainstream enterprises with skilled, high wage jobs, and the
periphery of low profit enterprises employing disadvantaged workers at
low wages. This thesis depends on the idea of a dual economy and a dual
labour market, a 'one-third/two-thirds society' (Therborn, 1989). This is
sometimes pictured as institutionalised in a new, information-rich core

employing the 'flexible' worker, and an unskilled, routine and increasingly casualised labour force on the margins (e.g. Murray, 1985; Castells, 1989, ch. 4). The division is seen as useful for capital in creating a pool of disposable, low wage labour power and in politically dividing the working class. This view is apparently supported by the fact that policies which are ostensibly for the 'periphery' – equal opportunities training, community business, coops, job-links, compacts, start-up and make-work schemes – are in most cases separately implemented from those for increased competitiveness (pp. 95–9, 109–10, 245–6). But is the effect of policy to harden and institutionalise the division?

The first problem is the one-third/two-third thesis. While income differentials and economic opportunity have indeed widened enormously over the past fifteen years, this is due to economic crisis rather than the emergence of an institutionalised dual structure (Harrison and Bluestone, 1990). Intensified competition is shaking out rigidities accumulated during the boom years. With greater competition between workers and an increasing premium on skill, wages are increasingly linked to the profits of the particular workplace, firm, industry and locality. Greater competition between firms increases the divergences of their profits and hence their wages (Gough, 1992a).

Dualism – or rather increasing differences – is not, then, simply institutional; and accordingly, local economic initiatives do not institutionalise dualism. On the contrary, they tend to move enterprises and workers up and down the various hierarchies. They tend to enhance fluidity rather than equality. We argued in the previous chapter against the view that there is a well-defined flexible core emerging, or that localities are falling into a stable hierarchy. The formation of a stable, high wage, high skilled core is constantly undermined by the intensification and splitting up of work, and strategies for cost reduction and labour discipline. Groups of workers move in snakes-and-ladders fashion in the labour market, and do so differently in the non-coincident dimensions of skill, conditions and security. TV technicians have been casualised, compositors have had enormous wage cuts, software writers have been deskilled (Ruggiero, 1989). Local economic initiatives enhance this fluidity in wage levels and differentials by tying wages more closely to the profits of the enterprise and to the local demand for labour, and by loosening up the labour market.

Local economic initiatives in the peripheral labour market tend to integrate it with, rather than distinguish it from, the mainstream. Even when they fail to get the disadvantaged into better jobs or ease them into the informal economy, they do not merely reinforce ghettos. Local initiatives push the disadvantaged and unemployed into the culture of waged work, albeit in a subservient position. Semi-compulsory work-fare, education compacts and Third Sector initiatives integrate dis-advantaged groups into the labour market. The diversity and social divisions between these groups paradoxically facilitate the creation of an increasingly homogeneous, competitive labour market. Even schemes which stimulate the informal economy do not necessarily create a ghetto: many people in this sector see their work as leading into the mainstream through part time jobs, contacts made in subcontracting, or family connections (Neary, 1989, p. 29). Initiatives in the periphery also affect the mainstream itself. The Youth Training Scheme, for example, was not simply a means of parking the unemployed, but an attempt to replace the apprentice system and thereby reduce the power of organised labour.

Nor do local initiatives for peripheral enterprises merely ghettoise them. Community employment initiatives can pioneer new, risky but low capitalisation sectors which ultimately become part of the main-stream, as has been the case with health foods, green products and some minority ethnic ones. Third Sector policies may lay the basis for future profitable investment in what were thought to be abandoned areas, through land and property preparation, labour market inte-gration and new welfare policies. Community enterprise may be a paradigm for future forms of industrial relations in knowledge inten-sive enterprises, paralleling developments in the most advanced trans-nationals (Maddock, 1991). Delivering welfare through community enterprise can help to change mass attitudes towards the state and the market. Again, support for the periphery both integrates it and affects the mainstream.

The effects of this integration depend upon the locality. In isolated areas with high unemployment, support for the low profit economy keeps the area and its labour force ready for investment at some time in the future. In contrast, in isolated labour markets with low unemploy-ment these initiatives serve to ease the tightness of the labour market. Within the highly uneven economies of cities and conurbations, they can both ease labour markets where they are tight *and* prevent the forma-tion of residential areas with cultures of unemployment. Both sides of this coin, the effects of integration on the mainstream and the margins, are important for capital accumulation.

Despite capital mobility, there are systematic differences in profit rates in the modern economy. Social, economic, and political con-straints exclude some enterprises from avenues open to others;

transnationals have the widest range of options and hence a higher-than-average rate of profit (Andreff, 1984); at the other extreme, coops and community businesses are strongly constrained sectorally and spatially. In the UK in 1977–81 the profitability (return on total assets) of small firms was around half that of large ones (Burns and Dewhurst, 1986b, pp. 66–9). Local policies for small enterprise may or may not perpetuate and institutionalise their low profits, depending on the approach taken. The initiatives of the Right tend to increase duplicate capacity ('extensive investment') in cost-competitive small firm sectors, exacerbating their poor productivity and profitability; at the same time, the Right benefits sectors that are already highly profitable such as property, banking and privatised monopolies (pp. 216–21); it therefore tends to perpetuate differences in profits. In contrast, the Centre can have a more dynamic effect on differences in profitability. Local small firm sectors can be shifted from low to high profits, both through attention to local socialisation and by encouraging leading-edge ('intensive') investment through a targeted approach. Here again, mainstream initiatives tend to combat rather than reinforce dualism.

Local policies are not, of course, always successful in integration; Berndt (1977) shows how community initiatives in the black ghettos in St Louis were aimed at integrating the workforce into the mainstream but failed to do so. However, their thrust can be towards integration. This is not to say that they create equality; in Chapter 10 we shall see that mainstream policies not only fail to increase equality but actually reproduce it. But they can increase fluidity and movement within a system of inequality. This is of benefit to capital: capitalist development spontaneously produces divisions and ghettos; but these are problematic for capital itself, in cutting off effective sources of labour power and enterprise, in insulating the mainstream from pressure, and in storing up political problems. A dual economy and divided working communities are not always in the interests of capital.

One cannot, then, separate the low profit and the mainstream economy, either in the way they are created or in the way that local economic policy affects them; they are two poles of a single system. Initiatives that sponsor low profit enterprises cannot be accused of supporting the ghetto economy or of legitimating decline. The real problem is that the low wage economy is not ghettoised, that it increases competitive pressure on existing enterprises and workers and on mainstream welfare. Mainstream initiatives tend to integrate rather than divide the community; but as they pull some up they drag down others.

Enterprise: the economic, the social and the individual

Enterprise appears as individualism, as the antithesis of community and socialisation. Yet policies for promoting it have centred on community and local socialisation, creating tensions in them. Understood as individualism, enterprise appears to be unambiguously pro-capitalist; but this individualism can cut across the wage discipline and other forms of socialisation sought by capital. Like the other community initiatives we have examined, policies for enterprise have to negotiate the conflict and interdependence of individualism and socialisation within capitalism.

'Lack of enterprise' is a consensus explanation of poverty; but psychological and social understandings of enterprise sit uneasily together here. Lack of enterprise has always been the Right's explanation of individual poverty. In the 1980s the scale of unemployment hardly allowed for individualistic explanations; localised decline was instead put down to unenterprising *communities*. But the Right has continued to see this in moral and psychological terms. Thus Birley and Bridges (1986, p. 4) reduce the economic problems of Northern Ireland to the psychology of the '"typical Ulsterman"': '"we don't like to grow beyond the comfort level"', '"we are a stay-at-home society"'. In the USA, 'spiritual decay' is a popular explanation for economic decline (Bluestone and Harrison, 1982, p. 12).

In more social accounts, these attitudes are a product of a vicious spiral of decline which produces and is deepened by a 'culture of poverty', or a product of the dominance of large workplaces, intensified by a dependency created by welfare. The social nature of these explanations make them plausible to the Left (for example Cooke, 1989a). They underpin a strategy of restoring enterprise through social and community policies rather than through incentives and deregulation (Hopkins, 1989).

These ambiguities in the meaning of enterprise have produced a melding, but also tensions, between material and moral means of promoting it, as well as a great diversity of policies. Understood as a coherent psychological trait, enterprise becomes a crucial condition for success in life. In this form it is incorporated into the school curriculum and into youth training. Enterprise here fulfils the same role that music does in other countries, a means of confidence building, group working and sensitivity to others. But because enterprise as an abstract psychological trait can be used for diverse social ends, different means used to produce it in young people can have quite different effects.

Enterprise also appears as the willingness to form small firms; a low density of small firms is put down to a local lack of enterprise. Some psychological meanings of enterprise are irrelevant in this context. Lack of ambition, for instance, is not a constraint, since small firm formation is higher the lower the income target of the entrepreneur: many minority ethnic businesses are formed precisely because of low expectations. Psychological explanations also underplay the material barriers to working class small firm formation, such as skills, assets, discrimination and the domestic responsibilities of women. Lack of entrepreneurialism can also be a rational adaption to an absence of opportunities for small businesses in the local economy.

Nonetheless, for given material constraints, small firm formation *is* affected by attitudes to responsibility, learning, independence and unpredictability. In these respects, hundreds of years of proletarianisation in Britain have made entrepreneurialism alien to most of the working class and much of the middle class. Exceptions are localities with traditions of small scale craft work and services such as parts of London and the West Midlands, and migrant communities from regions with an important small business sector. Capital's success in creating a subordinated proletariat is a barrier to certain forms of capitalist development.

Mainstream policies to change these historically embedded attitudes have a strong community dimension, though the Right, with its strongly psychological understanding of enterprise, is hesitant about such policies. We have seen how community control legitimates Third Sector entrepreneurship. Programmes to encourage small firms among specific constituencies (Afro-Caribbeans, women, poor estates) aim to construct self-conscious communities of these entrepreneurs. Even a sense of community duty is exploited; BiC (1987, p. 10) argues that redundant workers should not spend their pay-off frivolously, but use it to to set up in business. The aim is always not just to change individuals' attitude to their own entrepreneurship but to change its social valuation and status. However, as we noted earlier, community enterprise has the potential to embody a quite different meaning 'of enterprise: building services to meet needs outside the market in a democratic and innovative way.

Another meaning of enterprise is the formation of a political leadership in what are seen to be leaderless communities. After the 1981 riots, fostering of enterprise among Afro-Caribbeans was seen as a means of forming a moderating stratum. Support for community businesses in estates thought to be plagued by anomie has been seen as a way of giving them a political leadership. These community entrepreneurs also play an important role in organising welfare initiatives: enterprise as self-help. But we have seen that this enterprise is paradoxically compromised by deeply embedded patterns of individualism in social life.

For those in waged work, enterprise in the first place denotes competition. We saw earlier how capital–labour relations have been shaped by workers' attention to their own and their employer's competitive struggle, both of which are validated by the notion of enterprise. Enterprise can also denote the active initiative by workers which some employers and local economic agencies are keen to promote (pp. 152–3). The enterprise of the worker is here pictured as close to that of the small proprietor – the classic identity of the male craft worker. Once again, the Third Italy is a model: the committed worker respects the commercial pressures on the small employer, who in turn respects the dignity of the skilled worker, a mutual understanding reinforced by men moving between the roles of worker and employer (Brusco, 1980). This model provides a melding of enterprise-as-workers'-commitment and enterprise-as-entrepreneurship. Again, it is strongly community based.

But local economic initiatives also promote a different notion of enterprise in employment: subordination to managerial discipline. Enterprise-as-competition requires discipline; and enterprise initiatives accustom people to long hours at low reward. Enterprise then, appears as both sides of the employment relation: as the worker taking the initiative and as workers' subordination to the employer.

This points to a central contradiction in the project of promoting enterprise: enterprise as independence contradicts the needs for employers to maintain authority over workers. In the 1970s the labour movement's proposals for participation and the formation of cooperatives in large bankrupt firms exemplified workers' enterprise; but these initiatives were opposed by most of British capital as potentially eroding industrial discipline. (For another example, see p. 225.) The promotion of enterprise is therefore embroiled in the highly charged issue of authority and autonomy within production.

These meanings of enterprise come together in the notion of the enterprising locality. Through acting as a community, it can become enterprising (Rose, 1986b). Just as the individual enterprise creates self-respect, so the enterprising city generates civic pride, and can inspire its inhabitants, firms and government to be enterprising. However, if a city stakes its political stability on its economic success, that stability becomes vulnerable to commercial failure; the apparently naive cosiness of civic pride requires economic sophistication – and luck. Like the enterprise of the individual, the enterprise of localities is subject to disruptive external markets, and needs external support. We shall see that this leads to policies for socialisation at higher spatial levels (pp. 134–7); but these then threaten to undermine the Bootstraps individualism of the locality-as-entrepreneur. Again, the necessary supports for enterprise undermine its promise of autonomy.

Enterprise, then appears as a unitary quality, but in reality denotes diverse and even contradictory things. It appears as individualism and as a psychological trait, but is pursued through social engineering and community. It appears pro-capitalist, but can express opposition by labour to capital. Enterprise walks along the edge of the twin faces of capitalism, individualism and socialisation.

Conclusion: the problematic construction of locality

Local economic policy, then, in trying to construct coherent and competitive localities, faces multiple and interlocking contradictory pressures. We may summarise these as:

• *Production and social life* Profitable production depends upon social life, yet how far can local economic agencies intervene in social life, and how much responsibility can they take for it? The increasing separation of work and home and mobility of labour within and between localities make the articulation of initiatives across production and social life more difficult. The policy that brings work and society together most closely, community enterprise, suffers tensions precisely because of the conflicting demands from the two sides.

• *Mobility and immobility* The spatial mobility of capital and the openness of local economies to wider markets create pressures which can encourage a local community of capital and labour. But the same pressures also threaten to disrupt this collaboration and to disorganise the productive patterns of social life. Capital is therefore often ambivalent about making a local commitment. Because of the widely differing degree of spatial mobility among types of capital, commitment by one sector may be undermined by the behaviour of others.

• *Market and non-market reproduction of labour* The commodification of reproduction and the welfare state increases wage pressures and transfers profits from high to low risk sectors. It also tends to undermine both unpaid social reproduction and community social ties. Economic stagnation has further weakened these ties, with the result that the capacities and attitudes of labour deteriorate from the viewpoint of employers. Community initiatives based on residence are therefore hampered by individualism and anomie. The basis in social life for local and independent cultural production is weakened. The potential for political instability is also increased: the more goods and services workers have to buy, the more capital has to cushion the effects of unemployment; and the balm of social life as a haven from capitalism is weakened. Policies for equality run up against the recalcitrance of family and of exclusive community, which are partly underpinned by support from capital.

● *Individualism and collectivity*　Local economic initiatives have to negotiate the relationship between the individualism of firms and workers on which capitalist society rests, and the socialised forms which it has assumed. There is a fine balance between these two aspects: too much socialisation may undermine the private appropriation of profits, while excessive individualism inhibits efficiency. Thus policy seeks to improve the labour force through socialised means while putting these services on to a more fragmented and market-oriented basis. Similarly, enterprise has been promoted by encouraging group solidarity, which is countered by exposing the units so created to the market. Firms are encouraged to think of the overall relationship of capital to the locality, yet competition tends to make firms take individual decisions.

● *Cooperation and discipline*　The balance between collectivity and individualism is also hard to maintain within the firm. Firms require both cooperation and discipline from their workers. Initiatives are drawn both ways over the types of relations to promote within enterprises and the degree of commitment by firms towards local labour. The promotion of enterprise in particular may conflict with maintaining industrial discipline.

● *Long and short term interests of capital*　The production of skills, the maintenance of welfare services, and keeping the unemployed part of the workforce do not show short term returns but can be vital for capital in the longer term. While high unemployment can be an effective means of disciplining labour, the construction of collaborative industrial relations offers a more durable solution. Relocation can offer a firm a quick fix, but this may be less effective than long term social and political intervention in the locality. Rapid technical and organisational change and the short term pressures from internationalised finance make capital ambivalent about such long term policies. Even policies for socialisation have been undertaken in a short termist way; small firm policies were partly a political response to rising unemployment, but became less popular with the sponsoring firms when they were faced with the costs of continuing support. When capital does seek a long term response, it tends to try to pass on the organisation and costs to the state.

• *The state and market discipline* State welfare services emerged, in part, from demands of capital; but capital's inadequate control over them led to their erosion and to the development of community forms of provision. Yet for capital, these semi-market forms can be inefficient. Moreover, while capital may resent the ethos of the welfare state, it is often unable to step into the gaps left by its decline.

• *Legitimacy and profitability* The community solidarity which local economic initiatives promote helps to build a legitimate, consensual form of capitalism. Yet this harmony can be undermined by policies for increasing profitability such as restructuring, technical change and intensification of work. Measures to expand the scope of the market such as commodification of culture undermine local solidarity and, as with privatisations, can elicit outright conflict. Moreover, we shall see in Chapter 10 that maintenance of class harmony can have political costs for capital.

In each of these dimensions the two processes are not merely mutually opposed but mutually dependent. Local economic policy cannot simply support one process against the other but has to negotiate them. Successful initiatives are therefore typically very delicately poised.

The framework that we have developed here focuses not merely on conflicts but on contradictions. Growth coalitions, for instance, are commonly thought of as bringing together sections of labour and capital, each with well-defined interests which include local economic growth; the coalitions' problems lie in conflicts over the means of achieving growth (Molotch, 1976; Logan and Molotch, 1987). But the interests of each participant are themselves contradictory. Capital's interest in increasing profitability often contradicts its interests in growth and leads to cuts in output and employment. Nor is it the case that some sections of capital and labour are simply locally committed and others not; all, as we have seen, have contradictory interests both in local commitment and in remaining mobile. Moreover, local collaboration between labour and capital is not merely cement for the political coalition: it concerns the relations of production and reproduction and is therefore a substantial aim in itself. But these relations tend to conflict just as much as they tend to collaboration, so that growth coalitions are intrinsically unstable (Gough, 1992b).

Another popular view of local economic initiatives is that they are riding on an epochal change from Fordism to flexible accumulation, which fragments, decentralises and informalises not only production but social life and culture; the decentralisation inherent in local initiatives, and their fragmented and informal modes of organisation, appear to be running with the tide. In the previous chapter we argued against this view of economic change. In this chapter we have seen how the social relations said to be characteristic of post-Fordism – individualistic enterprise, egalitarian cooperation, harmonious industrial relations, localised culture – are in fact the product of everything that post-Fordism is said not to be, namely capital mobility, the centralisation of capitalist control, global markets and class conflict. At the same time, these two sets of tendencies undermine each other; that is why there is no sign of a new stable 'model' of localism. Local economic initiatives, then, do not mirror a pivotal change in social structure, but reflect the contradictions of local socialisation in the broad sense discussed in this chapter, and the way in which economic stagnation sharpens the differentiation and instability of localities and encourages local collaboration.

The multiplicity of tensions within local economic policy mean that there is space for different political–economic strategies. In Part IV we argue that the Right and the Centre-Left are two different ways of addressing these tensions with an aim of capital accumulation. The Right seeks to promote mobility of capital and labour, regulation by markets, individualism, discipline, and short term profit maximisation; the Centre-Left gives more weight to the local socialisation of production, fixity, non-market relations, cooperation and long term considerations. We shall examine how the underlying tensions erupt in both these strategies.

Further reading

Recent studies of local economic policy as social relations can be found in Cooke (1989b) and Harloe *et al.* (1990). The contradictory relation of community to capital accumulation is discussed by Cater and Jones (1989, ch. 6). The impact of capital mobility and uneven development on workers' organisation is graphically presented in Bluestone and Harrison (1982) and Beauregard (1989a). The construction of local collaboration of capital and labour is theorised as a 'growth coalition' in Molotch (1976) and Logan and Molotch (1987); the different conception presented here is developed in Harvey (1985), Cox and Mair (1989a), and Gough (1992b). The relations between local production, social life and gender are developed in Mackenzie and Rose (1983), Maguire (1988), Warde (1988) and Bagguley *et al.* (1990). The nature of 'locality' was extensively debated in *Antipode* in 1987–90. Some fundamental contradictions of locality and the local state are highlighted by Lojkine (1977) and articles in Dear and

Scott (1981); Johnson (1986) discusses their contemporary form and the resultant political choices for local economic policy.

Gough (1979) gives an account of the welfare state in relation to class interests, and Folin (1981) and McDermott (1991) of its relation to local accumulation. Burgess (1982) gives a critique of self-help initiatives. Much radical geography of the past fifteen years has been concerned with local variation in industrial relations; see Gordon (1978) and Storper and Walker (1989). Nichols (1986) discusses the specificities of British industrial relations, and shows (chs 7, 8) how they are embedded in a wider socialisation of production. The tension between workers' autonomy and discipline within production is discussed in the articles in Gorz (1976), particularly Pignon and Querzola, by Friedman (1977 and 1986) and Cressey and MacInnes (1980). Gans (1990) argues against the notion of a dual workforce and an 'underclass'. On the meanings of 'enterprise' see the articles in Burrows (1991). The view that local action is being underpinned by post-Fordism is put forward in Esser and Hirsch (1989) and, more critically, by Harvey (1987); for critiques along the line of our argument see Bonefeld and Holloway (1991).

7 Local Control in an International Economy

One of the strongest impulses behind local economic initiatives has been to increase control by 'the locality', however understood. In this chapter we examine the problems, limits and meanings of local control. Hopes for local control have been strongly focused on small, locally owned firms; we first examine the prospects for small firms, and then discuss what kind of control is given by small firm promotion. Part of the promise of local economic policy is to extend economic democracy by bringing economic decisions down to the local level; we argue that the effect can often be the opposite. We examine how the use of the local level causes policies to be deflected from their aims, and thus the problems of using local control to exemplify general economic strategies. We discuss the different spatial levels of economic policy – is local control sufficient to achieve the aims of local economic policy? Finally we look at the problems of coordinating local control with spatial policy within regions and the country as a whole.

Is the future small?

It is widely thought that both workplaces and firms are becoming smaller, and that this provides an increasing basis for locally controlled economies. We first argue that trends in ownership and control are more complex than this. In the next section we argue that even where local ownership exists, this does not necessarily provide a basis for 'local control' in any useful sense.

During the 1980s the number of firms in Britain expanded strongly, from 1.27m to 1.70m. In the cities, particularly, many localities have seen the replacement of all their large industrial employers by multiplying small enterprises (Meegan, 1989, p. 214). In employment terms the change was more modest but still substantial: the proportion of manufacturing jobs in enterprises with fewer than 100 employees increased from 19 to 25 per cent between 1980 and 1989. There are diverse, even contrary, pressures underlying this trend, but all are related to the conditions of economic stagnation. Fragmentation has been due in part to increasing specialisation: with intensified competition, firms have specialised in order to accumulate experience, concentrate their R&D effort, and achieve greater synergy between products ('economies of scope'). To a small extent, it may have been due to risk avoidance in innovation by large firms, allowing small firms to pioneer new markets and technologies. In markets where product variety and flexibility has increased (pp. 133–4), this does *not* necessarily lead to fragmentation: small units often produce standardised products, while large ones have greater capacity to produce diverse products (Sayer, 1989).

As market conditions have worsened, large firms have become more conservative about increasing capacity and instead have increased their reliance on small firms for overflow orders. Another result of stagnation is enforced, risky, low profit investment in small firms through lack of employment alternatives, leading to a proliferation of start-ups in sectors with low barriers to entry (pp. 92–3). Finally, small firms in some sectors have benefited from their greater ability to pay low wages and intensify work, because of the difficulties of union organisation in small units. Unemployment and firms putting out work to cut wages and intensify work also largely account for the rapid increase in self-employment and homeworking in the 1980s.

These explanations suggest that increasing fragmentation has not resulted in organisational or geographical decentralisation of power and control; on the contrary. Large firms have used subcontracting for risk avoidance and cost-cutting. Some have increased their control within subcontracting relationships through increased vertical coordination. Learning from Japan, corporations build up around them constellations of suppliers, marketing networks and partnerships, linked through long term contracts, partial shareholdings, joint R&D, and licensing and franchising agreements.

Moreover, the current advantages of small workplaces (as distinct from small firms) are being exploited by large firms internally through a combination of decentralisation and centralisation. Product groups or workplaces are given greater autonomy in business strategy and purchasing, thus better using their specialist knowledge; decentralised wage setting weakens labour's bargaining position; and production is split up and located in the most favourable localities – a form of fragmentation that large firms can carry out more effectively than small.

At the same time, sub-units are subject to tighter financial control from the centre, and benefit from corporate R&D, funding capability and political clout. Networking outside the corporation, and decentralisation within it, spread certain types of decision-making, but they centralise the most essential decisions (Sayer, 1989; Amin and Robins, 1990). Fragmentation of workplaces, then, is compatible with increasing centralisation of control.

Meanwhile, straightforward concentration of ownership among large firms has continued in many sectors (often accompanied by fragmentation among the sector's small firms). Economic stagnation has tended to produce concentration of ownership for financial reasons: low profits have facilitated or required takeovers and asset sales, and burgeoning funds which have failed to find profitable productive outlets have been available to make purchases. In most sub-sectors capital requirements are increasing through greater mechanisation and use of information technology, despite the falling unit costs of computing power. The investments now necessary for R&D in manufacturing are often colossal, particularly with the short life of IT products; Glaxo's new research centre is costing £500m. World-wide marketing and servicing networks are also very expensive. These costs are increasingly being shared through 'strategic alliances' between transnational corporations, marking a new stage in the concentration of ownership.

Increased concentration is also resulting, surprisingly, from increasing product specialisation. A focus on the 'core business' is motivated by the need to concentrate resources to meet intensified competition. One form of increasing specialisation is vertical disintegration. This is common in services that have been hard to organise on a large scale, either because they are dependent upon key skills, as in professional business services, or because they are spatially fragmented, as in cleaning and catering. As we suggested above, the first phase of this process is a proliferation of small firms; over time, however, these firms concentrate as specialisation shows the possibilities for economies of scale and scope through a detailed division of labour, deskilling and mechanisation. In both high and low skill services, then, subcontracting has led to the growth of large firms. Moreover, 'core businesses' are widening; in the media, for example, it now extends across TV, radio, newspapers, film, books, electronic publishing, information services, and printing, resulting in rapid concentration of ownership over the past ten years. Specialisation, then, while it divides a previous pattern of ownership, tends to *increase* concentration of ownership within larger specialist areas. Thus corporate concentration continues.

The scope for local control, in the sense of control by small business, thus has important limits. First, fragmentation among smaller firms is being accompanied by an increase in concentration at the global level. Second, at least part of the growth of small firms is transient in the medium to long term. Recessions eliminate overflow subcontractors; in sectors pioneered by small firms concentration often occurs with maturity either through acquisitions or through large firms moving into successful product lines. In the long term fragmentation is powered, not by a permanent shift to new 'flexible' production methods, but by economic stagnation; if growth and profitability regained their levels in the post-war boom, much fragmentation would be reversed. Third, fragmentation is often accompanied by, and is even the means to, greater centralisation of control by corporations.

Should local ownership be promoted?

Promoting local control through locally owned small firms has been a major thread of local economic initiatives. Such firms are thought to be more firmly rooted in the area and to have stronger local links than externally owned ones, producing a more stable, coherent, and autonomous local economy. Moreover, local economic agencies are seen as better able to influence the behaviour of small than large firms, therefore enabling greater local political control. Investment by externally owned firms is then, at best, a necessary evil.

The implications of local ownership are, however, considerably more complex than this:

• *Stability* Are locally controlled firms more stable? It is true that large firms are more mobile than small ones, since they are more likely to have the capital necessary to enter new sectors, and the resources for sectoral and geographical change. One should not, however, underestimate the mobility of the capital of small firms: they frequently make radical switches in their field of business; through disinvestment or as diversification they can channel their capital into the financial markets where it becomes internationally and sectorally mobile.

But the difference between large and small firms in this respect is a contradiction for local economic policy. If it supports successful small firms, these firms will grow, and their larger resources then make them more spatially mobile. It also makes them more attractive for takeovers. This is particularly so in Britain (and the USA), where growth tends to be by acquisition; few successful small firms grow to a significant size before they are bought out. The development of a locally rooted audio-visual sector in Tyneside is being undermined by takeovers of its successful firms (Goddard, 1990, p. 32). The current growth of venture capital deepens this tendency: with their short time-horizons and good contacts, venture capitalists tend to sell their stake earlier than an owner-manager would. The creation of new tiers to the stock market has allowed firms to go public earlier, increasing the transience of their ownership. In short, an integral part of capitalist success is to be mobile between different sectors and places; 'local success' therefore tends to undermine local rootedness.

● *Investment and profit rates*   Small firms may be locally 'loyal' investors, but this investment is often weak. We noted in the last section that a part of the expansion in numbers of small firms has been through technically backward investment and sweating. On the basis of the average return on capital, firms operating with little capital, as many of these do, can claim little profit. But problems of profitability are associated not merely with size but with local ownership itself. The more spatially immobile capital is, the lower the rate of profit it has to accept, and the smaller its available investment funds tend to be. Capital that limits itself to a particular locality, such as cooperatives, community business and credit unions, tends to accept a lower rate of profit as a result. Similarly, firms which are most loyal to their locality and industry may be so precisely because they are prepared to accept a low rate of profit. For example, Massey (1984, pp. 276–81) has argued that a large proportion of medium sized, family-owned British manufacturing firms keep going at a low rate of investment and innovation because they accept a low rate of profit: these firms are exceptionally 'loyal' to their sector, country and locality, but, by the same token, exceptionally undynamic. Again, local economic initiatives face a contradiction: local loyalty tends to mean lower profit and investment, and thus a limited future.

● *Control and hierarchy*   A motivation for a small firm strategy is that the locality can thereby escape the hierarchical divisions of labour organised by large firms, particularly the branch plant syndrome. But, as we saw in the last section, many small firms are subject to external control by corporations and a subordinate place in the division of labour through networking. This can be true even of manufacturers of proprietary consumer goods who are often dominated by the major retailers. Less widely recognised is that a hierarchical spatial division of labour can also be reproduced through markets, without being designed by large firms. The small clothing manufacturers of East London and the West Midlands are dominated by small design and trading firms based in central London, who control the sector and appropriate most of its profit. Small firms can be dominated even by other small firms! In all, local ownership is no defence against relegation in the hierarchies.

• *Local finance* The locality of ownership of firms is not as simple a concept as might at first appear. Small enterprises, including cooperatives, rely heavily on bank borrowing for working capital as well as fixed investment; given the internationalisation of British banking, a part of their capital is therefore externally owned and directly subject to the vicissitudes of the international economy. This has contributed to calls for local banking in Britain.

A community-based model of banking for depressed areas has been developed in North America. Credit Unions for business formation have long existed in the ghettos. Community bond corporations raise capital locally to fund locally owned businesses in selected sectors; in Saskatchewan some sixty towns have now registered such bonds. Some funds, such as the South Shore Bank in the black ghetto of Chicago, have raised their finance from philanthropic investors outside the area (Oxford, 1987, p. 158).

These locally based funds, through their local knowledge, are able more accurately to assess risk and are thus less risk averting than the majors; they are also less likely to stereotype potential entrepreneurs. But the major banks have quite sufficient resources to develop local knowledge and anti-discrimination practices if they so choose. Nor is a formally local structure sufficient: in the USA community banks have been set up because the laws inhibiting inter-State banking have proved insufficient. Rather, the key strength of some of the North American community banks is in their interventionist strategy: they do not merely discover market opportunities but, like the LEBs, seek to create them. The South Shore Bank has supported its clients with technical and management assistance and training. It has sought to improve housing in the area as a way of increasing business confidence. The key to the approach is not localness, nor finance by itself, but a programme of linked policies for the local economy including non-profit social programmes (Bingham *et al.*, 1990).

Another element of the North American approach is the use of community. Some US banks are adopting the Third World practice of group borrowing, in which micro loans are given to members of particular communities, often on an ethnic basis, using peer group pressure to ensure repayment since further commitments depend on the record of the entire community. Again, it is not the localness of the bank's ownership but the use of local socialisation which is important.

Even with this new approach, there have been no miracles. The South Shore Bank, despite giving a low return to its sponsors, reached reasonable profitability only after ten years operation; it is able to lend only a third of its funds available for minority enterprise. Some North American 'successes' have been through gentrification or lending to non-local middle class entrepreneurs. There is a danger of swelling the supply of uncompetitive businesses (p. 92): banks with low profit targets may lead to businesses with low profits. Again, local funding needs to be linked to policies for competition.

● *Coherence of the local economy*   The popularity of the industrial district model and the notoriety of branch plant economies has led to the idea that small firms tend to have denser local linkages and produce a more coherent local economy. But the crucial technological links of small firms are often non-local, sometimes through far-flung corporate networking. Conversely, large firms may build strong links with local firms as part of a just-in-time strategy. Large firms may promote a more coherent local economy in a wider sense: they are better able to train and retain skilled labour, and to elicit public infrastructure. Again, the size of firm is not the decisive question.

● *Wages and conditions*   Local ownership can be a problem for labour because the quality of jobs in small firms tends to be inferior to those in large ones. This is particularly the case where small firms have grown on the basis of absorbing market fluctuations, cutting wages and intensifying work. We have just seen that the localness of small firm ownership does not necessarily counterbalance these weaknesses by generating a stable and coherent local economy.

● *The influence of local economic agencies*   If control depends on incentives offered to the firm, local agencies can obviously influence a small firm more easily than a large one. But to the extent that small firms have a lower rate of profit and are spatially and sectorally less mobile, they are more vulnerable to the market; to this extent they are weaker vehicles for local economic policy, and the control that they make possible over the local economy, as opposed to individual firms, is less. Moreover, to obtain significant growth from small firms both individually and in aggregate, local economic agencies need to create local infrastructures and networks (pp. 90, 94, 107, 136); this is no less ambitious than influencing large firms' local investment.

The same point arises if we consider control of investment *between* localities. Public agencies or a trade union can negotiate with a multilocality company the spatial distribution of its investment. In contrast, if those same workplaces were owned by single-site firms there would be no central investment body with which to negotiate. A multisite firm already carries out conscious planning of the relationship between different areas, whereas with single-site firms these relations are governed blindly by markets. The division of labour between two Courtaulds factories can in principle be negotiated; that between the fragmented Leicester and West Midlands clothing sectors cannot. Local economies dominated by multisite firms are in this sense more easily planned than those dominated by locally controlled enterprises.

The argument of this section, then, is that if local autonomy is to mean anything, it means strength of capital accumulation or good working conditions, not local ownership. We have found that this local performance is partly shaped by the size of firms, though the *location* of a firm's control has not been important to the argument (Townsend and Peck, 1985, pp. 77–9). But the implications of the size of firm are complex and contradictory. Both large and small firms may, under the right conditions, undertake strong local investment rooted in the locality. The crucial variable is not the size of firm but the competitive strategies adopted: local autonomy is better pursued through strengthening the local socialisation of production than through promoting local ownership.

Can local economic initiatives extend economic democracy?

One of the virtues of local economic initiatives is said to be the way they extend economic democracy. The localness of the initiatives is seen as crucial in this: they involve grass-roots action; they circumvent large, bureaucratic organisations; and they are based on detailed and thus effective knowledge. They thus increase participatory, democratic control over the economy (pp. 10–11; Falk, 1978b; Ward, n.d.). What is the truth in this idea?

Right, Centre and Left all promise to increase economic democracy; but this means different things to each. For the Right, markets themselves embody economic democracy; local economic initiatives which remove non-market constraints enhance democracy by allowing individual workers and firms the maximum freedom of choice. The Right has pursued this aim largely by restricting local authority powers: it sees economic democracy as superior to local political democracy. The Right's economic democracy is not locally rooted: it is above all the right to enter and leave the locality rather than positively to shape it; market democracy is then necessarily against local political democracy since it must eliminate the local barriers to mobility.

But this has its contradictions: the Conservatives have weakened not only the political democracy of local electors but the economic democracy of local firms. Their local property initiatives have arbitrarily distorted markets; through weakening the local authorities they have reduced local business's ability to obtain the services and infrastructure they demand; and through nationalising the business rate they have removed the crucial lever of business on local councils. Even the Conservatives' own qualgos have weak representation of locally based business: the TECs are dominated by executives from large firms.

For the Centre and modernising Left, local economic initiatives extend democracy by subjecting firms to intervention by an elected local authority, or by an unelected local economic agency using consensus, and thus 'representative', approaches (only 6 per cent of qualgos in Sellgren's sample (1987, p. 56) had elected boards). These initiatives shift economic power from central government to local agencies, which are seen as inherently more democratic through being 'closer to the people'. They also develop a more direct economic democracy through Third Sector enterprises and enterprise planning.

We have argued that the small scale of the enterprises commonly targeted by local policy does not produce a greater degree of control or of local autonomy. Further, Centre–Left strategy leaves control of most of the economy in private hands, beyond the reach of democratic decision-making. It might be replied that this strategy *increases* the scope of democratic decisions, and that to increase it *further* would lead to economic inefficiency. But this large degree of private control also affects the quality of democratic institutions and procedures: the reliance of the Centre–Left on enhancing private profitability conflicts with the participation of labour and leads to bureaucratic decision-making. The promotion of workers participation, whether through enterprise planning, cooperatives, or workers' share ownership, can lead them to 'see commercial sense' and subordinate their interests to those of profitability more readily than they would otherwise have done (p. 199). An alternative effect is where democratic mechanisms are closed off so as not to interfere with profitability; for instance, workers have been excluded from strategic planning by LEBs when it involved restructuring detrimental to them (p. 198). In the first case, self-restraint under market pressures stops the use of democracy; in the second case, the institutional mechanisms of democracy are suppressed by capital.

These failures of democracy are rooted in the central thread of Centre–Left strategy, collaboration between capital and labour in order to increase the profits on which benefits to labour are to depend. Labour's inclusion in this politics depends on its renunciation of interests which conflict with profitability; this tends to exclude a wide debate by workers of alternatives addressed to their needs, since these are liable to go beyond commercial constraints. It is not surprising to find that labour's involvement in local economic policy is dominated by union officers, whose role is to find agreements rather than lead struggles. We are back to a politics of smoke filled rooms, even though they are local ones (Gough, 1986b).

The 'constraints of profitability', however, are not fixed. The greater the degree of public or cooperative intervention and ownership, and the wider it extends spatially, the more these constraints are mediated by political choice. The logic of the Centre–Left's conception of economic democracy is therefore towards greater intervention, including non-local intervention (pp. 207, 209, 255–8).

Another way that the democracy of local economic policy is circumscribed is the unscientific manner in which policy is often formulated (pp. 113–14): if aims are not explicit and effects are not examined then democratic debate is impossible. This arises, again, partly from pressures of profitability and private ownership. The lack of attention to the wider effects of policy results from the attempt of consensus policy-making to respond to the demands of firms, their private interests. The evasiveness of policy-making enables it to avoid awkward pressures from capital and labour which might disrupt their collaboration.

Saunders (1984) has argued that the local level is more democratic than the national; for this reason, in order to avoid pressures from labour the regulation of production is carried out at the national level – an assertion we have already criticised (p. 133). It is dubious that local government is any more democratically accountable and pluralist than the national (Duncan and Goodwin, 1988, p. 36); the turnout of voters in the respective elections, for example, suggests the opposite. At any rate, we have argued that local *economic* policy is often conducted in undemocratic ways. Indeed, it is precisely the localness of the policy which limits the pressures from labour and thus limits democracy: Bootstraps collaboration for localistic competition can subordinate labour to capital more effectively than national policy (Chapter 6; see further pp. 239–40).

It is not merely, then, the limited powers of local institutions that constrain local democracy. The pressures of competition on the locality cause self-censorship and suppression of democracy in the name of unity and profitability. The immediacy of local initiatives does not necessarily make them democratic.

What division of labour between local and national policy?

In the two previous chapters we argued that the local level has specific strengths for economic policy. But we now argue that the local level also has limitations which tend to deflect initiatives from their intentions: local policy slips through local fingers.

The mobilities of capital and labour across local boundaries are the root of many of the problems we have analysed in this book. The effectiveness of the EZs, for example, has been almost wholly negated by the inward movement of jobs from nearby locations, and by a rise in rents which greatly reduces their cost advantages: the mobility of production means that the geographical area of the policy is simply too small. A similar problem is when outer city residents take the jobs destined for inner city populations; again, the area of the policy is too small relative to the daily mobility of labour. Attempts by the Left to impose conditions on capital are similarly weakened by its mobility between localities. Policies can 'leak': firms which become more profitable, and workers who become more skilled, thereby become more likely to move out of the locality. Localities can use these leaks to 'free ride': southern England can economise on training through immigration of skilled labour. While these disruptive mobilities also operate between nations, causing analogous difficulties, the mobilities are greater between localities and the policy problems correspondingly more acute.

Product markets, too, can undermine local initiatives by diffusing beneficial effects out of the locality. Policies which facilitate a closure in a sector with overcapacity benefits all other firms in the sector regardless of location. Local policies for cost reduction often lead to price reductions, benefiting firms or consumers outside the area, rather than to qualitative improvements in local production. We shall argue in Chapter 11 that the potentially beneficial effects of local economic initiatives on profit rates and growth operate for the most part at an international level, diffused through both capital and product markets. Again, these leaks occur also at the national level, but are a greater problem for local policy because trade as a proportion of output is higher at the local level.

Non-local capital, labour and product markets thus deflect local initiatives from their aims. In some cases the policy then achieves nothing; in others its benefits are reaped elsewhere. The converse of these failures are false successes achieved through spatial mobilities. For example, policy may achieve increases in local employment through spatial transfers and thus at the expense of localities elsewhere. In many cases this achieves no justifiable aim (pp. 50–1, 244–5), but its local impact is always presented as proof of policy 'success'.

Local economic initiatives are severely limited by the lack of local state powers. While national policy can create jobs through monetary and fiscal means, local economic initiatives have to resort to spatial competition to achieve the same effect. The local modernisation of industry is constrained by lack of powers over capital flows, over company and investment taxation, for compulsion on firms to train, and so on (pp. 255–6). The Left is inhibited by lack of powers to take firms into public ownership. The economic powers of British local government could be increased in many ways, but subject to limits set by the nature of the nation state itself. Capitalist nations are constituted by the free movement of commodities and capital within their boundaries: local powers therefore cannot include capital and trade controls. Nation states are constituted by their control over the money supply; this requires the national government to have exclusive control over bank credit, aggregate public spending and borrowing and, hence, interest-rate policy. No national government will tolerate local money, favoured by the Greens, on any significant scale (Dobson, 1990, pp. 149–50). Nation states are constituted by their defence of private property rights; no major infringement of them by local authorities is allowable. Local powers can be unbridled only in supporting or directly undertaking production and reproduction, where the activity of the local authority does not differ in kind from those of private firms and individuals. This necessary division of economic powers between national and local government has been underestimated by those who emphasise their different roles (Saunders, 1984), by those who see these roles as historically contingent and fluid (Duncan and Goodwin, 1988), and by those who focus on their common class structures (Cockburn, 1977).

Non-local mobilities and markets and the constitution of nations, then, not only constrain but deflect local economic policy. Yet localness is integral to all the strategies we have considered; local economic policy rests in this tension. Moreover, non-local mobilities actually help the Right and Centre to construct a local subordination of labour (pp. 141–4);

these mobilities therefore play a highly contradictory role in the effectiveness of local economic policy.

It might be argued that the effectiveness of local as compared with national policy should not be measured by their tangible economic benefits, but by their ideological impact. This view of policy effectiveness has been influential on the Centre–Left (Hall, 1985b; Hall and Jacques, 1989). It does not matter that the EZs fail to create jobs or higher profits if they dramatise the theories of the Right and change local authority attitudes. But, in the long term, in order to be persuasive policies must have some of the effects claimed for them (Levitas, 1986, pp. 18–20); the failure of the EZs to produce these has reduced their effectiveness as ideology. Local economic initiatives are effective in changing ideas when they change ideology and material practice simultaneously and through each other, that is, when they change social relations.

A popular view of the effectiveness of local economic policy is that it has an 'exemplary' role, that is, that by showing tangible successes, albeit small scale and localised, it encourages the spread of the approach, right to the national level (Hodgson, 1984, p. 152; Moynagh, 1985). This differs from the view just discussed in assuming that the local policy is economically successful. But we have seen that the localness of policy can negate or deflect its aims: geographical scale is important. The local is not in any simple way a small scale testing ground for the national.

The need for non-local policy

The relation of local policy to higher spatial levels of intervention has received remarkably little attention; the Bootstraps promise of the local, the discrediting of centralised regional policy, and the absence of regional government, have focused attention on the local level. Since the early 1980s the Centre and Left have proposed regional authorities with economic powers (Mawson and Miller, 1986; Danson *et al.*, 1991), and the existance of an important unelected regional state has been registered (Duncan and Goodwin, 1988, ch. 7); but the relation between local, regional and national spatial economic policy remains unclear. In this section we look at arguments for a regional level of policy on grounds of national profitability, equality, and even the needs of strong localities. The articulation of the different spatial levels of policy is discussed in the next section.

First, there are the problems of local congestion and inflation, for which local policies are contradictory. A local anti-growth policy which restricts growth in the leading local sectors will damage the sectors' national performance. If it restricts population growth, it will exacerbate local labour shortages. Alternatively, local policy can attempt to accommodate strong growth. But the provision of extra infrastructures and housing is costly, and often runs up against opposition to change of land use. Local authorities can use land zoning partially to protect essential sectors from being expelled by high land costs; but in the absence of public ownership of land it is difficult to hold this line. These limitations of local policy suggest the need for policies within and between regions to redistribute some sectors away from the congested areas, thus also using underemployed infrastructure in depressed areas. This, admittedly, is not easy, because the sectors to be redistributed have high local socialisation, requiring the creation of alternative integrated local centres, with all the problems this entails (pp. 136–7; Murray, 1989).

A second reason for non-local policy is the competition of localities for high level activities, in which many inevitably fail (pp. 132–5). The problem here is not merely one locality stealing some jobs from another, but the wasting of infrastructural projects, and the location of firms in would-be special localities that never make it and where the firms are therefore less productive. This suggests the need for planning and rationing across localities of initiatives to attract high level sectors.

Third, at present the major spatial shifts of jobs are within regions. A solution to unemployment depends on national policy (pp. 50, 265–9); but if the aim is to make local unemployment rates *more equal*, then redistribution within regions is crucial. Such policy could aim to move either jobs or workers. In the first case, resources for creating employment could be concentrated on the weaker and denied to the stronger areas. Controls similar to the regional industrial and office development permits could be imposed on employment growth in the stronger localities, though these would shift jobs to other regions rather than to the inner cities unless the socialisation of the relevant sectors within the inner cities was addressed.

Given the difficulties of organising local socialisation, another possibility is to move workers to the jobs. One strategy is to improve transport links between localities with high and low unemployment, for example, by rapid transit systems. However, this is of little use to women with domestic responsibilities, and requires low fares to enable unskilled workers to travel the long distances. Rail systems with this aim would also be expensive since the employment mismatches are ever-changing.

A second strategy is to help workers to move to where the region's jobs are concentrated. Since inner city unemployment takes the form of a faster movement of jobs than residents out of the cities, why not speed up the decentralisation of residents (Buck and Gordon, 1987)? This is nominally the policy of the Conservatives ('on your bike'), consonant with their notion of perfecting markets by increasing spatial mobilities. In practice they have reduced labour mobility by their housing and social security policies, and have failed to increase it by weakening restrictions on residential land use (Chapter 9). Effective relocation of low skilled workers to jobs would anyway require much more extensive measures: post-war policies for decentralising workers did not benefit non-skilled workers (Hall *et al.*, 1973), and current conditions are even less favourable. Increased provision of owner occupied housing and even (on past experience) council housing in growth areas would be taken mainly by skilled workers; housing provision needs to be linked to job change (Moore and Townroe, 1990). Targeted training schemes and measures to change employers' recruitment practices would also be needed; though unskilled workers stand a better chance in Berkshire than in Hackney (Buck and Gordon, 1987), there are still large barriers to their employment there.

This necessarily high degree of coordinated intervention is one reason why a strategy of relocating workers has not been undertaken. But another is that, even for the Centre and Left, policies to redistribute jobs or people within regions smack of 'old-fashioned' planning and cut across the Bootstraps ethos. The Labour Party's (1991b) proposals for regional economic authorities envisage them providing resources, perhaps differentially, for local development, but not redistributing jobs and people between localities. This neglect of measures for labour mobility means, in effect, that capital accumulation in localities takes priority over reducing inequality in local unemployment rates.

Some important aims of local economic policy then, can, only be met through regional policy. The effective organisation of the local socialisation of production depends on coordination across local boundaries. Local control is not enough.

Coordinating local, regional and national policy

Local economic policy, then, depends on higher level policy. Yet this inevitably limits local control; how is this limitation to be organised? The different political currents have very different means and criteria for national coordination of local policy; yet there has been little debate on this issue. The Centre and Left in particular, because of their attachment to Bootstraps, have attacked Conservative local economic policy on the grounds of its local effects rather than its national rationality.

For the Conservatives, economic initiatives by local authorities have been crudely regulated simply by lack of powers and finance. But the government has still needed a criterion for distributing central funds to local economic agencies. This has increasingly been to obtain the maximum financial or social return on funding for each project (City Grant, Urban Programme), each agency (the TECs), or each local programme (City Challenge). National coordination is to be through a quasi-market which measures local initiatives against each other.

Though this appears as a neo-liberal criterion, in essence it is not very different from the cost–benefit analysis favoured by the consensus in the 1960s, or even the social auditing supported by the Centre and Left (Rustin, 1986; Geddes, 1988a): funds are allocated to schemes with the highest benefit/cost ratio. The Conservatives have been less systematic in accounting social benefits, though they have not ignored them. A deeper difference in national coordination by the Right and Centre–Left is that the Right takes little or no account of the coherence of local economies, reflected in the fragmentary units of its accounting. In contrast, within Centre–Left strategy a judgement has to be made about economic initiatives within each locality as a whole; the logic is to allocate funds to localities sufficient for them to sustain and enhance local coherence.

However, since the Centre–Left also wish to address socialisation at the national level, and possibly at the regional level (see previous section), there is a need to coordinate local with higher levels of socialisation. The aspiration is for policy at each spatial level addressing the socialisation specific to that level, each fitting snugly inside the next like Russian dolls (Ward, n.d.). But this coordination involves deep tensions. The most obvious is competition between the lower level agencies both for jobs and to be major sectoral centres. On Teesside, for example, subregional collaboration in economic initiatives has been disrupted by some District Councils wanting to compete against the others (Beynon *et al.*, 1989). This cannot be dealt with simply by the authority at the next higher level because spatial competition is based not merely on the interests of local agencies as bureaucracies, but on competition between sections of capital, and, through that, between sections of labour.

A further source of tensions is that the appropriate spatial level for addressing particular aspects of the socialisation of production is often unclear. Should technology transfer from academic institutions be organised at a local, regional, national or even international level? Training schemes should address themselves to labour requirements over what geographical area? If there are sectoral restructuring initiatives operating at spatial level x, should the training initiatives operate at that same level or another? Or consider plans to rationalise sectors with overcapacity: from the point of view of local specialisation or linkages, plant x should be preserved while plant y should be closed; but from the point of view of specialisation or linkages or technical superiority at the regional level, it might be the reverse – a tension familiar from disputes between the EC and nations about rationalisation projects. The organisation of socialisation in one area or at one spatial level often violates that in another area or at another spatial level (Harvey, 1982, pp. 426–31).

These tensions are compounded by the fact that the forms of socialisation are never static. A subregion invests in a rapid transit system in order to promote sectoral specialisation and unification of the labour market. But this harms the coherence of some local economies within the subregion: the central business district expands and disrupts its surrounding areas, suburban economies lose their captive supply of young female labour to the city centre, and so on. The spatial arrangement of socialisation is constantly reconfigured by the mobility of capital which socialisation itself promotes (pp. 249–51).

These contradictions inevitably lead to tensions between the economic agencies at the different levels. From an administrative point of view, these conflicts can be resolved by instituting a division of powers. But if this divides functions between levels (e.g. labour market policy to the local level, funding of medium firms to the regional level, etc.) it introduces artificial and harmful divisions between policies. If it takes the form of an administrative hierarchy, where all local action must be approved by the region, the region's by the national government, and so on, then the whole notion of local autonomy is undermined. In Chapter 10 we shall see that class relations too cause problems for the Centre–Left's articulation of policy at different spatial levels.

Whatever the strategy, then, there is no functional fit between local and national policy. For the Centre–Left, the spatial coordination of socialisation is threatened by mobilities and competition. The Right's project of adjudicating local demands through markets and quasi-markets is subverted by the need for local coherence. The problems of both the Right and the Centre–Left with coordinating local policy in the end have no administrative solution since they arise from the contradictory faces of capital in space, socialisation and mobility.

*   *   *

The idea of local control is thus much more problematic than appears at first sight. It is not necessarily furthered by local ownership; it does not necessarily further economic democracy; attempts at local control are deflected from their aims by non-local markets; local socialisation and more equal development of localities require policy at higher than local levels; and coordination between local and higher levels of policy is disrupted by tensions between local coherence and socialisation at higher spatial levels. As we shall see in Part IV, however, each of these difficulties is dealt with differently by different political currents: the possibilities and meaning of local control depend on politics.

Further reading

There is now a substantial literature on the relation of small to large firms; for theorisations see Bechofer and Elliott (1981) and Gerry (1985); Amin and Robins (1990) discuss the new networking. On the problems for labour of small firms and decentralised production see Murray (1983b) and Rainnie (1989), and those of homeworking Allen and Wolkowitz (1987).

Part IV

The Future of
Local Economic Policy

Introduction

Will local economic policy have continued relevance through the 1990s? The immediate economic problems to which local initiatives have responded – unemployment, deindustrialisation, lack of competitiveness – have not been resolved. At the world level, the austerity practised since the mid-1970s has not returned the capitalist economy to health. The 1980s expansion was powered by US military Keynesianism, which failed to resolve the USA's ever-widening trade and federal budget deficits and accumulated debt, and its unprecedentedly low rate of profit. No stable system of world regulation has emerged to replace the US dominance of the post-war boom. The changes in Eastern Europe offer no quick fix for capitalism. The enormous debt creation of the 1980s leaves a continuing problem. The traditional response of writing it off through inflation is unlikely at present; if it is slowly paid off it will be a long term drain on productive capital, preventing recovery. There is a continuing danger of widespread defaults, jeopardising the world financial system.

In Britain, some indicators of performance in the 1980s seemed to show a halting of long term relative decline. Between the peaks of 1979 and 1988, output and productivity increased more rapidly than in the EC as a whole, and productivity increased as fast as it did in Britain during the post-war boom. Britain's share of world manufacturing exports stopped its long term decline and stabilised between 1983 and 1990. At a local level the boom was most noticeable in the central area and waterside redevelopments of the big cities, and in some phoenixes such as Corby and Consett. Towards the end of the 1980s, many areas were faced with overloaded infrastructures and skill shortages, and policy was redirected towards these 'problems of success'.

But the relative decline of Britain has not been halted (Green, 1989; Costello *et al*, 1989, pp. 81–9). Manufacturing output grew less than 10 per cent between the peaks of 1973 and 1989. The recession of the early 1990s was the most severe of any of the advanced capitalist countries. The failure of the Conservatives' policies was signalled by real interest rates remaining at historically high levels and real wage increases continuing even during the recession and, most ominously, the balance of payments remaining in deficit, no longer cushioned by a surplus in oil.

Underlying these problems was the weak investment in manufacturing. There was no growth in manufacturing investment between the peaks of 1979 and 1989. The 37 per cent increase in annual investment in that period was wholly in finance, business services and distribution – no surprise that city centres looked 'confident'; but these sectors cannot compensate for the increasing trade deficit in manufactures (Hirst and Zeitlin, 1989, pp. 270–2). R&D continued its relative international decline, and did not rise during the 1985–8 boom. The most successful manufacturing was generally in niche markets with limited prospects of expansion, a traditional retreat for British manufacturing; high volume manufacturing continues to be 'hollowed out', with high tech production, particularly, being shifted overseas (Williams *et al*, 1991a). While profits on industrial and commercial capital peaked in 1988 at their 1970 level of 10 per cent (having fallen to an unprecedented 3 per cent in 1981), this is still a historically low rate, and it did not result in expansionary investment. Both profit and productivity increases were due in a large part to the scrapping of backward capacity – 20 per cent of the industrial capital stock was scrapped between 1979 and 1981 alone, and net investment in manufacturing was negative between 1980 and 1984.

The Thatcher boom was to a large extent based on expansion of credit to companies and consumers. Lack of manufacturing investment meant that this resulted both in the increasing trade deficit and mounting inflation; the apparent success of the mid-1980s was unsustainable. The following corrective deflation differed from the previous recession in having a proportionally greater impact on the South than the North, because the expansion had been so strongly based on consumer and property credit. But the greatest casualty was again manufacturing. The recession also exposed the shallowness of the 'small firm revolution': the British traditions of volatile bank lending and high interest rates reasserted themselves with a vengeance, resulting in unprecedentedly high attrition of small firms. Two deep recessions have meant that the growth rate in the past fifteen years has been the most *unstable* amongst the OECD countries; this has not only wasted much potentially profitable investment, but has reduced investor confidence and contributed to the low overall investment rate.

World economic stagnation and ever-declining British competitiveness are thus likely to provide continuing motivation for local initiatives in the 1990s. Moreover, further European integration will intensify the problems of many localities. There will be a tendency for Britain to become increasingly used as a low wage, low skill assembly location; yet membership of the ERM would make a strategy of price competition more difficult by inhibiting devaluations. The economies of regions and localities will increasingly be defined within a European rather than national division of labour – a 'Europe of the regions'. Some areas with high value added or specialist economies will benefit from increased access to European markets; but others will suffer from a concentration of specialist activities into fewer centres at the European level. Given that the South is already more competitive at the European level than the North, and geographically better placed, the North–South divide will be exacerbated, particularly in producer services (Howells and Green, 1988). Both capital and skilled labour will be able more easily to leave the weaker areas of the country. Increased European integration will therefore tend to deepen the uneven development of localities and regions within Britain, eliciting further demand for local initiatives.

A continuing debate on strategy

Continuing economic problems reflect continuing problems of strategy. Despite the consensus in local economic policy in the early 1990s, the role of local initiatives as a part of different national strategies will not disappear. There has, it is true, been an increasing political consensus on national economic policy. Aspects of the Conservative programme in the 1980s are widely accepted as successful and necessary: the weakening of the trade unions, most of the privatisations, the reorientation of welfare services, and a need for 'enterprise'.

But this consensus contains acute tensions. One with profound implications for local economic policy is between Britain's Atlanticism and its integration into Europe. In the 1980s the traditional orientation of British capital was deepened by world financial liberalisation, accelerated export of capital, and the continued role as junior military partner to the USA. But important sections of British capital also looked increasingly to Europe: many manufacturing and consumer-service multinationals, but also the City itself, anxious not to lose its dominant position in Europe.

In the early 1990s the advocates of a stronger European orientation also tended to be critics of the Conservatives' record; these were not only the opposition parties but also from within the Conservative Party itself. The worsening economic situation, the debate on Europe, and criticisms of their strategy led to the downfall of Thatcher and a cautious but marked shift to the Centre and towards Europe. The change in domestic policy concerned the socialisation of production in its widest sense, including the stability of class relations. There was concern about organised and disorganised rebellion against widening poverty, clearest in the reform of the poll tax, but also in concern about the explosion of crime; it was acknowledged that equal opportunities might need more than market mechanisms; the government dipped its toe into industrial policy; infrastructures and large scale land use planning might need more attention. Debate re-emerged on classic themes of the British disease. The banks' hardened policy towards small business in the 1990–1 recession was criticised as reverting to type. Despite the weakening of the unions, industrial relations remained as controversial as ever. Though employers had achieved a more thorough dominance in the workplace, real wage rises had not been contained, and talk of non-statutory or tax-based incomes policies re-emerged. The European model of formal management–workforce consultation and a framework of legal rights was increasingly canvassed against the traditional liberal British model which the Conservatives had maintained. Thus the consensus approach which had dominated local economic policy during the 1980s began to appear at the national level. With the marginalisation of the socialist Left and a discrediting of Thatcherism, the Centre–Right appeared to be unchallenged.

The new consensus is however riddled with dilemmas which will come to the fore as the oil runs out and as Britain's competitive weakness is further exposed by European integration. The tension between Atlanticism and Europeanism, far from being resolved, is deepening, and further complicated by the events in Eastern Europe. European monetary integration restricts many social and infrastructural initiatives which the Centre would like to take. The dilemmas of Centre strategy at the local level are exemplified in the debates within the TECs and between them and the government (p. 111). The difficulty of a Centre strategy was reflected in the tentativeness and '*ad hocery*' of the policy making of both the Conservative and Labour Parties. We shall argue later (Chapters 10 and 11) that the tensions of a Centre strategy run very deep.

Moreover, Right and Left strategies retain a real social basis in Britain. For the Right, the liberal traditions of British capital retain their power, and chime in with world trends towards neo-liberalism. As we shall argue, behind the Right's manifest failures is a real political–economic logic; and the British Centre has itself shifted towards the

right. As to the Left, the trade union movement has been weakened but
has not been rendered powerless: the proportion of workers unionised
remains high, and new realism within the trade unions is not unchallenged. One therefore cannot rule out a resurgence of the Right or
Left; certainly these strategies will be attempted in some localities, and
any consensus will periodically incorporate elements of them. In the
remaining three chapters we therefore consider the future not only of
the current consensus but also of the Left and Right.

8 The Left: Modernisation or Class Struggle?

The retreat of Left initiatives during the 1980s was due in a large part to external pressures; but it also involved the intrinsic ambiguity of the Left's strategy. We saw in Chapter 3 that the strategy had two strands: on the one hand a defence of workers' interests and extension of their influence, and on the other a project of 'modernising' the British economy. There is an evident contradiction between these two projects. The first is prepared to pursue workers' interests for their own sake, irrespective of their negative impact on competitiveness; the second pursues them only in so far as they are compatible with, and indeed increase, competitiveness. The first seeks to organise struggle by labour against capital, while the second seeks the maximum collaboration of labour with capital, provided the latter is 'productive' (Weaver, 1982; Cooke, 1989a; Meyer and Boyle, 1990). This tension caused failures, and was increasingly resolved in favour of the modernising project. Since we are concerned with the future prospects for Left local initiatives, we shall not focus on the national pressures that derailed the Left but rather on the internal contradictions of the strategy itself, and how these might be overcome.

Social objectives versus profitability

Attempts at defending workers' interests were damaged by the confusion between the two strands of the Left's strategy. In Chapter 3 we noted many failures to achieve its 'social' aims – improvements in wages, conditions, unionisation, workers' participation and equality. These failures often appear as due to obstruction by bureaucracy, failures of political will or inadequate resourcing (Benington, 1986, p. 21; Mackintosh and Wainwright, 1987, Introduction). But this timid approach to social aims itself needs explaining. It arises from the Left's strategy of seeking social benefits through, or in tandem with, improve-

197

ments in efficiency and profitability: the fundamental problem is that the firm may not be able to afford to grant such benefits. This problem manifests itself in a number of different forms:

● *Social cost versus survival*   The LEBs have been inhibited from pressing social aims on client firms because of extra costs which include not just improvements in wages and working conditions, but also in training, improved recruitment practices and the time involved in enterprise planning. This problem was exacerbated by the weak state of most of the LEBs' client firms, a problem that is endemic since they tend to act as a lender of last resort. Thus LEBs have been reluctant to coerce firms into improving their employment practices, even where they have the power to do so. A similar problem arises in contract compliance and with employment legislation: the firm can threaten, sometimes justly, that compliance will jeopardise its future, and workers may then also oppose enforcement. If the local authority threatens to remove a purchasing contract for non-compliance, this too can jeopardise jobs.

● *Promote the good or push the bad?*   Should one support firms and sectors with poor employment practices in the hope that increased competitiveness will lead to improvements, or support those with better employment conditions? There has been pressure to sustain local sectors and firms with good wages and unionisation, but this does little for the worst-off workers. But it is difficult to upgrade the profitability and employment practices of sweated sectors. The informal management style of these sectors makes it difficult for a LEB to engage with them; improvements will be from a low level, with little prospect of the employees' participation which the Left wished to exemplify. Similarly, with contract compliance there is a dilemma as to whether to buy only from good employers, or to put pressure on poor employers. Moreover, the experience of the LEBs is that improvements in employment practices depend on monitoring and continuous pressure from employees; this cannot happen without unionisation. Social policies are therefore hardest to pursue where they are needed most.

● *Management control versus participation*   Attempts by LEBs to promote greater worker involvement in aided firms have experienced resistance from management, despite arguments that it can increase efficiency. While this is often put down to their conservatism, it has its roots in their fear of a loss of control (Hyman and Elger, 1981), in commercial confidentiality, and, where survival is precarious, maintaining the confidence of suppliers and customers. LEBs are often involved in cuts in capacity, and here management fears the reaction of its workforce. The London LEB's restructuring of the furniture industry is illustrative: workers were kept in the dark about the plans because they could have exposed the lack of honesty and realism in managements' proposals (Furniture, Timber and Allied Trades Union, 1986). Thus the Left's strategy was harmed not only by its small resources and the weak firms in which it was implemented, but by contradictions in the industrial relations it aimed to promote.

• *Participation and self-exploitation* The effects of participation can be the opposite of those intended. Workers' stake in coops, combined with market constraints can lead to self-exploitation. The same problem arises also in other forms of workers' participation. Low profitability, especially in times of high unemployment, always puts pressure on the workforce to make concessions; LEBs' intervention may increase this pressure because of workers' support for their political project and because of their sense that they have a stake in the enterprise (Mackintosh and Wainwright, 1987, ch. 6). The employee share ownership schemes of the LEBs add to this pressure. The Left's 'flexible specialisation' strategy (p. 80) leads to a less institutionalised form of this tendency. Workers are to be flexible with respect to job tenure, hours, tasks and wages as part of a strategy which is to deliver high wages and high profits; the corollary is that they accept low wages, intensification and job loss when profits are low, which they would not otherwise have done – the reverse of the social aims professed by the Left.

The same conflict between social aims and profitability therefore appears in different forms and in different policies. The virtuous circle hoped for by the Left – better conditions and greater participation by workers leading to greater competitiveness leading to further advances for the workforce – is a theoretical possibility, and has occurred at certain conjunctures; but in Britain in the 1980s the level of profits and the traditions of the local economies with which the Left was dealing virtually ruled it out.

Social aims have suffered in the conflict with commercial ones. Programmes to enforce employment law had to pull their punches. The LEBs and providers of collective services progressively softened or dropped their social aims in the second half of the 1980s. In some cases where commercial policies failed to achieve integral social improvements, separate social policies had to be introduced; for example, Greater London Enterprises set up a fund to give grants for social gains in client firms. This returned to the classic social democratic separation of policies for production and redistribution which the Left had set out to overcome (GLC, 1985a, pp. 15–19).

The conflict between social and commercial aims also generated bureaucracy. The Left had hoped that its strategy would open up a *dynamic* process of increasing workforce involvement and self-confidence. Enterprise planning was not to be a static formula but an open-ended process. In contract compliance the threat to jobs posed by effective policing was to be resolved by workers using the pressure from the local authority to strengthen their bargaining position. In the most radical versions of the Left strategy, conflicts between workers' control and profitability would stimulate workers' collective action. The outcome, however, was the opposite. Attempts at dynamic enterprise planning were replaced by *prior* social conditions being placed on funding, and the better firms selected in a static manner. The balancing of the conflict between social benefits and profitability was achieved, in time-honoured fashion, through negotiations which excluded the workers. Thus the Left failed in one of its central aims, to exemplify an alternative to bureaucracy.

Could the Left's strategy have a different outcome? A virtuous circle of increasing productivity and increasing workers' control implies a profitable local economy. It is questionable whether the Left could maintain the necessary militancy under these conditions of prosperity. Moreover, if the strategy was not to be limited to the most prosperous areas, it would require radical change in structures of the British economy, and unleash sharp opposition from sections of capital (Chapter 10). Alternatively, the Left could pursue the defence and extension of workers' interests effectively if it dropped the productivist strand of its strategy and its concern to maintain enterprises' profitability. But there would then be the problem of employers' disinvestment and bankrupcies, requiring greater financial resources and greater powers to take over firms than local agencies currently possess.

The new guild socialism

The productivist strategy is flawed by its divisiveness. High wages and strong union power are to flow from skilled production, a perspective rooted in the strong craft tradition within British unionism. In the 1970s this policy took the form of defence of skilled, unionised jobs in manufacturing. From the early 1980s it took on a more forward-looking form: technological, design and organisational innovation would reap higher-than-average profits from which good wages could be paid, and require skills which would strengthen labour's bargaining position (Murray,

1985). The former strengths of the steelworker and miner are to be transferred to the flexibly specialised engineering worker, the cultural worker or the software writer.

This reliance on skill produces a type of power that is inegalitarian because of its basis in production, its labour market mechanisms and because it is anti-collectivist (Rubery, 1978). First, we saw in Chapter 5 that, even in an advanced capitalist country it is inconceivable that low skill tasks can be eliminated; promotion of skilled work tends to increase the differentiation of skills rather than their overall level. Moreover, even high skill tasks often fail to reap high profits because of the vagaries of technological and design competition and of market demand; the stable technical rents which existed in the nineteenth century are increasingly rare because of an increasing rate of technological change. The strategy is therefore inherently uneven between groups of workers and unstable over time.

Second, the bargaining power endowed by skill depends upon its supply. Clothing machinists, for example, have little bargaining power partly because their skill is so widely produced. The Left believes in the expansion of training; if this occurred, the bargaining power of skill would depend on other barriers to entry. Historically, skilled workers have erected barriers to entry on the basis of age, race, gender, family ties and locality; since the 1970s the struggles of black people and women, and the interests of some employers, have tended to break up such arrangements. But informal discrimination, and barriers to skill acquisition produced within social life, mean that skilled jobs still tend to be taken overwhelmingly by white men from skilled or middle class families (pp. 243, 246). The skills which women have are often ones acquired in the home, which are not only ideologically devalued but produced too widely to be a bargaining counter. The logic of the Left's strategy, then, is to connive in the perpetuation of these inequalities, and even to construct systematic (if covert) forms of discrimination.

Reliance on skill is also anti-collectivist. Where the bargaining power of skill – and the power to define it as 'skill' – rests on union organisation, this is inherently sectional and tends to be parochial, as British craft unionism shows. Particularly when it is in short supply, skill can appear to make any collective organisation redundant; the culture of skilled manual and professional southern England in the 1980s is an example. Thus, while deploring divisions by race and gender, the Left was reproducing them; while denouncing traditional white male unionism (Hall and Jacques, 1989), a new labour aristocracy was being proposed. This continuity from manual craft to professional élitism was facilitated by the increasing role of professionals in the Labour Party, continuing the traditional domination of the party by better-off workers. The reliance on skill contributed to the abandonment of support for collective action by a part of the Left: for many professional workers the new high tech, high culture city offered advancement without collectivity (Mulgan, 1989).

As Cockburn (1983) has argued, the Left should define desirable labour processes not in terms of 'skill', whether substantial or politically defined, but in terms of their health and safety, the variety and interest they afford, and the sociability between workers which they allow. Bargaining strength would have to depend on collective organisation rather than exclusionary skill; but the commonality between workers of the desirable qualities of jobs would be a basis for solidarity. Beyond this, a real increase in skilling consists in workers running production and making investment decisions (Braverman, 1974, pp. 443–6), which also requires the development of the inherently non-individualistic skills of collective organisation.

The coy politics of socially responsible production

The tension between the Left's two strategies – defence of labour and the modernisation of production – is graphically exemplified in attempts to promote more socially responsible production. The Left promoted alternative uses for sensitive sites, the development of socially useful products and of production processes which are sensitive to the needs of labour. These policies provide a vivid illustration of an alternative: different political philosophies are directed on to a piece of land, a product or a machine, which becomes a focus for struggle.

The Left, however, was ambiguous about the basis of the alternatives. On the one hand they were presented as anti-capitalist, meeting human needs irrespective of profitability; on the other they were said to increase productivity and profitability and therefore to be more rational paths for capital. The choice between these was avoided by focusing narrowly on the artifact – the piece of land, product, or machine, implicitly presenting it as a solution in itself.

Although the aim is to promote different social relations, in order to present the policies as realistic the economic and political obstacles have been downplayed. Community land campaigns, for example, press for developments employing manual labour; but their focus on the availability of land and buildings ignores the fact that inner city manual jobs would often require revenue subsidies and/or heavy investment. Similarly, support for product innovation assumes that the problem is lack of technology; but in most cases monetarily effective demand is inadequate. In some cases a sympathetic public body can be found as purchaser; but often a campaign is needed to change the priorities of the public body: use of the road–rail bus developed by the Transport Technology Network in London clearly involves a major change for transport operators. The emphasis on technology as such meant that the Technology Networks largely failed to develop this kind of campaigning role (GLC, 1985c; for an exception see Mackintosh and Wainwright, 1987, p. 207).

The underestimation of these barriers led the Left to believe that they could be innovators within the market. The campaign in London's Royal Docks, for example, argued that the port operators were overlooking the potential for profitable short haul traffic, and downplayed the fact that relocation of the docks was partly aimed at weakening the unions. The Technology Networks often sought to create new markets via product innovation, while the problems are essentially political. Proponents of human centred machinery, for example, have presented the problem of good jobs as being about machine design. The latter is sometimes a constraint, but often the problem lies in the use employers make of given machines. The alternative machine can be as productive as the standard, but employers may oppose it because of the control over the labour process which it gives to workers, and because of the price of skilled labour. Proponents of human centred machinery thus paradoxically end up picturing production as a question of technology and productivity, neglecting its social relations. Similarly, the GLC's campaign for combined heat and power stations stressed its cost and ecological benefits, but neglected the way in which it would entangle the power industry in complex planned relations with consumers and firms. These elisions tend to underestimate the political obstacles to the alternative proposed and thus the need for collective struggle to achieve it.

The concentration on the artifact also neglects the wider effects of policy. When they were part of a socially useful alternative, the Left accepted production conditions that it would otherwise have opposed. The London Docklands strategy envisaged encouraging clothing and lampshade manufacturing, without policies which could effectively change their working conditions. Wages in some alternative production sectors such as community printing were ignored. The London Technology Networks have worked with companies with poor working conditions, which were not considered a relevant issue (GLC, 1985c). The alternative could also be divisive: land use campaigns have often pitted manual against office jobs, neglecting the fact, *inter alia*, that the latter are generally a better option for young working class women; this follows from focusing not on jobs as such but on the use of a piece of land. The inevitable contradictions of alternative initiatives are not addressed because of the *deliberately* narrow focus adopted.

Because of the lack of clarity over political aims and wider effects, policies tended to fail or move to the right. A GLC report on the Technology Networks found that most of their products were not 'socially useful' (ibid., ch. 2); since 1986 the Networks have become increasingly geared to commercial product innovation and consultancy, similar to mainstream innovation centres. These failures and shifts arose partly from external pressure, but also from the internal ambiguities of the policies.

A focus on a concrete social alternative can be a powerful stimulus for struggle and can widen the scope of socialist politics, as happened to some extent in the Royal Docks campaign (Newham Docklands Forum, 1983; Mackintosh and Wainwright, 1987, pp. 308–16). But this can only happen if these alternatives are understood as challenges to capitalist social relations. They therefore cannot base themselves on productivist employers or market niches, but require collective struggle; this collective development of the alternative should be seen as a virtue, not a problem.

Localism and the retreat from public ownership

Public ownership could address many of the problems of the Left which we have discussed. Public production is often more efficient than private (pp. 145, 214–16). The virtuous circle hoped for by the Left – of better conditions leading to greater worker commitment and higher productivity, allowing improved conditions – would have a greater chance of working under public ownership: the public sector can take a long term view by accepting a lower rate of profit on capital, by accounting social benefits, and by the possibility of subsidy. Public ownership, rather than the planning agreements made by LEBs, would make it easier for a local authority both to institute strategic planning and improve working conditions, especially if it had a monopoly in the local sector. The tendency to tailor social alternatives to short term commercial pressures could better be resisted.

In view of these strengths, it is striking that municipal enterprise has not played a larger role in Left local economic policy. Its only significant expansion has been in nursery provision; even this has not been undertaken to replace profit-making enterprise, but rather as an expanding, subsidised social service (but see Mawson and Miller, 1986, pp. 174–5).

The *de facto* rejection of municipal enterprise has for the most part not been due to legal restrictions; though disallowing some types of public enterprise, these allow far more scope than the Left chose to exploit. There are many sectors in which local authorities could have expanded it without interference from the government, which have relatively small capital requirements, and indeed which can be profitable (Chandler and Lawless, 1985, ch. 10)

One reason for this lack of interest was an ideological retreat in the face of the Right and of most sections of British capital, which supported privatisation rather than further public ownership. But another element was the Left's belief in decentralisation (Geddes, 1988b). The Left in the 1980s was hostile to the bureaucracy of existing public ownership; the more decentralised forms of ownership and control promoted by its local economic initiatives, such as planning agreements, worker participation and partial ownership, and the Third Sector, were seen as more efficient; many argued that they were more attuned to a supposed new period of 'flexible accumulation' (pp. 169–70). There was a conceptual slippage here: a belief in fragmentation – a question of scale and spatial arrangement – was said to justify a change in the form of ownership.

The view of municipal enterprise as cumbersome and old-fashioned was reinforced by the intensification of work, wage restraint and redundancies carried out by Labour authorities from the mid-1980s, which tended to discredit the idea that local public ownership could improve working conditions and provide better services. The argument for this strategy was that local, detailed and 'creative' management of austerity was preferable to a nationally coordinated resistance aimed at getting more central government funds; again, the local was preferred to the national. Thus, in two ways, an ideology of local control and decentralisation played a major part in the decline of support of the Left for public ownership.

Unravelling the Left

Through the 1980s the tension between the two strands of the Left was increasingly resolved in favour of the modernising project. Left policies converged with the Centre: both aimed to increase the efficiency of capitalist production through addressing its local interdependencies and by dealing with various British peculiarities; both aimed to advance the interests of workers and the disadvantaged through this modernisation. The productivist Left was as careful as the Centre to avoid policies such as public ownership which few sections of capital could be persuaded to support. The policies of the modernising Left were more ambitious and far-reaching than those of the Centre, but they did not differ strategically. Our discussion of the future of the productivist Left is therefore continued in our discussion of the Centre in Chapters 10 and 11.

We shall argue that the productivist Left faces severe problems of class relations in its project of modernising British capital. We have seen in this chapter that the productivist strand also led to many of the Left's policies having results which were unattractive for labour: bureaucratic organisation, needs subordinated to profit or managerial control, and deepening of divisions in the workforce. These resembled traditional labour movement practice, and weakened the initiatives' popular appeal. In the early 1980s, the Left hoped that the small scale of its resources would be compensated by the 'exemplary' character of its initiatives: workers elsewhere would take the examples as a yardstick and achieve the same gains through pressure on their employer (Palmer and Wainwright, 1983). This failed to happen partly because of the defensiveness of the trade unions during this period. But it was also due to the unappealing features of Left initiatives resulting from their productivist aspirations.

The socialist Left whose aim is the defence and extension of popular interests therefore needs to free itself from the modernising project. The low profitability of British industry and its effects on workers' living standards makes a modernisation strategy a constant temptation to the Left; but a strategic alliance with modernising capital may be unrealisable (Chapter 10, 11), and attempting it derails popular collective organisation and aims. What, then, would a socialist local economic strategy freed from a project of modernisation look like?

Socialist local economic strategy

A central question is the location of economic power in the contemporary economy. To many socialist commentators local initiatives are irrelevant since power in a capitalist society is overwhelmingly located outside the locality, at corporate headquarters, in national government and in international markets. But this neglects a crucial sense in which capitalist power is rooted *within* each locality: the management and control of labour in order to extract surplus value takes place within each enterprise, and is eminently 'local' (Gough, 1991a; Ruccio *et al.*, 1991). Accordingly, this power is strongly influenced by the activities of local government. As we have seen in this chapter, the local power of capital can derail the Left's initiatives; but it also means that socialist strategy can, and indeed must, challenge capital at the local level.

There is another side to this, however. Precisely because the capital–labour relation is not external to localities but is ubiquitous, capital is mobile; and this mobility constantly threatens local gains made by the labour movement. Socialist strategy must therefore include collective action across localities, in tandem with local action.

This interplay of local and global action is complex. Encroachment on the power of capital proceeds through collective action of workers and residents to impose their interests, sincc, as we have seen in this chapter, attempting to realise these interests through improving the competitiveness of capital is uneven and unstable (Beauregard, 1989a). This collective organisation is always strongly local. The immediate experience of economic problems is local by definition. Because a large part of most people's economic knowledge concerns their locality, and because of the logistics of organisation, solidarity between workplaces and industries is easiest to organise at a local level; the major examples of workers' councils in the twentieth century have been city-based. Consumption too is still largely local, and its local problems expose the links between everyday life and capital accumulation (Chapter 6). Not merely the inadequacies but the *contradictions* of capitalism, especially that between the socialisation of production and private decision making, can manifest themselves clearly at the local level (Chapters 5 and 6).

There is, then, potential for local collective action against capital, involving people as residents as well as workers. Since the mid-1970s, when the Left in Western Europe has been weak at a national level, local economic issues have produced some militant and popular locality-wide mobilisations with support beyond the industry immediately affected. The most spectacular of these – Lorraine in 1979, British coal mining areas in 1984–5, Spanish steel and shipbuilding areas in 1986, Dortmund in 1987 – have centred on the contraction or closure of large, strongly unionised workplaces; but the potential is not limited to such cases.

Locally based collective action is not necessarily anti-capitalist. We have seen that, by virtue of being local, it can easily involve self-exploitation and an *anti*-social dynamic; as a worker-director at the long-established cooperative, Scott Bader, said when one of its factories closed, 'we had no boss to blame, only ourselves' (Channel 4, 15 July 1987). It can be divisive: the Loyalist workers' strike in Northern Ireland in 1974, organised on a community basis, is a classic case. Geographically uneven development militates against shared experiences, while local community organisation can defuse opposition to capital (pp. 143–4, 158–9). The *aims* of local collective action, then, are crucial.

The overriding aims in local socialist economic policy should be political: to strengthen collective organisation and solidarity and combat divisions within labour. Right and Centre strategies are at base strategies of class control (Chapter 6; pp. 211–17, 239–40); sometimes, as in enterprise policies, this aim is quite conscious; socialists should have the same approach. Thus it is not enough for social aims to be added on to investment policy; they should be what investment policy is for (Gough, 1986b; Massey, 1987b). Particularly important at the present time is to combat the increasing fragmentation of workers' organisation through subcontracting, individualisation of employment contracts and increasing differentiation in the use of different sections of the workforce. Though these are strong trends, they are not uncontradictory and unstoppable (Pollert, 1991; pp. 161–3). Local authorities can oppose this fragmentation both through their direct employment and through their influence on the private sector. Local organisation is important in extending unionisation, including to the unemployed. The local level is also central to the defence, extension and transformation of welfare services, and for linking these to workers' organisation in production; this linkage is essential to address divisions within labour, particularly of gender and age. The most powerful local popular mobilisations in recent European history, those in northern Italy in 1969–73, involved mutually reinforcing offensives within production and around housing, transport and social facilities (Red Notes, 1979).

On some issues the socialist left will find itself making similar demands to sections of business which are dissatisfied with neo-liberal policies and wish to address the local socialisation of production and reproduction (pp. 71, 74, Chapter 9). Disagreements within capital can make left campaigns easier. However, business and the left will eventually diverge on implementation. Both may support more council house building; but they will differ on whether this is to be provided universally or to key workers, on the types of household for which housing is designed, on the means of subsidising it, and so on. Moreover, no section of business is aligned with socialist policies on all issues. Unlike the productivist strategy, then, the socialist Left cannot form an alliance with modernising business.

Socialist campaigns can start on a local basis, but they have to become national or international if they are not eventually to be undermined by the spatial and, increasingly, the sectoral mobility of capital. Whereas labour lags behind capital in international organisation within industries, it has even less control when capital switches sectors at the same time. As we suggested in the previous section, socialist local economic strategy cannot ignore the issue of public ownership and planning, unfashionable though these are. It is the regulation of the economy by private profit which limits the Left's ability to improve conditions of employment, and, as we shall see in Chapters 10 and 11, to stabilise investment, increase equality, and resolve the economic crisis. Private ownership eventually undermines any secular increase in social control of the economy, even where this could in principle benefit capital accumulation, because of capital's political fears of excessive socialisation (pp. 256–8).

A form of social ownership which is strongly local and decentralised is market socialism, in which enterprises are controlled by their workforce and may be owned by them or formally in public ownership (Selucky, 1979; Hodgson, 1984). Despite claims for democracy, this does not resolve the problems of private ownership, since the economy would still be regulated by the pursuit of profit by independent, and effectively private, units. The spatial and sectoral mobility of capital might be reduced, but spatially uneven development via markets in goods and services would remain. The aggregate patterns of the economy would be immune from democratic control, particularly the aggregate rate of investment and hence the level of employment; once again, more local control does not necessarily mean more democracy. Overcoming uneven development, and achieving productivity growth in each locality, requires national and sectoral allocation of investment (Devine, 1988).

In the present situation this may appear an academic point; but it has implications for socialist local economic policy now. It is not enough to build collective organisation and pursue democratic control of the economy in each enterprise or each locality separately; the forms of control have to extend nationally and beyond. Democracy does not have meaning without effective power and control, and these cannot be mainly local.

Further reading

For critiques of the Left strategy compatible with ours see Levidow (1983), Harris (1986), Gough (1986b), Nolan and O'Donnell (1987) and Cochrane (1988). Swartz (1981) shows the political silences and ambiguities of the productivist Left. The resistance of management to the gradual extension of workers' control envisaged by the productivist Left is explained in Hyman and Elger (1981), and a critique of workers' share ownership is given in Centre for Alternative Industrial & Technological Systems (1987). Socially responsible product initiatives are criticised by Clark (1983) from the left and Rustin (1986) from the right. Pickvance (1977) and Urry (1985) analyse the bases for local popular collective action.

9 How Can Markets be Freed?

We have seen that the Conservatives' local economic initiatives have been relatively weak: they tolerated, and over time shifted towards, consensus policies (pp. 72–5). This is a result of a fundamental tension in strategies to revive capitalism: on the one hand they have to increase the mobility of capital and the freedom of markets, while on the other they have to organise the socialisation of production (pp. 122–3). The freeing of markets and the circulation of capital sought by the Right are not ensured merely by removing barriers; they depend on profitable and efficient production, which requires the social organisation of production addressed by the Centre. This dilemma has often surfaced in debates between the Conservative government and its business supporters; it means that neo-liberalism is constantly vulnerable to pressure from the Centre. In this chapter we show how this contradiction will shape the future of the Right's strategy.

Neo-liberalism promises to deal with the stagnation of the global economy by using economic crisis as therapy. At the centre of stagnation is an excess of investment capital chasing too few profitable outlets; the crisis destroys capital values and enables the remaining capital to obtain a higher rate of profit, illustrated by the increase in profitability in Britain after the large destruction of capacity in the early 1980s. Prices of goods and services, of labour power, and of capital assets, which tend to depart from their real values during times of prosperity, are brought back into line as the crisis destroys accumulated rigidities. High unemployment enables wages to be held down and the intensity of work to be increased. These processes can lay the basis for increased rates of profit and a renewed boom in investment.

The Right adapts these processes to present-day conditions. First, deflation brings prices into line with true values. Inflationary fiscal and monetary policies, public and private sector monopolies, and state subsidies are attacked, speeding up the destruction of capital values through bankruptcies and scrapping of capacity. Second, the Right aims

211

to maximise the mobility of capital between sectors and locations. During the period of economic prosperity, interdependencies between firms and between parts of the economy were *institutionalised*, partly by government economic and social policies, and partly by private or mixed private–public arrangements (industry training boards, common research and marketing organisations, and sectoral collective bargaining). These arrangements constituted temporarily profitable forms of socialisation of the economy. They did not, however, amount to a coherent system of regulation, and economic stagnation has arisen partly from the tensions of these institutionalised arrangements. Stagnation has highlighted their costs to firms both directly and in taxation, and restructuring has put into question their appropriateness. The Right therefore aims to destroy many of the existing institutionalised forms of the socialisation of production in order to remove constraints on the free deployment of capital. This has been the motivation for deregulation, privatisation, and cuts in support for industry.

Third, the Right does not prescribe the new avenues into which capital should flow after it is freed, except that privatisation provides new fields for investment of surplus capital. A weakening of state industrial policy has been a common feature of neo-liberalism worldwide. But it has taken an extreme form in Britain. As Gamble (1981) argues, the wide sectoral and geographical opportunities for investment by British capital during its period of world dominance have produced a deep culture of economic liberalism: free markets, interests coordinated only by markets, and maximum mobility for capital. The contemporary British Right is within this tradition, and has therefore rejected industrial intervention particularly firmly. Contrary to an influential view (Anderson, 1987), these characteristics of British capitalism do not mean that it is misformed, backward or aristocratic (Wood, 1991): international mobility is perfectly capitalist and is a strength which runs with the grain of contemporary world trends towards capital mobility. Its defence by the Right is therefore not reactionary.

Fourth, the Right seeks to break down institutionalised groupings of workers and to fragment the labour force through workplace bargaining, widening regional– and job–wage differentials, and individual contracts. These in turn imply changes in social and cultural attitudes. The importance of labour markets for the Right is indicated by the Conservatives' switch in industrial spending from subsidies for fixed capital formation, notably in regional policy, to labour market initiatives. The cheapening and intensification of labour inevitably elicit resistance and are necessarily authoritarian; while neo-liberalism and traditional authoritarianism are sometimes seen as heterogeneous strands in Thatcherite urban policy (Hall and Jacques, 1989, Introduction; Anderson, 1988), they are logically related.

From these elements flows the essence of the Right's local economic strategy: to maximise mobility of capital and labour both within and between localities. Institutionalised forms of the local socialisation of production, embodied in the local state and non-market regulation of factor markets, are to be broken up. The spatial mobility of capital is to be used to discipline labour within both the workplace and the labour market. This local discipline may be enhanced by non-local employers (Liverpool is now cleaned by a French firm); but locally owned enterprises can also exert discipline, through fragmenting labour or through self-exploitation (as in the coops formed by former council workers to bid for cleaning contracts). Local differences are to be *exploited* through abandoning national regulation and national wage bargaining; but local differences are also *eroded* by breaking up varied local socialisations, tending to make localities more homogeneous. This breaking-up also allows enterprises, even those in the public sector, to reorganise production at new spatial scales which were previously institutionally blocked; compulsory competitive tendering means that Leeds City Council caterers are now doing work for the NHS, while Manchester's Direct Labour Organisation is doing building work for Salford.

The coherence of the Right's strategy lies in its use of the intrinsic therapeutic processes of capitalist economies to remove obstructions to markets. But in pursuing this, it ignores the social organisation of production. In the rest of the chapter we examine how this contradiction will shape the future of the Right's local strategy.

The chaotic devaluation of capital and labour

Devaluing capital and devaluing labour power – in the form of unemployment – have their functions; but, carried out in an unplanned way, they have penalties for accumulation. It is often the wrong capital and the wrong labour which is devalued. Efficient capacity may be scrapped because of the firm's financial weakness, and because of conflicting interests of creditors (GLC, 1985b). A firm with a high target rate of profit may scrap plant which another firm would have continued to operate. In other words, the contingencies of finance interfere with natural selection by efficiency and productive profitability.

The scrapping of capital also breaks up important interdependencies between firms and sectors such as subcontracting chains. Bankruptcies in an industrial district may take it below its critical mass. Similarly, where capacity is lost from a locality, part of the local infrastructure, both private and public, is devalued even though it may be efficient.

High unemployment in many localities has little value to the Right. The unemployed often fail to ease local labour markets or to discipline the employed because they have the wrong skills, are in the wrong location, or are what local employers regard as 'the wrong gender'. They may have minimal impact on the employed because of labour markets being internal to firms. When the unemployed lose a 'positive attitude to work' through repeated rejection, their threat to the employed is correspondingly reduced.

The anarchic geography of devaluation in Britain in the 1980s meant that labour and infrastructure were 'freed' in some areas while shortages of them damaged the economies of others. Production and labour are not transferred because the socialisation of production within both declining and congested areas has been neglected. The markets do not work because the organisation of production has not been addressed.

Deregulation, wage cutting and intensification of work: the problems of cutting costs

Deregulation of factor markets aimed to reduce prices; in this it has been disappointing for the Right. Land release, freeing labour markets, and simplifying the planning system were to cut the costs of inputs to local firms; privatisation of council services was to remove 'inefficient' work practices. In many cases, however, these policies have led to increases in prices paid by firms; the deregulation and privatisation of housing, for example, have increased its price, putting upward pressure on wages and reducing the spatial mobility of labour. The problem is that regulation or public ownership may be necessary precisely to organise effective supply of a factor and thus hold down its cost (Barnekov et al., 1989).

The Right's aims of cutting factor costs and intensifying work reflect its belief that competition is concentrated on price (pp. 36, 38); but this is a naive view of competition in the advanced capitalist countries. In capital goods and a considerable part of consumer goods, design, production quality and back-up service are vital; cost cutting can harm this quality. Wage cutting and intensification can be effective strategies in some sectors where mechanisation is hard to introduce, such as clothing and some assembly work. But these sectors in Britain cannot compete by repeatedly reducing wages because of minimum subsistence costs, which are not only demanded by workers but which are necessary to produce them *as* workers: the social nature of production means that wages are not indefinitely flexible downwards. Nor can producers cut costs by endlessly intensifying work: in contrast to raising labour productivity through new processes, there are physiological limits to how much productivity can be raised through increasing the work rate. For these reasons, much of these labour intensive sectors have shifted to the Third World. The limits of intensification are shown by the 'British productivity miracle' of the 1980s: virtually the whole rise in productivity was due to new process technology and reductions in overcapacity, and a negligible amount to pure speed-up (Bennett and Smith-Gavine, 1987). Increased managerial power has affected productivity not in enabling pure intensification, but in helping management to accelerate process and product change.

In Britain, the profits to be made by technological innovation far exceed those to be made through cutting factor costs. The policies of the Centre, which focus on the social organisation of knowledge and innovation, are addressed to this task. In labour intensive sectors, British workplaces may be able to compete through high quality or through rapid response to market change, capabilities which are again addressed by Centre strategies (Steedman and Wagner, 1989).

State promotion of cost cutting may not only be irrelevant but may actually make matters worse: firms are encouraged to continue to compete on price alone and thus neglect innovation and quality. Local sectoral studies have shown this to be a weak competitive strategy (e.g. GLC, 1985a, ch. 3). In the USA cost cutting is the dominant approach (INSEAD 1991), reflected in spatial competition centred on cost comparisons (p. 35); the outcome is that the balance of trade in manufactures has experienced continuous long term decline, remaining stable only in high tech goods; the Conservatives' favoured source for ideas on local economic initiatives does not have an enviable record.

Generous and bureaucratic subsidies and featherbedding

The government has retained many subsidies which it inherited, and has introduced new ones, though often disguised. While these subsidies have a logic in the Right's programme, they also create problems for it.

Because the Right does not acknowledge the high level of socialisation of modern societies, it believes that taxes can tend to zero, a similar logic to its view of wages; this is reflected in its local tax cutting initiatives. All advanced capitalist societies, however, have high levels of taxation, ranging from around 35 to 60 per cent of GDP. Socialisation requires a minimum level of state expenditure; any level of tax below that cannot be generalised. Thus the mechanism of the EZs is essentially subsidies rather than lower taxes, since firms in them depend on tax-financed services. Deregulation and privatisation, too, give hidden subsidies.

Because these subsidies are not acknowledged as such, let alone informed by an industrial policy, they distort markets in quite arbitrary ways from the point of view of business. Privatisation of consumption sectors such as bus services, water, energy, telecommunications and housing, and abolition of the Wages Councils in consumer service sectors, have transferred profits to these low risk areas and tended to increase wage costs for higher risk industries. This is the opposite of a policy for internationally competitive industry. Many firms and property owners have complained of the arbitrary subsidies of the EZs, the director of property investment at the Post Office pension fund declaring them 'a disaster' for this reason (*Financial Times*, 1984; see also *Estates Gazette*, 1980). Because the subsidies are not considered as such, they are not finely tuned and thus give rise to large deadweight. For example, the EZs in easy areas could have attracted development with less subsidy, while those in difficult areas have needed more.

The Right presents leveraged subsidies as minimising interference in markets. But, in order to set the grant, the state must have an informational capacity at least as good as the firms that it is validating, exactly what the Right wishes to dispense with. It also needs to be able to guess how the firm estimates and discounts risks and the opportunity costs of their capital, and thus its acceptable rate of return. This is very much a poker game, and it is impossible to arrive at an objective assessment, as shown by the substantial and varied estimates of deadweight in the Urban Development Grant (p. 88–9). This contradicts the Right's aim of transparent accounting of state expenditure. Leveraging is also at odds with the Right's aim of minimising uncertainty in markets, since the net return of a project will only be known after the completion of negotiations with the state. From this point of view, predictable, non-discretionary subsidies, such as those under the Inner Urban Areas Act, are preferable to leveraged grants and to the secret and *ad hoc* land subsidies given by the UDCs. This uncertainty probably accounts for the low take-up of the Urban Development Grant (Martin, 1990).

For the Right, then, the possible economies of leveraging are contradicted by the increased uncertainty for both firms and the state.

The bargaining of community benefits from developers favoured by
the Right is a 'leveraged tax', with the same informational difficulties for
the state as leveraged subsidies. These difficulties are suggested by a
review of leveraged benefits by New York City, which estimated in a
sample of schemes that the City had given away $108m-worth of extra
profit to developers in exchange for $5m-worth of community benefits
(Frieden, 1990, p. 426). Again, public policy 'attuned to the market'
requires a sophisticated bureaucracy and is necessarily subjective and
unpredictable.

The effect of many of the Right's subsidies is directly contrary to its
aim of shaking out surplus and inefficient capacity, tending rather to
featherbed it. Most of the help given to small firms and in property
subsidies takes no account of existing capacity. Moreover, many of the
beneficiaries of government policy – the former Wages Council
industries, much of the small firms sector – operate with low levels of
productivity. This type of production needs actively squeezing in order
to encourage a higher rate of productivity increase in the economy as a
whole and remove the claim on profits of undynamic capital. The Right
is guilty of the sin of which it accuses its opponents, that of featherbedding production which should be shaken out.

The Right's subsidies therefore contradict its own aims of transparent
markets and state spending, shake-out of the inefficient and the mono-
polistic, and reduction of state bureaucracy. All this might be justified if
they advanced an industrial strategy; but that is precisely what these
policies attempt to avoid.

Failure to promote entrepreneurialism and popular capitalism

The Right wishes to encourage risk-taking and entrepreneurialism. This
responds to a central element of a period of crisis, a constant build-up of
uninvested money capital; if investors can be encouraged to take greater
risks and accept lower rates of return, then the rate of productive
investment can be raised. The Right has also aimed to make free
enterprise popular in the way that it is in the USA, which would mark a
major shift in British workers' attitudes. Moreover, even with existing
attitudes, enterprise can be a popular card for the Right to play. Local
economic initiatives promised a fertile field for the Conservatives' enterprise initiatives; yet these have been a signal failure.

First, the Conservative government has left intact some of the major burdens on small firms: the tax and benefit status of the self-employed, lack of protection from the poor payment practices of large firms, and ineffective regulation of monopolies. The government has not introduced the kind of substantial economic privileges enjoyed by small business in other countries, such as the guaranteed entitlement to a fifth of US public procurement, or the close to zero taxation of very small firms in Italy. Incentives to savings and investment, such as TESSAs, have not been angled towards small firms, or have been channelled mainly into property as in the Business Expansion Scheme. Most damaging has been the government's policy of a high exchange rate and interest rates; whatever the long term benefits, the immediate burden falls disproportionately on small businesses because of their high borrowing and reliance on domestic markets, while the beneficiaries are the banks and firms that invest abroad.

Second, the Conservatives have eschewed support for the local business infrastructure which is necessary to sustain small enterprises. We saw in Chapter 4 that small-enterprise support agencies have found the need for many-dimensional, selective and even strategically guided intervention. The Conservative government has not provided the resources for this, and its attacks on local government have prevented it from filling this role (pp. 70–2). This absence has been particularly serious for spreading enterprise to the disadvantaged, important for the Right's idea of popular capitalism, since this needs particularly strong support. The Enterprise Allowance, the Conservatives' major initiative for new enterprise formation, has not been linked to any substantial locally based support, and as a result has a poor record: only 57 per cent of enterprises survive three years, and each survivor employs on average only 1.1 people (National Audit Office, 1990); the scheme has advertised not productive entrepreneurialism but cowboy capitalism. The government-supported Enterprise Agencies have reduced their help for enterprise of the disadvantaged because of the difficulty of implementing it with very limited resources.

Particularly striking is the Conservatives' failure to reorient finance towards local investment in small enterprise (Advisory Council on Science and Technology, 1990). The Loan Guarantee Scheme has increased funding to small firms but has not encouraged any *qualitative* change in the banks' practices towards being more strategic or locally directed (p. 90). Financial deregulation has produced new instruments for funding industry, but they have not changed the relation of the City to industry as they are constructed around ease of exit and maximum flexibility. Venture capital remains focused on management buy-outs and low risk projects; this contrasts to the USA where venture capital funds have detailed local and sectoral knowledge and long time horizons (Saxenian, 1989); in Britain there is still a shortage of true risk capital (Mason and Harrison, 1991). Deregulation has encouraged the concentration and de-regionalisation of financial institutions such as the building societies and the Scottish banks. The insurance companies and the pension funds, which would be crucial to developing local equity funding, have been steered in the opposite direction by the Conservatives' relaxation of exchange controls which has intensified their international orientation. The Conservatives have not introduced any really substantial schemes to enhance small business funding comparable with the German two-tier interest rates, worth £5bn p.a., or US-type legislation to compel banks to preferentially invest locally. These failures arise from the fundamental agenda of the British Right – to make capital more mobile; this has accentuated the traditional restlessness of the City, and militated against the development of local funding.

Nor have the Conservatives emulated the community banking initiatives in North America (pp. 177–8). Despite their praise for philanthropy and the existing support in Britain for ethical funds, they have not sought to channel socially conscious funding into local businesses. The Conservatives' lack of action probably derives not only from a belief in mobile finance but also from the fact that the North American funds have usually required guarantees from the state to attract deposits, and have operated wider interventionist policies (Oxford, 1987).

The Conservatives' failure to develop popular entrepreneurship is thus partly a consequence of their refusal actively to support risk-taking, something which has been taken up by the Centre. It is also rooted in their failure to develop localism: they have not facilitated the formation of local finance but rather its further internationalisation, and they have deepened centralised control of local government. This centralisation of both finance and state has prevented them from promoting local entrepreneurship.

Failure to develop a risk-taking property sector

Following the US example, the Right's local initiatives have centred on property. Implicit is the idea that risk-taking and capital mobility have been inhibited by the organisation of land and property development. The Right has tended to blame the state for this: a restrictive land use planning system and land hoarding by public agencies. But the British property industry itself is strongly risk-averting; this is reflected in chronic shortfalls in the provision of higher-risk categories of property (p. 100). An entrepreneurial property sector would develop property for the needs of particular sectors, and collaborate with innovative firms in developing new building types. It would pioneer new growth areas, and second-guess market needs and infrastructural development. The record of the sector in the 1980s was very different. The activity of the majors remained strongly focused on city centres, with smaller developers concentrating on the central area fringes. Oakey (1991, p. 142) found that science parks developed by the private sector offer nothing to high technology small firms except high rents. Even in London Docklands, with its strong location and high subsidies, the first developers were small builders; only when the returns were illuminated in neon did institutional investors – many overseas ones – come in.

The Right has failed to challenge this conservatism. Urban Development Grants and the UDCs nudge the developers with leveraged subsidies which fit in with, rather than challenge, its risk-averse valuations. According to a DoE advisor, 'the assumption that UDGs would persuade [the institutions] to take risks has proved almost entirely wrong' (Hamilton Fazey, 1988). The geography of the Conservatives' property initiatives has itself been risk-averting, with spending heavily concentrated in London Docklands: between 1981 and 1990 this received 60 per cent of the funds going to the eleven UDCs, while the EZ in the area, from its designation until 1988, received 55 per cent of public sector land acquisition grants and 28 per cent of infrastructural investment within the EZs (Turkie, 1991). The targeting of these initiatives on areas has meant that other forms of conservatism of the sector have not been challenged. Nor have the Conservatives used the tax breaks given to the institutions to push them towards a more entrepreneurial property policy. In contrast, innovative property development has been stimulated by the more interventionist policies of the Centre: the public and non-profit sectors particularly have created markets in new, risky types of property and in marginal locations (pp. 100–2).

The beneficiaries of the Conservatives' property policies have not been risk-taking users. Much of the subsidy to the EZs has been appropriated by the landowners (p. 66). The same is true of reductions in the business rate, which in most cases lead, in the medium to long term, to corresponding increases in rents and land values (Kirwan, 1986, p. 203). While some of the EZs and UDCs are in difficult locations, the activities in them are mostly low risk ones which are covered by their assets, such as hotels, retailers, tourism, and luxury housing. Because of their narrow property focus, they have done little for high risk manufacturing. Where EZs have attracted manufacturing firms, they have been unrelated, without agglomeration economies and often with a fast turnover – no more than an industrial estate. The failure to address socialisation within the areas has meant that they have not become the 'mini Hong Kongs' which were promised.

The Right's initiatives have also amplified the volatility of the development industry. Developers tend to pile into fashionable, apparently low risk, sectors, leading to a particularly sharp cycle, which is now being exacerbated by increasing international investment. Government schemes have worsened this tendency: tax relief for small business units in the mid-1980s led to large oversupply. The Right's liberalisation of finance has made it easier for funds to flow into commercial and residential property, accentuating speculative booms.

The industry's conservatism has been sustained by Britain's strong land use planning system, particularly the Green Belt policy, which creates limited and therefore highly profitable nodes for development. The Conservatives' restriction of infrastructure investment has reinforced this by focusing development on existing nodes. Partly for this reason, their release of public sector land and weakening of development control have scarcely eroded the spatial monopolies, and have actually facilitated low risk redevelopment to higher rent uses in the central area fringes. The failure radically to deregulate the land market, to resemble the USA for example, possibly reflects pressure to guard the profitability of the property industry. In continuing the restrictive land use planning system while liberalising finance, the Right either does not go far enough, or goes too far, in weakening state regulation of property.

The underlying problem is that the Right has been unwilling to challenge the risk-averting role which property plays in British capitalism (Ambrose and Colenutt, 1975). The sector's conservatism reflects its dominance by the institutions, which invest heavily in property for its apparent safety and inflation-proofing, as a response to the low returns and high risks in British manufacturing. Particularly in a period of stagnation, property is a haven for surplus capital which cannot find other investment opportunities and is attracted by self-generating speculative bubbles (Harvey, 1982, pp. 218–20). The patterns of property investment, then, reflect the strategies of British finance under conditions of crisis, which the Right is ill-equipped to resist.

Key Conservative policies, then, have penalised entrepreneurs while benefiting risk-averting sections of capital. It is consensus policy that has recognised that enterprise is a collective rather than an individual attribute; here, the future of the Right's aspirations lies with the Centre.

The recalcitrant politics of infrastructure

The Right has two key policies for infrastructures: first, to privatise their construction and operation, in order to provide new avenues for capital accumulation; second, to charge the full costs to the users or beneficiaries. This marketisation of infrastructure has been spurred by the tendency for its relative cost to increase in the long term, reflecting the difficulties of raising productivity in one-off production. Market pricing seeks to remove the lack of transparency of the cross-subsidisations when infrastructure is paid for out of taxation. Business has become increasingly resentful of cross-subsidisation, especially given the diversity of business needs in most local economies (pp. 130–1). Public underinvestment in infrastructure over a long period has led to undersupply and thus potentially high returns, encouraging private investors to enter the field.

The essential problems with this strategy are similar to those we have already encountered. First, the Right neglects the complex interdependencies of local economies which are particularly strong in the case of infrastructures, and hence neglects the adverse effects of marketisation for capital itself. Second, the Right assumes that the removal of state interference will result in free markets in infrastructures, whereas this depends on their efficient provision which is a social process.

Marketisation exacerbates the tendency towards underinvestment in infrastructures in capitalist societies (Harvey, 1982, pp. 236–7; Gough, 1991b). Infrastructures with large fixed capital are inherently risky because of the long and uncertain payback period and the lack of flexibility in switching markets. Moreover, these risks have tended to increase because of infrastructures' increasing relative costs, and because many types of production – and thus the infrastructures' markets – are becoming more footloose and unstable; economic stagnation adds to these uncertainties. Thus although investors may currently be interested in infrastructure, reliance on private capital is likely to exacerbate rather than solve the current bottlenecks. This is serious for the Right because of infrastructure's role in elaborating the spatial division of labour and countering inflationary pressures in areas of strong growth.

Privatised physical infrastructures still require state intervention such as compulsory purchase of land. Privatisation here enables the state more easily to ignore non-market criteria by hiding behind the private sector's demands for profitability. But since the state has to act on terms dictated by private investors, privatisation makes this role more politically exposed, as exemplified by the Channel tunnel rail link – exactly the reverse of the Right's intentions.

A paradoxical result of the Right's failure to grapple with the social organisation of infrastructure is that even projects with a high direct return fail to be undertaken. For example, combined heat and power is potentially very profitable, but its realisation depends upon cooperation between private and public sectors. This failure contradicts the Right's aim of enabling capital to flow into high return investments.

Making the beneficiaries pay for infrastructures, as in the contribution to transport links made by the Canary Wharf developer, comes up against their social logic. How can the state assess future benefits and capitalise them among the beneficiaries? As with leveraged grants, the process involves a poker game in which each player calculates the others' costs and benefits in each option; the 'market solution', where the beneficiaries and builder obtain equal returns on their subscribed capital, emerges only fortuitously. Nor can future beneficiaries contribute. Dependence on a few beneficiaries perilously exposes infrastructure provision to the cyclical vagaries of the market.

Charging beneficiaries also often requires the state to engage in tough, *ad hoc* bargaining with them, paradoxically the kind of 'harassment' of business which the Right opposes. A notable example is the way in which local authorities, under financial pressure, have increasingly tried to extract planning gain from developers, usually in the form of infrastructures; in effect they have attempted to charge the beneficiaries according to the best Right principles. The developers, however, have not been happy about this, and in 1981 the Planning Advisory Group recommended that planning gain should be outlawed; again, charging beneficiaries does not create a market but rather a new form of politicisation. Caught between these contradictory pressures, the government, after two years' deliberation, restricted but did not abolish planning gain.

Marketising infrastructures, far from balancing supply and demand, often results in either insufficient or too much revenue relative to benefit. It may be insufficient because of the impossibility of charging for indirect benefits, such as the improved labour supply and lower wages for firms resulting from public transport investment. On the other hand privatisation can create private sector monopolies such as BAA which charge high prices and fail to invest, to the cost of other firms.

The marketisation of infrastructure may increase costs to labour, which, depending on labour market conditions, can generate pressure for higher wages; this happened in south-eastern England during the 1980s with the cutting of subsidies to public transport. Though the Right regards this as an improvement, since prices and wages more closely reflect costs, local firms become more likely to attempt to influence the price and quality of services, as with the CBI's ever-increasing complaints about infrastructure in the South East. By becoming politicised, infrastructure is then less attractive to the market.

Marketised infrastructures thus create new problems for the Right: they shift profits from one group of firms to another rather than on to labour; they can result in low investment and poor quality, damaging growth; and politicisation is not avoided but merely given new, perhaps less tractable, forms.

One-dimensional industrial relations

The Conservatives' national labour market policies have had a major impact on industrial relations in every locality. This climate has influenced the local economic policy not only of the Right but of the mainstream. The prioritised types of enterprise – small firms and community businesses – are those where the collective organisation of workers is weakest. Union representation has been marginal not only in the UDCs and TECs but also in the Enterprise Agencies and Economic Development Companies. The Centre has not tried to oppose the weakening of labour organisation; indeed, the local competition which it promotes has tended to intensify the subordination of workers to management (pp. 141–3).

But however influential, the Right's approach to industrial relations suffers from major problems. First, the reliance on unemployment runs up against its uneven geography, which the Right does nothing to address. Second, the Right's wish to create a homogeneous, deskilled labour force does not correspond to real trends (pp. 134–5), leading to serious national and local skill shortages which have strengthened the bargaining power of skilled workers.

Third, we have seen that, for management, pure discipline in the work process is not enough: active cooperation can increase productivity and production quality, especially in task-flexible and skilled work. Such cooperation is formalised, in different ways, in the two most successful capitalist countries, Germany and Japan. The project of the British Right, so far, has been simply to impose managerial discipline. This fits with its strategy of low innovation, cost-competitive production. It has perhaps also been a necessary stage for British capital in dealing with what was, from its viewpoint, excessively militant labour; but employers generally have not yet felt strong enough to build on this and engage in active cooperation with labour, and their ability to change work processes has suffered as a result (Holloway, 1987). The Conservatives have attempted an element of incorporation through their enterprise initiatives and, indirectly, through wider populist projects; but as we have seen, these are far from having established a solid new form of class collaboration, and in some ways actually cut against it (pp. 163, 166).

These weaknesses are strikingly exemplified in London. The city should be a show case for the Right: since the mid-1970s unionisation in manufacturing has dropped precipitously; many sectors consist of small, non-unionised firms; and among a large proportion of manual workers the Thatcherite attitudes parodied by 'Loadsamoney' flourish. Yet this has not created productive industrial relations: employers have complained of productivity and costs being worsened by high labour turnover and by the 'indiscipline', 'lack of cooperation' and 'unwillingness to learn' of manual workers (Leigh *et al.*, 1982). Behind these lie the skills shortages, high living costs and lack of labour mobility exacerbated by the Conservatives' policies. Effective discipline, and sometimes active cooperation, have probably been best achieved in London in fragmented sectors employing disadvantaged groups, such as clothing, catering and cleaning (GLC, 1985a, chs 4, 18); but these sectors are the least significant for capital accumulation. These problems show that the Right does not necessarily create either a disciplined or a cooperative workforce for employers.

The one-dimensional quality of the Right's industrial relations has been partly mitigated by collaborationist initiatives by individual firms and by the local Centre. At some point in the future the Right may feel that the labour movement is weak enough for a wider, national collaborationist project to be undertaken. But the subordination of labour to management using the coercion of the market is fragile; it can be undermined if national or local unemployment falls or by skills shortages. The Right's future industrial relations policy will therefore depend both on employers' strategies for organising work and on the course of industrial struggle.

Muddled intervention, lack of industrial strategy, and the weakness of the Right

The Right's rejection of industrial strategy underlies many of the failures discussed so far: ineffective cost competition, featherbedding of the inefficient, inadequate and expensive infrastructure, and failure to support risk-taking and entrepreneurialism. Yet, paradoxically, the Conservative government has been highly interventionist in many fields (pp. 60, 72–3). A large amount of this intervention has been wasteful: the benefits have gone to risk-averting, undynamic sectors and firms, to oligopolists, and towards inflating overcapacity. This is not simply political muddle: it derives from fundamental weaknesses of the Right's strategy. Lacking any framework of industrial strategy within which to reject claims, the government is susceptible to business lobbyists. More profoundly, the Right lacks any project which could unite the classes – and competing fractions of them – around active collaboration aimed at productivism and community, and which might persuade both capital and workers to forgo short term benefits for long term gains. The Conservatives therefore crudely resort to hand-outs to buy off discontent, appealing to the fetishisation of instant cash which is part of British economic liberalism (Gamble, 1981). They tend to place spectacle before substance ('just look at the cranes in Docklands!'). Lacking any positive industrial strategy that would make demands on their spending, they are content to use public funds for pacification.

The Conservatives have thus been easy game to pressure, particularly from the traditionally powerful sectors of capital, but also from fear of working class unrest. Lobbying from the property sector resulted in the inclusion of non-industrial uses in the EZs, though this greatly inflated their cost and was irrelevant to stimulating innovation (Anderson, 1988). The relatively mild deregulation of the land market which we noted above was a response to pressure from the retail and development sectors. Under pressure from public opinion and the 1981 riots, the Conservatives have wanted to be seen to be doing something about the inner cities; but lacking an industrial strategy, this was only possible through stimulating spectacular property development in small areas. The government's lavish spending to reduce the unemployment figures, via training schemes and the Enterprise Allowance, came from political defensiveness, a fear of brazening out high unemployment.

The lack of coordination between the local economic initiatives and urban policies of different government departments, often remarked on (Morison, 1987, ch 5; National Audit Commission, 1989), is not primarily an organisational question but arises from the Conservatives' lack of industrial strategy and their resulting susceptibility to pressures (Haughton and Roberts, 1990). Handouts such as continued mortgage tax relief are often seen as a purely electoral weakness. But the Conservatives are also weak in the face of pressure from business, and this is a logical outcome of their strategy rather than an inconsistency.

Responding to these immediate pressures, the Conservatives paradoxically failed to develop the kind of subsidies favoured by consistent neo-liberals. The latter argue for help to firms, rather than to inputs to production such as property, since factor markets are less sensitive to final demand than firms are (Oxford, 1987). Neo-liberal theorists favour universal subsidies as of right, since these provide a 'level playing field' giving minimum distortion to markets (*Financial Times*, editorial, 13 January 1988). In contrast, the Conservatives' policies have been highly selective on a project basis (City Grant, regional grants) or area basis, or have followed along behind the Centre's selective schemes.

The Conservatives have also been susceptible to pressures arising from vital and widely shared interests of employers. Sections of business at the workface have been more aware of the socialisation of production than the government has, and have accordingly supported Centre-type local economic initiatives. The logic of these policies for business, and the Right's lack of any concepts with which to think them through, has dragged the Conservatives into unsystematic support for them.

The Conservatives have an image, shared by admirers and detractors alike, of being tough in destroying the 'bad old Britain' and impartially imposing the rule of the market. In a sense their project *is* clear: to shake out overcapacity and old forms of socialisation, and impose managerial discipline and work intensification. The single minded pursuit of these aims has no doubt been necessary to push them through. But the crude conceptualisation of markets and enterprise has prevented any response to new forms of socialisation, and has given the Conservatives no political defences against interest group pressures. The outcome has been a weak and vacillating Right.

Selective intervention is not less intervention

A shift from universal and nationally uniform welfare services to selective ones has been a central strand of local economic initiatives. They promise a more flexible response to varied forms of local socialisation, and a shift from state control to community based enterprise (pp. 146–8).

They have been particularly important for the Right given its desire to relieve the pressures of both labour and capital on local government welfare services.

An important aspect of selectivity is concentration on the most needy. Here again, a pruning of the state fails to generate or even enhance market mechanisms. Concentration of spending on the worst-off decreases differentials among manual workers; the 'poverty trap' deepened during the 1980s. This is directly contrary to the Right's aim of tying rewards more closely to effort. As with leveraged subsidies, selectivity distorts markets more than universalism does.

The Right hopes that selectivity and local variation will depoliticise welfare (Piven and Cloward, 1984); but again, the result can be the opposite. First, welfare provision becomes more unstable: the LDDC, for example, suspended welfare programmes financed by its land dealings when that market collapsed in 1988. For the Right this can be politically salutary if residents and workers see local decline as remediable through their own greater effort; but often local decline derives too obviously from non-local developments – the Docklands land market being a case in point. In the contemporary highly internationalised economy, it is not so easy to develop localised expectations, particularly, as the Right does, relying solely on markets.

Second, if services are no longer universal, then each social group has to lobby for them, focusing attention on the nature and quality of the service. Local variation can generate pressure for the generalisation of successful experiments to other areas. Privatisation of services, motivated in part by its potential to allow councils greater selectivity, has made explicit the standards to which they are delivered and the trade-offs between quality and cost; these were not so clear when the services were performed in-house. Explicit standards in contracts could, paradoxically, lead to greater uniformity between authorities. The Right's contract state, far from imposing market discipline, tends to increase politicisation of service delivery.

The Right's notion that selectivity increases responsiveness to local needs rests on a misunderstanding of universal services. 'Universal' has never meant either 'equal' or 'indiscriminate'. 'Universal education' has delivered quite different education to different social classes: it has been flexibly tailored to the differentiated demands of the labour market. Council housing has been provided selectively to different income and social groups within the manual working class. The Conservatives' attacks on local government erode this flexibility for capital: council housing does not now respond to any of the differentiated demands of employers – for non-skilled or skilled workers, for women workers, for workers in the inner city and in growth areas, and so on. As we have seen (p. 148–9), the selective community based services which have partly replaced local government ones often cannot meet the demands of local employers.

It is true that traditional services are 'inflexible' in that they go to many people whose labour power would be adequately produced without them; but no amount of selectivity can target only those for whom support is necessary. Long term future labour-power requirements are impossible to predict. The freedoms of workers to move their employment and residence mean that support cannot be narrowly targeted to the local needs of employers. Focusing training on the 'most needy' has left an enormous gap in skills supply; to correct this, the state would have to support the training of workers for whom employers could in principle pay. Moreover, the labour power of one worker can be influenced by welfare services to another: for example, the housing costs, and thus wages and location, of better-off workers are influenced by social housing for workers with lower incomes. Selectivity therefore worsens the supply of appropriate labour power.

Localised, selective welfare thus distorts labour markets, is ineffective in meeting employers' labour requirements, and tends to politicise welfare provision in new ways. This explains why its introduction has been slow and uneven. Yet the promise of selectivity makes it likely that the Right will continue to experiment with it.

Business is bad for business

We have seen that the Conservatives' aim of giving business the leading role in local economic initiatives has been resisted by business itself (pp. 69–70). The Conservatives modelled their approach on the USA; but the structure of British business is different. National firms, banks and utilities are far more regionally based in the USA than in Britain. Pittsburgh is not a steel city like Sheffield: it has corporate headquarters, substantial local financial capital, a local big bourgeoisie and private foundations. Britain lacks locally based banks and utilities, the backbone of US growth coalitions, and corporate headquarters are heavily concentrated in London. In the age of the professional manager, the institutional shareholder and the multi-site firm, most British executives have weak ties with their localities.

The Conservatives' policies have actually increased these differences between US and British cities. Neo-liberal policies on trade, capital flows and takeovers threaten the local basis of the few major firms remaining with headquarters outside London. The old Quaker firms have suffered, with Cadburys falling to Schweppes and Rowntrees to Nestlé, while the new status of the building societies makes it likely that their archetypal paternalism based in the northern towns will be lost. The shift of manufacturing overseas by British industrial corporations, facilitated by the Conservatives, weakens their ties to their traditional towns. There is still a basis for local interventions by corporations, but these depend on particular local conditions and corporate strategies (pp. 156–7, 263–4).

Small and medium business is equally ill-equipped to take up a leading local role. Poor economic cooperation between firms is associated with a lack of organisational and political cohesion, the Chambers of Commerce being weak compared with their continental counterparts. This reflects the individualistic traditions of British industry, which, again, are encouraged rather than combated by the Right.

Moreover, when business *has* become involved severe problems have arisen. Control by executives over local economic and social services is taken by many critics to mean that these services will be 'geared to the interests of business'; in fact, it tends to mean a poorer response to business's needs.

First, the awareness of executives tends to be as partial as their interests. This is a problem because of the great variety in the use of the locality by businesses and their ties to it. The prominent role of development companies in running the UDCs tends to accentuate their narrow property-led strategy. Politicians are better able to develop an overview of local business needs, and to mediate between the distinct and often conflicting needs of different sectors and firms. Business is timid in challenging other capitalist interests, yet there must be losers and beneficiaries in any strategy for capital as a whole. In Britain, these problems of control by business are exacerbated by its priority to immediate profit over long term strength. Thus many fear that the TECs' activity will centre on the short term skill demands of local business (Peck, 1991).

Nor does the independence of agencies make them more sensitive to business needs than a local authority. While the Right criticises the state because it does not operate in a market, nor do most local economic agencies. In the 1980s some of the UDCs found it easy to be 'responsive to the market' since this was strong and they had lavish funding; but they have not shown themselves capable of sustaining that momentum in more difficult times. When they have adopted a more comprehensive and balanced approach (pp. 73–4) they have been as beset with delays as local government.

Second, the way in which the Right has enlarged the role of business has fragmented local economic policy. Each area of policy is to be controlled by a separate *ad hoc* board dominated by business, and even a single function such as small business support can be undertaken by a multiplicity of agencies in one locality; this makes it extremely difficult to coordinate the different aspects of policy. For instance, to alleviate the negative effects of the housing market on business in southern England would require local agencies which could not only provide social housing but also coordinate it with transport, training and land use policy. This is precisely the traditional role of the local authorities: they are more flexible than *ad hoc* agencies in the crucial sense of being able to integrate services.

The time horizons of fragmented agencies are also often a problem. The Right tends to picture the problems of localities as being due to 'disequilibrium'; short term measures can jolt them back so that markets clear (full employment, full use of land, etc.). The local agencies favoured by the Right are therefore typically of limited duration: those funded from the Urban Programme, for example, are expected to stand on their own feet after four years funding, presumably on the basis of a local economic revival. But local economic problems are due to systematic uneven development, not disequilibrium (Chapter 5, pp. 248–51), and are therefore very seldom resolved in the short term. Moreover, short term agencies are inclined to neglect necessary long term investments.

Competence and efficiency are more difficult to ensure in small and often temporary organisations, and the experience accumulated in them is continually lost. Some firms have complained that the UDCs are the most inefficient bodies they have ever dealt with (Brownill, 1990, p. 149). Corruption is an even greater problem in qualgos than in local authorities, since the procedures for monitoring are typically un-developed. Colleges of Further Education have accused TECs of taking their designs for training courses and farming them out to cheaper providers (an example also of the Right's sacrifice of quality to price) (Nash, 1992). Disruption can result: the *ad hoc* body running the World Student Games in Sheffield had to be taken over by the city council only nine months before they started because of misaccounting. The traditions of local government are misread by the Right: much of its 'bureaucracy' and 'inflexibility' is necessary to develop competence, accountability and honesty.

Local economic initiatives directed by business are inevitably frag-mented. If all the powers relevant to the local economy were put in the hands of a single business-dominated board it would have all the powers of a local authority. Such a board would be seen as a local dictatorship of business, with no legitimacy, in contrast to a plethora of boards which does not appear so dictatorial. The extent to which unelected business interests are regarded as legitimate does of course vary between societies. In the USA there is a long-standing consensus that 'business knows best', and there is no working class based party analogous to the Labour Party. But even there, the business-run development corpora-tions are typically limited to the physical aspects of city centre re-development. In Britain the authority of local economic initiatives has to some extent been enhanced by their being directed by 'the people who know'. But this legitimation is sensitive to economic circumstances: the ability of business-dominated development bodies in inner city areas in the mid-1980s to cross-subsidise community uses disappeared with the end of the property boom.

Business involvement, then, is high risk. If politicians fail to regener-ate a local economy then their policies or party will be blamed; if business fails then its class may be blamed. The political exposure to which business is subjected in running local services, and the greater ability of the state to mediate such pressures, was one of the reasons for the development of local government services. The pressures on local government can certainly be intense too; this is why the Right has tried to restructure it. But transferring the pressures on to business represen-tatives does not alleviate them.

Paradoxically, then, if local economic initiatives are to reflect busi-ness' needs, business itself needs to be kept at arm's length. Because of local interdependencies, a pro-business policy can never be reduced to the interests of individual firms. The costs of democracy decried by the Right reflect not merely pressure from labour but the necessary com-plexity of planning the local socialisation of production.

Centralisation and local initiative

The Conservative government has continually increased its control over local government in general and its economic initiatives in particular. While the Conservatives doubtless privately recognise the aspirations of most local authorities to help business, they fear that this help will be delivered with too high a public sector subsidy and too much control

(Rowthorn, 1983): we saw in Chapter 1 how local economic initiatives transplanted welfare attitudes to support for small firms. Because of the strong cross-party tradition of welfare in Britain, the Conservatives have not trusted the local authorities to cut spending merely under the pressure of local business and residents. Centralism has been successful in shifting local authority policies further to the right; and it attempts to deal with the pressures on local authorities – from business as well as residents and workers – for higher welfare and economic spending.

The Conservatives have formally decentralised much local economic policy implementation to its own qualgos and to voluntary organisations. But this was intended to weaken the local authorities rather than decentralise power, and the Conservatives have maintained a strong control on these agencies. The voluntary organisations funded by the Urban Programme are subject to political selection and pressure from Whitehall. The TECs have their main programmes determined centrally, and their funding regime pushes them towards the Conservatives' cost cutting strategy (p. 111). We have seen that some of the UDCs and local training agencies have managed to pursue policies significantly different from those of the government, but central direction is strong. The relations between the government and the local agencies is consequently highly bureaucratic and consumes enormous administrative resources (National Audit Commission, 1989, pp. 23–6); the measurements used by Whitehall to control the spending of local organisations, such as the 'output' measures for the TECs, are inevitably crude and obstruct local creativity (Peck, 1991). The Conservatives have not trusted the independent agencies, even its own creations, not to succumb to Centrist temptations.

The principal casualty of the Conservatives' centralism, however, has been the local authorities. As we have seen (pp. 70–2), this has damaged the Right's own policies. Centralism not only prevents the local authorities from using their powers on behalf of business; it prevents the local political process from developing collaboration between business, residents and workers. This again shows the problems in 'removing obstructions to markets': eliminating what was a barrier to certain operations of capital does not by itself create new opportunities. Because it ignores local socialisation, the Right does not see the penalties in attacking the institution which is best placed to address it.

Ironically, in the USA, whose urban regeneration policies the Conservatives claim to emulate, the local authorities play a large role. Although largely confined to property and environmental initiatives, this role could not be achieved with the powers available to British local authorities. Since the mid-1970s, the role of city government in central area redevelopments has *increased* relative to that of the Federal government and the private sector (Frieden, 1990). City government has played a key role in land assembly, infrastructure and environmental improvement, and in winning public support (Logan and Molotch, 1987). Some US development authorities release land on to the market to avoid cyclical movements, keep land prices low to encourage developers to make public improvements, and avoid social contrasts by upgrading the surrounding housing. They typically take an equity stake which reduces the windfall profits to the private sector and gives the public sector a measure of control in the future. The extent of the state's role is reflected in low leverage ratios, only 1:2 in Baltimore for example. US practice is therefore often more interventionist than the Conservatives allow.

The British Right might reply, correctly, that this interventionism is 'disciplined' by a different political tradition and a more powerful local capital. But the Conservatives' solution, to shackle the local authorities, cannot reproduce the US pro-business growth coalition. We have seen that British business is not prepared to undertake this role directly. Centrally appointed boards such as the UDCs and the TECs do not have the legitimacy, nor so far the powers and autonomy, to take it on.

The Conservatives' attempts to change the agency of local regeneration through business involvement, fragmentation, and shackling of the local authorities, have therefore weakened pro-business local economic initiatives. The Conservatives attempted to remedy this by sponsoring local coordination and urging local economic agencies to develop local strategies (p. 74). But this cannot fill the gap left by the weakening of local government. This leaves difficult choices in the future. As with the trade unions, the Right may feel, at some point, that the local authorities have been tamed and can be allowed some stronger role in economic policy. But, given continuing national and local economic problems, the Right must fear a resurgence of demands on local government. Any letting up on the local authorities walks this tightrope.

The contradictions and future of Right local economic policy

The central problem of the Right's local economic policy is that, in increasing capital and labour mobility and working with the therapeutic effects of crisis, it ignores the local socialisation of production; it thereby fails to enhance the freedom of markets and capital.

The Right's misapprehension of the nature of the state is closely connected to this: the local government which the Right seeks to weaken is a response to the local socialisation of production. The integration of different services within local government reflects the interdependence of their economic functions. The separation of local government from business reflects the difference between the individual interests of business and the profitability of the local economy as a whole. The Right's attempts to reduce the role of the state through deregulation, privatisation, selectivity and leveraging end up by muddying markets more than the forms of intervention which they replace. Business is reluctant to become involved with socialisation on the terms of the Right: it is wary of the complexity of the task and the difficulty of isolating its own vested interests.

The Right's attack on local government is aimed not simply at cutting public expenditure but at depoliticising society. But we have seen in discussing deregulation, infrastructure and localised welfare that privatisation and the contract state can lead to new forms of politicisation. This is because the reality of, or pressure for, local socialisation remains; the state is not so easily dismantled.

Flowing from these lacunae, the Right has a one-dimensional project for local class relations: to establish the untrammelled rule of management. This neglects the way in which cooperative class relations can enhance productivity, not only within individual workplaces but across the local economy, by strengthening its integration and pushing employers towards high value-added strategies. The reliance on market discipline and absence of integrative strategies also leaves the Right politically vulnerable. The local socialisation of production continues to break through in demands from both business and labour, for which the Right lacks a strategy.

Ironically, the mobility and concentration of capital promoted by the Right in the long term tend to increase the pressure for policies to address local socialisation. This pressure comes both from agencies representing localities and from capital itself. Increased capital mobility intensifies pressure on localities to find new ways of competing, of stabilising their local economy, and of preventing the devalorisation of local public and private sector capital. We have seen that the most promising means for pursuing this competition and tying down capital in the locality is through enhancing the local socialisation of production.

From business's point of view, the Right's removal of barriers to competition, and the greater resources for competition possessed by internationalising capital, give any local differences which can be exploited a particular importance. These are not simply spatial price differences, as is often thought, but qualitative local differences created by varied local socialisation. In tourism and retailing, for example, increasing scale of production and geographically expanding markets put a premium on creating unique local environments. Precisely in order to use its mobility effectively, capital needs local socialisation. The progressive extension of neo-liberal policies thus tends to elicit increasing demands to address local socialisation. The Right's policy unleashes its opposite.

These tensions, however, do not show that the Right has a 'hidden agenda', or that it holds to an antiquated economic theory: the problems are results of a strategy which performs vital tasks for capital – destruction of old forms of socialisation, disciplining of labour and local government, and enhanced mobilities. The Right's problems should therefore be seen as *contradictions* of a strategy for raising profitability.

These contradictions mean that the future of the Right's local initiatives is open. Under a government of the Right or Centre–Right, there are two possible trajectories. The first is that local economic agencies operating a consensus strategy could continue and even deepen their degree of intervention, responding to the pressure, which the Right's policies themselves increase, to address local socialisation. This seems the most likely evolution under the Major government, with its cautious and uncertain attempts to address socialisation. But the further this proceeds, the greater the problems of agency would become. The local authorities are the best vehicle for organising local socialisation; but, under conditions of stagnation, the government will find it hard to go back on its weakening of local government lest demands on it once again explode.

One possible resolution would be for the government to allow greater economic intervention by local authorities, but under a strongly centralised regime in which localities were allocated particular roles in the spatial division of labour and budgets to achieve them – a new regional policy. The local authorities would manage the local detail, but local demands would be kept in check by centralised allocation. Alternatively, the government might attempt to use non-elected local bodies to organise local socialisation, perhaps through increasing the powers of the TECs. But either arrangement is a purely administrative approach to maintaining discipline: as we shall argue in the next chapter, to address seriously the socialisation of production tends to open the floodgates of demands from both capital and labour, jeopardising the discipline which the Thatcher government imposed. Maintaining local consensus policy is therefore a high risk strategy.

The fear of such demands may push the Conservatives in the opposite direction: towards restrictions on consensus local economic policy and a reinforcement of distinctly Right initiatives. This outcome depends on the national economic situation and conflicts between different orientations for British capital. In the event of continuing deterioration in the domestic economy, the export of capital is likely to accelerate, and the traditional dominance of banking, trading and property interests to intensify. This would lead to continued neglect of local socialisation, in turn accelerating deindustrialisation in a vicious circle. Local economic policy would be increasingly confined to central city property and prestige projects to attract business services, and quasi-workfare for the rest. These possible scenarios are explored further (pp. 272–3) after we have examined the consensus strategy.

Further reading

The logic of the Right's strategy for dealing with the present crisis is analysed by Mandel (1978a, pp. 165–80), Itoh (1980, chs 4–6) and Clarke (1988, chs 10–12). Szelenyi (1984) contains articles from the Centre–Left criticising the Right's local strategy. The inadequacy of pure cost-cutting and the search for static comparative advantage is discussed by Best (1990) and, from a marxist standpoint, Jenkins (1984). The problems of infrastructure investment and the state's involvement in it are discussed in Folin (1981) and Harvey (1982), and those of training by Ashton *et al.* (1989). The contradictions of the Conservatives' industrial relations strategy are analysed in Hyman and Elger (1981), Nichols (1986, Part 4) and Holloway (1987).

10 The Future of the Consensus

We now turn to the future of consensus local economic policy. This has become increasingly dominant in Britain over the past ten years: will this dominance continue? We first analyse, in greater depth than we have done so far, the promise of this strategy and the basis of its growth. This enables us to examine the problems and tensions of the consensus which will condition its future.

The core of consensus local economic strategy is a recognition of the local socialisation of production and the need for collective action to deal with it, thus addressing the problems of the Right discussed in the previous chapter. It seeks to strengthen long term relations between finance and industry; greater private and public investment in skills and infrastructures; cooperative industrial relations; and, at its most ambitious, long term planning within firms and coordination within sectors.

These internal interdependencies are particularly weak in Britain because of its tradition of high sectoral and geographical capital mobility established during its period of world dominance. Inter-firm organisation and the productive roles of the state are weak compared with countries where capital had fewer options, notably Germany and Japan. The Centre seeks to counter this one-sided emphasis on capital mobility, and its perpetuation by the Right, by strengthening the socialisation of production and thus rooting capital more strongly in Britain and its localities.

Through making capital somewhat less mobile, the Centre makes it more dependent on national and local political conditions, and is therefore more concerned than the Right to establish cooperative class relations. It is thus more strongly nationalistic and localistic than the Right, both in favouring 'home' investment and in fostering the social unity of nation and locality.

The Centre shares with the Right the aim of making markets free and facilitating capital mobility; it supports the Right's use of the therapeutic mechanisms for overcoming crisis, including the use of unemployment

238

and limitation of public spending. Even public works schemes are justified by the Centre on the basis that they do not increase public spending or wage pressure (pp. 112). But the Centre argues that effective organisation of production, which must be partly collective, is necessary precisely in order to make markets work. It also sees the Right as unnecessarily confrontational and potentially fragile (pp. 225–7), and thus seeks more cooperative class relations. In a sense, the Centre seeks not to replace but to supplement the policies of the Right, by strengthening socialisation.

The Centre, then, addresses the socialisation of production only in so far as it furthers private capital accumulation; it does not take socialisation to its logical conclusion, which is a planned economy. But it shares important policies of the modernising Left. It supports attempts to reorganise the relations between finance and industry and to stimulate sectoral planing; and it supports the Left's participation and equal opportunities policies providing they do not harm profitability, which has largely been the case in practice (pp. 198–9).

The Centre's combination of socialisation with freeing of markets embodies a delicate dialectic of apparent opposites: it promotes greater integration of disadvantaged groups which also increases competition in the labour market; more training which at the same time weakens the monopoly power of skilled workers; more cooperation in the workplace which also strengthens managerial authority.

Localism is central to this subtle politics by enabling political tensions to be contained. The Centre supports the Right's national policies for disciplining labour, and like the Right, it wishes to mobilise localistic competition to gain workers' acceptance of employers' projects. But the Centre argues that wage stability and increasing productivity require, not the cowed worker that the Right seeks, but industrial collaboration, as was attempted by some large firms in the 1970s (Beynon, 1983; Newton and Porter, 1988). It seeks active initiative by labour and a local community of capital and labour involving mutual obligations. The market alone cannot create the desired relations: 'The same trusted friend which pushed sterling up to the glamorous levels of \$2.40 and induces "realism" in wage bargaining can, if irked, just as easily send the pound tumbling and propel the looters on to the streets' (Marsh, 1981).

But this approach poses the danger to employers that labour may take *too* active a role (Rowthorn, 1983). This danger was shown by labour's involvement in national economic policy during the post-war boom, which contributed to economic efficiency, but at the cost of strengthening labour's bargaining power and raising popular expectations. In this way it contributed to the industrial, legislative and welfare offensives of labour in the late 1960s and early 1970s. Locality limits this danger: local collaboration may raise labour's expectations, but its explicit premise is to raise the competitiveness of the local economy. Local competitiveness is a sharper discipline than national competitiveness because capital is more mobile between localities than it is internationally. Unlike the corporatism of the 1960s, the local collaboration by the Centre is therefore not embodied in general norms (such as regular annual real wage rises) nor in general rights (such as the universal welfare benefits). On the contrary, it links wages to individual effort and local profitability; and the Centre, like the Right, favours increasing selectivity and self-help in welfare to reduce expectations and limit state expenditure. Pressure from labour is fragmented by locality; and employers and local authorities can resist it by pointing to the need for the locality to remain competitive. As Piven and Cloward (1984, p.40) put it, 'popular economic demands [are] deflected from the national political arena and channelled into an increasingly competitive State and local politics'. A *local* Centre strategy can therefore hope to manage the contradiction between the encouragement of workers' enterprise and the maintenance of managerial discipline (pp. 152–3). It can gain the benefits of labour's participation, while avoiding the dangers for capital to which national systems of collaboration are prone.

Localness also limits pressures from employers. The Centre's policies for helping firms and sectors, providing infrastructures and coordinating restructuring can unleash increasing demands from capital, as happened in the 1960s and early 1970s. By appealing to the pressure of localistic competition and the need to limit expenditure, local economic agencies can respond to firms' demands in a pragmatic way.

Consensus local economic strategy, then, has had a subtle relationship to a national government of the Right. The Centre professes the same aims – important during a period of neo-liberal ideological offensive – yet presents more subtle policies for achieving them. Attention to socialisation promises to address many problems neglected by neo-liberal governments since the mid-1970s.

However, it is *because of* national deflationary policies that it has been possible to undertake Centre local initiatives without running into 'excessive' demands from capital and labour. Consensus local economic policy has thus counteracted the neglect of socialisation in national policy, while at the same time using and reinforcing the market disciplines being imposed at the national level.

The consensus partnership of business and local government

The Centre appreciates that local government can play a positive role for business. By highlighting localistic competition the Centre believes that local authorities can be kept in bounds without the Right's crude coercion (Hutton, 1990); it is aware that most councils, including Labour ones, have long been accommodating to business because of *local* pressures. Moreover, strangling the local authorities prevents them from being entrepreneurial and responding to business's needs and thus from building a collaborative relationship with it; accordingly, the Centre supports greater economic powers and autonomy for local government. It then rejects the Right's attempts to marginalise the trade unions and local government for essentially the same reason: it believes that they can be contained, and thereby play a positive role.

We have seen that large firms and employers' organisations by-and-large support a consensus approach to local economic policy, both to address local socialisation and to foster political stability (pp. 144, 155–8, 227, 233–4). They do not, therefore, seek the marginalisation of local government – though they may support some of the pressures put on it by the Conservatives – nor do they seek to take over the local authorities' activities (Association of British Chambers of Commerce, 1989). Business is aware of the coordinating and mediating roles of the local authorities, of the problems when business manages agencies, and the danger of the most powerful firms becoming dominant. However, it does not want to leave local economic initiatives entirely in local authority hands, recognising that business involvement can help to keep them on the political straight and narrow. Business is also aware that non-state agencies can sometimes be more innovative, and that where these are business run they may have greater legitimacy than local authorities, certainly when the clients are businesses and possibly when they are community groups.

The relationship of corporate initiatives to the local authorities is therefore complex. Their independent initiatives have been undertaken through agencies that are formally independent, in order to limit their political exposure, to combine firm's contributions, and to receive state funding. Firms have, however, expressed dissatisfaction with inefficiencies and fragmentation of these agencies, and on occasion have even questioned their rationale. One response has been to attempt greater coordination between them (pp. 74, 94); another has been for business-dominated agencies to work more closely with the local authorities, as the TECs appear to be doing. Collaboration between business and the local authority may be coordinated either by the council, by a private body, or by a voluntary one such as the Civic Trust. The *ad hoc* nature of these arrangements ensures that excessive expectations are not raised: the contributions of the local authority, business and the voluntary sector are to be negotiated case-by-case, always with local competitiveness as the overriding criterion.

A model of this approach is Lowell, Massachussetts, an old textile town. The central area has been turned into a National Park, not only bringing additional finance but state regulation of the land market, making it possible to develop a sector strategy for tourism. Nine local banks formed a fund for central area development, and by this collective approach reduced their risks and the interest rates charged. A development corporation funded by other local business has undertaken initiatives in secondary and higher education, public transport, environment and culture, coordinating them with economic development. Attracted by this Bootstraps dynamism, Wang located a facility with 12 000 jobs, using a Federal leveraged grant which it is giving in instalments to the development corporation (Dutton, 1991). This intimate melding of strong public intervention with business involvement and local commitment is characteristic of the Centre approach.

In Britain, this approach has been used in the most ambitious of the corporate initiatives, the dozen or so community-based town renewal projects in small towns such as Neath, Ripon, and Thorne. These are organised through networks in which local authorities play an important though not dominant role. They have integrated the physical and social elements of change, and subsidised community uses from the profits of commercial development (CBI, 1988). Through this approach they have constructed a strong local consensus. The delicacy of business's involvement is suggested by the fact that these programmes have been carried out in small, isolated towns where job options are very limited and where it is easier to generate a sense of cooperation, in some cases reinforced by Methodist traditions. Business has been more hesitant about collaborating with local authorities on large scale renewal in the inner cities.

*   *   *

Despite this promise, the consensus contains major tensions, to which we now turn. Its attention to local socialisation often does not go far enough to ensure stability of the local economy or better opportunities for the disadvantaged. The fragmentation and pragmatism of consensus strategy tends to weaken each policy. But the problem goes deeper than this: in enhancing local socialisation, the Centre may actually increase capital mobility and local instability, and may increase inequality between areas and between social groups. These failures lead to pressures to deepen policies to give them greater purchase. Moreover, to be effective local consensus policy needs congruent national policies and a move away from neo-liberalism at the national level; yet this would unleash further pressures from capital and labour – a Pandora's box. The consensus approach therefore has a rocky political future.

Equal opportunities and the 'people based strategy'

A central aim of the consensus has been to improve employment opportunities for disadvantaged groups. This aim, however, has not been achieved. As we saw in Chapter 4, the Centre has separate policies for increasing competitiveness and for tackling disadvantage. Policies aimed at competitiveness usually do not have integral mechanisms for either the distribution of the jobs or their quality, and therefore tend to benefit those who are already well placed in the labour market. For example, the self-employment which local initiatives have promoted tends to reproduce inequalities: between 1980 and 1990, self-employment of men rose from 11 to 17 per cent, for women from 4 to 6 per cent. Employers in aided firms generally favour experienced workers, and discriminate against the unemployed. This can take a locational form: many aided jobs located in or near residential areas of high unemployment are taken by residents of 'less needy areas' (Buck *et al.*, 1986). Indeed, Centre policies to enhance profitability are sometimes explicitly regressive, such as policies to attract professionals.

A second problem is that measures to redistribute jobs to the disadvantaged are often ineffective. Training programmes aimed at groups such as the long term unemployed often fail to reach their target, or cream the groups at which they are aimed for the most marketable (Robinson, 1988, p. 80; Davies and Mason, 1986); the Youth Training Scheme, for example, has reproduced gender, racial and income disadvantage (Rigg and Miller, 1991; Banks *et al.*, 1991). These failures may partly arise from the training agencies wanting to make their task easier, or from their discrimination. But, more fundamentally, it results from employers' preferences: the training agencies want to give themselves the success of their trainees finding jobs. It also arises from a higher take-up of courses by the better qualified. The majority of Centre policies, then, worsen the position of the most disadvantaged by consolidating the competitiveness of the better qualified.

These failures have been emphasised by the proponents of 'people based planning' (Royal Town Planning Institute, 1985; see also Lovering, 1988), who argue for a radical version of the Centre strategy. They criticise local economic agencies for being vague in their aims (cf pp. 113–14), and urge them to make the economic welfare of the disadvantaged their priority through stronger job creation and distributional policies, and through development which uses the skills of the unemployed and incorporates unskilled jobs. Local agencies should directly influence the recruitment practices of employers through contract compliance and even equity holdings. They favour locally controlled enterprises as a means of increasing democracy and thus equality; however, they are critical of the job quality and recruitment practices of conventional small firms and therefore give great weight to the Third Sector. The failings of equal opportunities policies have thus led to pressures for a more radical strategy and stronger intervention (for example, Basset *et al.*, 1989, p. 66).

Deeper problems of equality

The people based strategy, however, does not overcome the problems of the consensus approach to equality, and indeed in some ways intensifies them. This is because there are weaknesses in the consensus approach beyond those highlighted by the people based critique:

• *The geography of redistribution*   The effectiveness of equal opportunities policies is limited by their local organisation. There is no coordination of these policies across District Council boundaries, for example, through policies for reverse commuting or for movement of labour between labour markets (pp. 185–6). The emphasis of the people based strategy on local control exacerbates this problem.

• *Redistribution by social group or area?*   There are strong arguments for redistribution to benefit oppressed social groups. It can be justified through the notion of rights, or respect for persons, and reduced inequalities tend to improve relations between social groups by eroding status distinctions (Baker, 1987). The case for redistribution to benefit poor *areas* is quite different. Discrimination against women and black people is due to their social position and creates an oppressed identity, which is not the case, or only weakly so, for people living in a particular area. Area targeting frequently fails to reach the most needy because they are insufficiently spatially concentrated. It has nevertheless been justified on the grounds that poor areas experience cumulative economic and physical decline, and a negative local culture of unemployment; or that the individual's experience of unemployment is worse if neighbours are also unemployed. These arguments are debatable and dependent on many contingent circumstances; the case for spatial redistribution is less clear than that for social redistribution.

While redistribution to disadvantaged groups is valid in itself, it creates harmful side effects and is undermined unless it is combined with policies to reduce unemployment and improve the quality of jobs. This shows itself in a number of problems:

• *Shuffling the disadvantaged* Unless the quality of jobs is improved, better opportunities for one group will result in their poor jobs being filled by another group, usually also a socially disadvantaged one (Turok and Wannop, 1989).

• *The losers from redistribution* If the quantity and quality of jobs are left unchanged, then their redistribution will be at the expense of more privileged workers. Moreover, Centre policies rely on increasing the competitiveness of the disadvantaged in the labour market, and this puts downward pressure on wages and conditions. This problem is particularly acute in the people based strategy, since this explicitly urges that positive action measures should be taken irrespective of the demand for labour (Howl, 1985, p. 72). In many cases the process of redistribution is hidden, particularly when it takes place via the market; where the transfer is evident, the measures are usually resisted by the losers.

• *Worsening the quality of jobs* The conditions of the specially-created jobs in 'enterprises of the oppressed' and in targeted job-creation programmes are on the whole poor. This may be justified on the basis that they are better than no jobs at all. However, like positive action in the labour market, they exert a downward pressure on conditions of existing jobs (pp. 161–2). Again, this problem is worse in the people based strategy since it argues for a blurring of the distinction between informal, Third Sector and mainstream enterprises, and between paid and unpaid work (Howl, 1985, p. 75).

Centre policies usually set out to benefit the disadvantaged without considering these knock-on effects. Yet if these policies start to have an impact, there will be pressure to avoid these effects by combining equal opportunities with job creation and policies to improve the quality of jobs. But this breaks down the separation in Centre strategy between policies for redistribution and production, and requires greater controls over production. The logic of the Centre's redistributional policies is thus towards more comprehensive intervention.

● *Permanence, cumulative advance and collective organisation* How durable are the effects of equal opportunities policies? The Centre hopes that employers will realise through experience that it is in their interest to employ disadvantaged groups, as the costs of positive action programmes will be offset by reduced wages and labour turnover. But this is only sometimes the case, depending on the sector and labour market conditions. Good practice has to be sustained by pressure from unions, community groups and organisations of the disadvantaged. The Centre is prepared to consult with such groups but does not seek to increase their power, since they may push for positive action measures which conflict with competitiveness, or which try to improve the number and quality of jobs: their demands may go beyond the balance between competitiveness and welfare which the Centre seeks. But unless there is a significant redistribution of power, gains are unstable.

● *Inheritance and family* Most fundamentally, consensus initiatives do not address the social barriers to equality. The use of training schemes is itself strongly affected by class background and by gender; inequalities in inherited social position affect the take-up of the very forms of welfare which are supposed to ameliorate it. This has long been known of traditional welfare services, which are most used by the middle class and the better-off working class, but it is true also of the new redistribution policies of local economic policy. The problem is that both consumption and the acquisition of skills are active processes in which the individual's existing social resources are brought to bear. The Centre does not tackle this problem because its policies for equal opportunities venture only weakly into the social sphere, and are not linked to the self-organisation of oppressed groups. It holds back from disturbing the structures of family and inheritance on which capital accumulation depends, and which reproduce gender, racial and class differences of opportunity (p. 145; Barrett and McIntosh, 1982; Gough and Macnair, 1985, pp. 60–6). Thus although the Centre addresses the social nature of production, it does not venture far enough to be effective. Again, the logic of the Centre is towards more comprehensive intervention.

Consensus strategy deepens inequality

But the problems go deeper: the consensus strategy actually reproduces inequality. The Centre's answer to poverty is based on promoting high innovation, high productivity economies, benefiting from local socialisation, which on this basis will provide good jobs for all. But by linking wages to profits, this strategy exacerbates wage inequality.

First, the high profits from productivity differences and from technical and design innovation which the Centre promotes are inherently uneven between firms and unstable over time. Moreover, differences in the profitability of firms tend to increase during a period of economic stagnation. Since these profits are to determine wages, the consensus strategy tends to increase wage differentials.

There is also no automatic link between high profits and high wages, as the hotel and catering industry shows. High profits may result in high wages if workers have strong bargaining power. But the Centre opposes this in order to prevent labour from taking an 'excessive' share of profits. On the other hand, it favours linking wages to profits through profit sharing schemes, which produce a downward flexibility in wages when profits are low. Overall, then, the Centre's strategy leads to greater dispersion and instability of wages.

The Centre's attention to the production of labour power can produce a more inegalitarian outcome than the Right. Whereas the Right's training policies are focused, albeit ineffectively, on the unemployed and the unskilled, the Centre gives higher priority to 'real training' which is disproportionately taken up by better qualified workers. It has been more active than the Right in eroding the degree of cultural autonomy present in education and bending it more to requirements of production. As with wages, the Centre's attention to socialisation makes it more effective than the Right in subordinating workers to profitable production.

The Centre strategy also promotes spatial inequality. We saw in Chapter 5 that, in addressing local socialisation, the Centre can only make so many areas 'special'; in helping some areas to attain or maintain a high position in the spatial division of labour, it recreates geographical inequality. Thus, even amongst large cities, Centre policies for capturing business services through addressing their high local socialisation are creating new hierarchies between them (Leo, 1991). Among the Japanese Technopolises, a supreme example of private–public planning, those in the core of the country are attracting R&D and high level activities while those in the peripheral regions are developing as branch plant locations (Tabb and Yokota, 1991). Murray's (1989) proposal to create an integrated high tech economy in the north of England explicitly concentrates expenditure into the Manchester–Leeds axis at the expense of the rest of the region.

The Centre's emphasis on non-market mechanisms, then, is not egalitarian but the opposite, since it is designed to make markets work more efficiently. This is perhaps why, during the 1980s, income differentials increased as much in interventionist France as in the neo-liberal USA and Britain. The effect of consensus local initiatives is to perpetuate and sometimes exacerbate inequalities, though they shift local economies and segments of their labour forces up and down the hierarchies.

Failure to localise capital

The consensus promises greater local economic stability. Production is to be anchored by the ties of local socialisation. Resources are to be saved from wasteful devaluation, and interdependent sectors preserved. Capital should not flow too fast out of sectors or localities, or shift on the basis of short term profitability. But the Centre cannot prevent local instability; and this is due not simply to its policies being too weak, but also to their very success. We look in turn at these two sides of the problem.

Local socialisation undermined by the mobility of capital

We have seen that the Centre's policies for the socialisation of production have little purchase on large fields of production which have only weak local interdependencies, in which cost competition and deskilled labour predominate. Even sectors with strong local socialisation are liable to internal disruption which weakens their local ties (Chapter 5). Moreover, policies for local socialisation are liable to be undermined by the individualism of firms. The Hackney Fashion Centre, for example, invested in a £250 000 computer-aided design and cutting machine which could have improved the quality of production of local clothing firms. However, there was insufficient matching investment within the local firms to enable them profitably to use the new equipment, and the facility was closed. A socialised facility failed to deflect firms from their accustomed short term outlook. This problem produces pressure in two contrary directions. Either the socialised investment is not made since the future private investment is unpredictable; or in order for the socialised investment to be used, greater control is attempted over the corresponding private investments, as when the GLC attempted to invest in clothing firms which could use the Hackney Fashion Centre. Thus policy is pushed to the right or the left.

The undermining of socialisation by capital mobility is intensified by a long period of stagnation (pp. 143–4; Harvey, 1985). Capital becomes less willing to be tied down to structures which promise only a long-term return. Increase in liquidity intensifies the need to find new avenues of investment. Firms try to force their way into established areas, breaking up existing institutional arrangements. Thus in Japan life-time employment in the major corporations is being dismantled, despite its central role in their previous success, as they shed labour to increase short term profits and export capital (Douglass, 1988). The holding company system of firm ownership, which has blocked stock market pressures towards short-termism, is now under severe pressure from US capital wishing to enter Japanese markets. Thus pressure for capital mobility arising from economic stagnation is tending to dismantle the high socialisation on which Japanese success was based.

For these reasons, other advanced capitalist countries are moving closer towards the liberalism and capital mobility of Britain (Anderson, 1987). Moreover, the particularly strong individualism and mobility of British capital is constantly renewed by the individualism and mobility of capital as such (Murray, 1983a). Thus the Centre's attempts to tie down capital have to combat its uneven degrees of socialisation, local disruptions, firms' individualism, and the mobility engendered by stagnation – and these are not merely British quirks.

Local socialisation promotes capital mobility

It is not merely that the Centre's socialisation does not go far enough to stop capital mobility: it also undermines itself by *encouraging* that mobility.

We have already seen this process at the level of individual firms: where Centre policies make possible the growth of local firms they tend to become more spatially mobile, often through external control (pp. 175–6). This kind of process also operates for whole local economies. The Centre's promotion of local economic specialisation is also a promotion of spatial hierarchies (Chapter 5), and encourages capital to shift to the privileged locations. Consider the consensus policy of increasing investment in advanced telecommunications and telematics. They are used more by large firms for their internal and external networking than by small firms for their mutual communication (Goddard, 1990, p. 21). Consensus policy therefore tends to strengthen the hierarchical divisions of labour between localities being developed by the large firms, and further reinforce the specialisation and dominance of the South-east (Goddard, 1990, p.25; Goddard and Gillespie, 1987). In addition high level specialisation involves higher-than-average profits, often through oligopolistic prices, which are charged to firms and consumers in other areas, producing a drain from weak to strong areas. Thus consensus policies do not merely perpetuate inequality between areas, as we argued in the previous section: they encourage the flow of capital and expenditure from weak to strong.

Moreover, strengthened socialisation, through overcoming local barriers to profitable investment, encourages the inward flow of capital; for example, where there is strong growth, Centre policies can reduce inflationary bottlenecks. Enhanced local socialisation can also facilitate the flow of capital out of areas where major sectors are in decline (pp. 156–7). Massey and Meegan (1979) found that the modernisation and rationalisation carried out by the Industrial Reorganisation Commission in the 1960s facilitated movement of production both within Britain and from it. The Lancashire Enterprise Board has invested in a business park in China, whose first tenant was a Blackburn firm in a joint venture to produce glasses; the LEB's attention to socialisation leads it to invest on the other side of the world.

From the point of view of a locality, policies for increasing socialisation may promise enhanced stability; but with many localities pursuing such a policy, the robust as well as the weak will be strengthened, deepened specialisation and unequal development will be promoted, and the overall effect is likely to be *more* mobile capital. This point is often missed because of the popular concern with capital flows from high to low cost locations. But since socialisation is as important to profitability as factor costs (pp. 214–15), it can promote the mobility of capital just as powerfully. In Western Germany since the 1950s, for example, there have been large shifts of capital between regions not just despite, but also because of, strong local coordination of investment by regional and local government (Hausermann and Kramer-Badoni, 1989).

The Centre and modernising Left see themselves as the champions of production against finance; British industry is seen as damagingly dominated by the accountant; the GLC presented the essence of its programme as giving priority to production (1985a, p. 17). The Centre–Left see this priority as making their strategy geographically stabilising: 'production' is relatively immobile plant, infrastructures and labour, in contrast to the mobility of money; it is particular and locally rooted in contrast to the homogeneity and universalism of money. But finance and production are more interdependent and mutually constructing than this view implies. The two are institutionally more separate in Britain than in other advanced countries. But even in Britain the major industrial companies increasingly combine production and financial activities, the latter often arising out of their industrial activities; they have sophisticated treasury units, and in some cases financial services subsidiaries. The fluidity over these boundaries illustrates that rooted production and mobile finance are not simply opposites; the process of production is a flow in which capital takes the forms successively of productive factors, then internationally traded goods and services, then money. While some countries may specialise in one stage of this cycle, it forms a whole (Murray, 1983a). The Centre's strengthening of local production therefore implies an intensification of international trade and financial flows.

As consensus local economic policies build up a track record, then, they are likely to come under pressure. On the one hand, their frequent failure to channel private investment decisions will lead to pressures either to abandon policies or to strengthen them. A survey in Northern Ireland found that most chief executives find the system of generous but undirected grants inadequate, and call for strategic and coordinated industrial planning (*Financial Times*, 1988). On the other hand, the way in which consensus policies promote capital flows to stronger areas is likely to cause increasing resentment: Sheffield will protest against Leeds's interventionism, Barnsley against Sheffield's. A key element in the support for the consensus, that it helps weak areas, may come into question.

It is frequently said that the Right promotes free markets while the Centre balances the market with welfare (Chandler and Lawless, 1985, p. 31; Benington, 1986), that the Right seeks merely to create wealth while the Centre attempts to redistribute it (Brindley *et al.*, 1989, p. 9). Our argument shows that these distinctions are misleading. The Right does not succeed in freeing markets (Chapter 9), while the Centre's policies are designed to do just this (pp. 238–40). The Centre's welfare policies are not anti-market but improve the functioning of the labour market. We have just seen that the effects of Centre policies are not necessarily more egalitarian than those of the Right. In thinking through the implications of Right and Centre strategies, the conceptualisation we have developed is a better guide: that these strategies represent different ways of dealing with two elements which are both interdependent and contrary – the production of markets and mobile capital on the one hand and the organisation of the local socialisation of production on the other.

The fragmentation of consensus strategy

We have seen that the fragmentation of the Right's local initiatives causes problems (pp. 231–2). But this is also a major problem for consensus strategy, although for different reasons and with different results: it pursues in isolation policies which are dependent on each other. In Chapter 4 we saw that consensus policies for stimulating small firms have been weak because of their separation from policies for technology and sectors; that property, area initiatives and science parks in isolation do not meet the Centre's aims; and that technology policies are weak without an appropriate local economic–institutional setting. In this chapter we have seen how Centre policies for equality are weakened by their detachment from policies for production.

The fragmentation of local policy has strong roots. Some are common to local economic policy of all political stripes. The limited statutory powers and resources of local agencies mean that coherence and strategy come second to practicability. The fragmentation of agencies makes coordination of initiatives difficult. There is political pressure to carry out policies with visible results, even if they do not contribute to any strategic aims. Narrowly focused policies for particular types of enterprise, factors and sectors seem by themselves to promise much (Chapter 2). And we saw in Chapter 1 how local economic initiatives developed as part of a rejection of the strategic planning attempted in the 1960s in favour of the incremental and the pragmatic.

In the case of the Right, these problems are exacerbated by putting business in control and by the weakening of local government; in the case of the Centre they are exacerbated by its theory of policy-making. Both the Right and the socialist Left have theorised, comprehensive strategies which link together their individual initiatives: for the Right, the promotion of free markets, for the socialist Left, moving towards a planned economy. The Centre has no such grand project: it just wants to make competition and redistribution 'work better'. Its policies therefore tend to be narrowly about the thing which is 'not working'. For example, because high growth in southern England or California is correlated with a large weight of small firms, the Centre believes that small firm stimulation in other regions will increase *their* growth. In contrast, the Right sees the low rate of formation of small firms in those regions as a result either of interference in markets or of comparative advantage, while to the Left it reflects structural weaknesses of the regional economies. The Centre does not theorise these interconnections, and thus treats problems in isolation.

Consider firms' complaints that skills shortages limit their ability to innovate. The Centre's response is to improve training provision; yet this may miss the roots of the problem. Skill shortages are embedded in a set of interrelated traditions: short-termism, a low rate of productive investment, lack of sectoral coordination, poor management, and strategies based on low skill and cost competition. Shortages of skills may not constrain innovation. White (1988) found that innovating firms in engineering had no more skilled labour than non-innovators, but organised it more effectively and made innovation a priority in all decisions. Formal skills are often less relevant than training on the job, careful organisation of change, and harmonious industrial relations. In many production processes, skills shortages can be circumvented by fixed investment. Thus directly addressing skills shortages may miss the mark because of the strong connections between different aspects of firms' and sectors' activities.

The Centre's tendency to focus on a particular issue as *the* solution to the British disease is politically appealing but simplistic. It has made local economic policy vulnerable to fashions (p. 116) – training, for instance, was the fashion in the early 1990s. Isolated policies for single aspects of the economy are often the worst of all worlds, since their lack of connections produce failures and thereby discredit any attempts to address socialisation.

The internal connections of local economies are such that simple cause and effect are meaningless (Forrester, 1969). Consider again the policy of meeting skills shortages through training schemes. In many localities skills shortages are produced by housing and transport provision. In others, local firms have encouraged emigration by failing to use existing labour, by paying low wages, or by repeatedly making skilled workers redundant. Gender relations are often an important constraint. This and the previous example show that Centre policy has to address a whole nexus of problems that constitute the British disease. This produces constant pressure on the Centre to widen and deepen its spheres of intervention. For example, the partnership set up for the Nottingham Lace Market (p. 101) has not only undertaken integrated policies within the area but has proposed a light rail system which would serve both the area and the rest of the city, and has proposed programmes to deal with poverty throughout the city in order to head off social instability which could frighten off capital (Duffy, 1989); effective intervention spreads.

The Centre's usual fragmentation of policy results from determining its strategy from the demands made by firms. But, as we have seen, a firm's view of its needs depends upon its strategy, which may not be the most suitable. Different strategies produce divergent views among firms as to what action is necessary; Davies and Mason (1984) found that among IT firms there was great variety of views as to which skills were needed, whether more training was needed, and whether the private sector could do it alone. Firms usually have short time-horizons: in upturns they seek action on labour shortages and infrastructure, but drop these demands in the downturn. Responsiveness to firms' perceptions has been a further cause of instability in local economic policy. Firms usually have little appreciation of the roots of their problems in the locality as a whole, and therefore wrongly diagnose them.

In Britain these problems are exacerbated by the poor collective organisation of business. Given the weakness of the Chambers of Commerce, business is not sufficiently organised at the local level to debate and arrive at a common policy, so that local agencies receive unmediated the demands of diverse local firms and sectors. Firms seldom consider solving their problems through collective action, and therefore tend to make demands on the state. In responding to local business demands, the Centre is therefore acting on anecdotal, partial and superficial evidence. An independent and long-term view is required which rests on the interconnections of a problem. But the Centre would then have to get tough with business, by often refusing to go along with its demands and by implementing policies which sections of local business found perverse.

The Centre has responded to these problems. It has taken more direct forms of control, as in small firm policy; it has increased co-ordination between previously fragmented policies, in seeking to provide a complete local infrastructure for small business and a technological infrastructure through the innovation centres. The people based strategy aims to link welfare and competition policies. BiC has attempted to coordinate central government and locally initiated policies through its 'One Town' initiatives. Just as the modernising Labour government sponsored the formation of the CBI in 1965, so local economic agencies of the Centre have encouraged business to strengthen its local collective organisation (Bennett, 1991). These show the dynamic of consensus policies towards more comprehensive intervention. Yet this demands strategy; it means *not* responding to many demands of business; and it undermines the incremental and 'common sense' approach to policy making which has been the Centre's political strength.

Taking on business for its own good

To address the local socialisation of production effectively requires the Centre to become more independent from business and take a more objective view of local vested interests, at times opposing the real or perceived interests of sections of business not only locally but nationally. This leads into deep water.

The extent of national problems in local strategies is suggested by Saxenian's (1989) analysis of the problems of the Cambridge electronics industry: lack of domestic demand due to low investment in new technology, a management gap, exclusion of small firms from military contracts, the drain of technologists by military production, and a lack of technological infrastructure. The organisation of local interdependencies requires their articulation with regional, national and international socialisation. Yet we have seen (pp. 187–8) that this inevitably leads not only to conflicts between economic agencies at the various spatial levels but also to their becoming embroiled in conflicts between different firms and sectors.

Lack of coordination has been a major contributor to the failure of past Centrist governments to 'modernise' the British economy. During the reform period 1958–74 there was little connection between policies for sectors, technology, training, higher education, infrastructures, nationalised industries, regions and public purchasing (Pollard, 1969, ch. 8; Blackburn and Sharpe, 1988). Even the publicly owned sectors were not coordinated at a national or local level (Mackintosh, 1987). Most was achieved within the nationalised industries, where control was greatest.

Underlying these failures of coordination has been British economic liberalism, which is not merely an historical hangover but is perpetuated through vicious circles of causation. Over the past hundred years, lack of attention to socialisation has resulted in productivity growth and rates of profit lower than the average for the advanced countries. These low profits have encouraged further export of capital and neglect of the domestic economy, discouraged the banks from forming closer relations with domestic industry, and encouraged speculative activities. They have made it difficult to persuade industrial firms to collaborate in cutting capacity, swapping product lines and agreeing specialisation, since each firm is unwilling to shoulder any extra costs or to renounce any opportunities (Stout, 1981); in Japan, by contrast, agreements for rationalisation have been facilitated by high rates of profit and promising opportunities for diversification.

Low profitability and consequent fiscal pressures have harmed the provision of social infrastructures. Modernisation programmes tend to be abandoned in times of austerity when the squeeze of profits intensifies; the development during the 1960s of increasingly comprehensive Centrist subregional planning was effectively scrapped in the recession of 1973–5. Financial pressure on the TECs is endangering their commitment to training. The cooperative industrial relations promoted by the Centre can come under intense pressure in recessions: the paternalistic industrial relations of the 'American Way' in the 1920s were broken up by the depression of the early 1930s (Piore and Sabel, 1984, Ch. 3). Inherited low profitability and world economic stagnation are difficult conditions for the Centre.

A comprehensive Centre policy, then, would have to take on powerful interests. The role of London as a world financial centre would have to be radically curtailed, since its corollary is weak regulation and policies favourable to capital export. The conservatism of the pension funds and insurance companies would have to be ended, requiring a wholesale reorganisation of savings. Britain's exceptionally high level of military spending, linked to its overseas investment orientation, would have to be cut in order to stop its drain on public spending, on the balance of payments, and on scarce technological resources. This would require taking on the electrical engineering majors in order to wean them off their cost-plus habits; it would mean putting in jeopardy Britain's most successful region, the Sun Belt, with its heavy dependence on armaments. It would require taking on other sections of British business such as agriculture, house building and commercial property which are long accustomed to receiving subsidies while not submitting to any industrial policy in return. This century is littered with instances of the state abandoning restructuring initiatives after meeting opposition from business. Effective restructuring would mean getting tough not only with large corporations but with the small and medium firms; in the inter-war years, for example, the modernisation of the cotton and wool industries failed because of opposition from those mainly medium firms which might have lost from rationalisation (Dunford and Perrons, 1983, pp. 310–18). It would require higher taxation to finance improved infrastructure. Such a stance would be a major change from the current consensus in local economic policy, of treating small and medium firms with kid gloves, of a 'pro-business' stance which offends nobody.

The Centre's relation to business is therefore extremely delicate. To be effective, it has to extend its control over increasing aspects of business practice, and has to attack sectional business interests. It has to

do this under the most unfavourable conditions of low national profitability and international economic stagnation, and sustain the policy
over a long period to allow the virtuous circles time to work. These
difficulties explain the failure of successive national modernisation projects since the mid-nineteenth century (Newton and Porter, 1988). The
articulation of national and local policy is equally delicate. We have
seen that the consensus approach is based on its localism; yet to be
effective it has to become a national project.

The Pandora's box of interventionism

The Centre has equally difficult relations with labour. A collaborative
relation with labour inside and outside production is fundamental; and
to take on entrenched sectional business interests in the way just discussed would, in a country like Britain, require the backing of labour.
Yet the Centre's strategy necessitates being as tough with labour as with
capital.

To carry through painful industrial restructuring successfully requires
measures to raise the rate of profit in the medium term, both to fund it
and to prevent firms' opposition re-emerging; the only obvious way of
doing this is through some form of incomes policy (Hirst and Zeitlin,
1989). Capital would push all the harder for such a policy if Centre
policies were successful in reducing unemployment, with resulting upward pressure on wages.

Worse, the Centre's strategy tends to elicit ever-stronger demands
from labour. As the British Social Attitudes surveys show, the expectations generated by the welfare state have not been eradicated. The
Centre's promise to deliver welfare through improving competition
encourages demands for stronger intervention into production, as we
have seen with the people based strategy. Because consensus policies
fail to tie down capital and increase equality between areas and social
groups, they encourage labour to press for more far-reaching measures.
In linking local production and social life, however weakly, consensus
strategy begins to question the autonomy from production of housing
and education, of gender, and of social problems such as anomie and
crime, and challenge the fragmentation of policy towards these areas.
The Centre can also strengthen labour's bargaining power: the highly
integrated local economies it promotes are particularly vulnerable to
disruption by union action (p. 128).

If Centre policies were extended from the local to the national level, which we have seen is necessary, the successful interplay achieved in the 1980s between collaboration with labour at the local level and discipline of labour by national neo-liberal policies would be endangered. National coordination of local economic policy to develop a more rational spatial division of labour and to allocate policy areas to different levels of government would be needed; but this would tend to weaken Boot-straps, politicise the role of local initiatives, and once again encourage demands on central government for more resources. A national incomes policy would once again politicise the process of wage setting, as well as endangering the link of wages to individual unit profitability and to local costs which has been developed in the 1980s.

A consistent Centre strategy, then, faces major problems with both capital and labour. Notice that these class pressures arise not simply within production but also within consumption and in its connections to production, contrary to Saunders (1984) (see also Chapter 6). These pressures threaten to fracture the consensus and common-sense nature of local economic initiatives. Indeed, the essential reason for the re-placement of the Centre policies of the 1950s and 1960s with neo-liberal-ism was to deflate the increasing demands from both capital and labour which Centre policies encouraged (Clarke, 1988). Resisting such demands is made more difficult by the British predilection, shared by capital and labour, for 'money now', and the *rentier* tradition of inte-grating sections of labour and business with hand-outs (Gamble, 1981). Both capital and labour have to be persuaded to forgo their immediate interests and step outside the vicious circles which perpetuate liberal-ism, for a gain which could appear only in the very long term.

These problems of a consistent Centre strategy can already be seen in the hesitancy of local economic agencies in increasing their coordination and adopting real local strategies, and in the slowness of the Chambers of Commerce to develop a substantial intervention. It is true that the Centre has scored some successes in freeing its interventions from traditional political constraints; a notable example is the adoption of an expensive sports-centred strategy with unclear beneficiaries in that bastion of manual unionism, Sheffield. Yet these strategies are still weak compared with those of many European and US localities: Sheffield's sports programme is modest compared with that of Indianapolis.

Some Centre policy-makers propose to deal with the sectional pressures they face by concentrating decision-making in a strong city leader. Michael Heseltine, for example, has proposed transferring many of the powers of local councils to an elected mayor. It has been claimed that US urban regeneration has benefited from 'charismatic' leaders

(Judd and Parkinson, 1990). The utility of strong leaders does not lie in their genius, but rather in the way in which they can more easily resist sectional pressures than can a legislature. Once again, the logic of Centre policy is away from, rather than towards, greater democracy (pp. 180–1). A strong city leader would, however, be more difficult to realise in Britain than in the USA because of Britain's class-based political parties; the nearest historical examples in Britain have, perhaps, been in one-party areas, such as T.Dan Smith's leadership in Newcastle in the 1960s. British business is also less willing than that in the USA to entrust a single leader with such powers because of its lesser cohesiveness at the local level.

The strength of consensus local economic policies, then, has been to organise the local socialisation of production in a way which avoids excessive pressures from capital and labour; but if consensus strategy is followed through consistently enough to be effective, these pressures will re-emerge and require new responses. Different ways in which these tensions may be handled are considered further in the final chapter.

Further reading

The Centre orientation of most of business's local initiatives has been extensively discussed by Moore and Pierre (e.g. 1988) and Moore and Richardson (e.g. 1989). Baker (1987) shows why equal opportunities policies fail to produce equality. The overall argument of the chapter, that socialisation is both necessary and problematic for capital, has not been made in the context of local economic initiatives, but is made at a general level by Mandel (1978b, ch. 8), Habermas (1976) and Aglietta (1979, especially pp.149–50); a similar thesis with regard to urban planning is developed by Roweis (1981). A key aspect, the contradiction between capitalist discipline and state support for accumulation, is developed by Clarke (1988). The tension between pragmatic policy-making and stronger, holistic intervention is reflected in methodological problems analysed by Wright Mills (1970, ch.4). Wood (1991) shows that the barriers to British modernisation are not merely national historical hangovers but are inscribed in capitalist dynamics, indicating the utopian character of modernisation projects.

11 The International Economy and the Future of Local Economic Policy

We have stressed the importance of international trade and capital flows for local initiatives. In this final chapter we consider three key international issues: the possible Europeanisation and Japanisation of the British economy, and the relation of local initiatives to world economic stagnation. We finish the book by considering the political future of local economic policy.

1999 and all that

The British Centre has traditionally been parochial in seeking to turn British capital towards the domestic economy; the other side of this, however, has been an admiration for foreign models, particularly those of Germany and Japan. Increasing internationalisation now appears to offer new routes to modernising Britain by incorporating European and Japanese methods directly. We consider these two variants in turn.

For mainstream local economic agencies increasing European integration promises to bring greater social and political consensus to economic policy. We have seen that economic policy in Britain is marked by a tension between the international mobility of British capital and the coherence of the domestic economy, which is reflected in a lack of consensus on a national policy. By contrast, in most other EC countries, there has been a substantial consensus, since the recession of the mid-1970s, around a more 'balanced' strategy which combines liberalisation of markets with attention to at least some aspects of·socialisation. This approach has been implemented not only at the national level, but by the EC on the one hand and local agencies on the other. The European model has been neo-liberal in fiscal and monetary policy, supporting privatisation and competition for state contracts, and liberalising international trade and capital flows. On the other hand, long-standing traditions of industrial planning remain, including strategic planning by firms, close relations between industry and finance, sectoral planning by banks and the state, and inter-firm collaboration within sectors. Infrastructural investment, in particular in training, is higher than in Britain. Subsidies to industry have been pruned but are still used in the rationalisation of declining industries and to support technological innovation.

We have argued that these interventionist policies can support but also conflict with the freeing of capital and markets. This tension has presented fewer problems on the continent than it would have done in Britain, because of the lower degree of internationalisation of capital in the continental countries, their longer traditions of strategic planning, and their ability to contain pressures from capital and labour because of their higher profitability.

For mainstream local economic strategy, the hope is that greater integration of Britain into the EC will introduce the continental consensus to this country, with a number of beneficial effects. First, it would give a greater legitimacy to policies addressed to the socialisation of production, in particular at the local level. This promise is reinforced by the fact that local and regional government on the continent generally has stronger economic powers than in Britain (Labour Party, 1991b). Second, a national consensus on the main lines of economic policy would facilitate coordination between local, regional and national policy, reducing the sharp policy differences between them which have obtained in Britain. Third, adoption of the continental approach promises to improve British performance and thus mitigate the political pressures which Centre policies face. A Europeanisation of Britain therefore promises greater harmony between the classes, within economic debate, and between local and national policy.

The reality, however, is likely to be very different. First, liberalisation of trade and capital flows will reinforce the patterns of uneven development within Britain (p. 194). It will become more difficult for localities to become special or to resist relegation down the hierarchies, because of increasing specialisation by locality at the European level and because the organisation of local specialisation is stronger on the continent. European integration is likely to lead to increasing concentration of production, ownership and effective control, making some aspects of small firm policies more difficult. These economic problems will add to the political impetus for mainstream local policy while hindering its implementation.

Second, adoption of continental practice, while it would reinforce a local level of policy in some respects, would weaken it in others. Stronger national industrial planning would regulate local policy, in order to prevent wasteful competition and conflicting interventions (pp. 187–8); this is why local government in Germany has been quite restricted in its economic powers (Johnson and Cochrane, 1981). On the continent, power within trade unions is less locally based than in Britain, and convergence would erode the localism of British unionism (Woolcock *et al*, 1991). We have seen that the latter has been an important base for collaborative and productionist local economic policy. Integration of the EC is leading to heavier regulation of non-EC immigrants, affecting all black people; this will hinder local policies attempting to combat racial exclusion.

Third, however, increased formal integration does not necessarily harmonise economic–industrial practices. Better opportunities for overseas investment and increased imports will reinforce key mechanisms through which British weakness has been propagated. Moreover, the notion that continental practices will be imported pictures them as a factor of production which can be transferred from one country to another. But these practices are part of wider social–economic processes, including particularly class relations and international linkages; continental companies and Europeanised British companies and managers will not necessarily behave in the same way in Britain as they do in Europe.

Fourth, the EC is often stronger in enforcing the neo-liberal elements of its strategy, such as attacking informal trade barriers, cartels and state subsidies, than in spreading interventionist practice such as the Social Charter; EC institutions will tend to block local Centre policies more than those of the Right. The outlawing of 'anti-competitive' industrial subsidies could block the Centre–Left's plans for expanding the LEBs. In 1991 the EC judged that Derbyshire County Council had transgressed its directives against subsidies to the motor industry by selling land to Toyota at less than market value. Coordination at the international level often cuts across coordination at a local or regional level.

Fifth, especially given long term British decline, all forms of monetary integration produce a highly valued exchange rate and a deflationary bias, and thus block Centre strategy. Over most of the last century the policy of a strong pound has served to discipline labour, leading to the neglect of more active policies for collaboration. It has failed to push producers into shifting from cost to quality competition, but has encouraged the export of capital. Moreover, because of continuing balance of payments problems, a Centre programme of industrial restructuring is likely to require devaluation, which is consequently more difficult. Strong sterling will put particular pressure on localities which are confined to cost competitive international markets. Not only does monetary integration inhibit national reflationary policies, but the European monetary system is itself being established within a strongly monetarist framework (Williams *et al*, 1991b).

In sum, it is by no means clear that increased integration into the EC will make Britain more similar to the continent, or increase the opportunities for consensus local initiatives. The neo-liberal elements in EC policy are likely to have greater purchase in Britain than the policies reinforcing socialisation because they run along the grain of the British economy, and because its competitive weaknesses inhibit it from taking advantage of European-wide socialisation.

A Japanese local consensus?

Another path with attractions for both the Centre and the Right is Japanisation. Britain has so far been the main recipient in the EC of Japanese manufacturing investment on the basis of its low wages and the relative absence of nationalistic industrial policy. The industrial relations of the Japanese transnationals combine discipline of labour – complete managerial control of tasks, no-strike agreements, harsh penalties for absenteeism and sickness, selection of recruits for maximum maleability, and 'continuous improvement' – with elements of collaboration – use of workers' suggestions, single-status contracts, and eliciting of dedication to company profitability. These industrial relations have been decisive in Japanese industrial success. They have not merely made possible task flexibility, but have given management a stable framework in which to carry out long term plans; product and process innovation, for instance, is often planned over many years, in contrast to the riskier 'big bang' approach of the West. Moreover, because of this dominance Japanese capital can adopt bold and integrated responses to problems, avoiding the fragmented policies of the British Centre and the reactive and indirect policies of the British Right. The Japanese corporation often has a strong involvement in local socialisation, both in constructing a system of local suppliers and in providing elements of welfare for its workers. The strong discipline of labour is appealing to the Right. But the model is closer to the Centre: attention to production efficiency, a strong local involvement, 'classless' industrial relations and active employee involvement; these promise to organise the local socialisation of production without unleashing uncontrollable demands from labour.

Aspects of Japanese industrial relations are being copied by many British firms and supported from the Centre by the electrical and engineering unions (Oliver and Wilkinson, 1988). Yet the support for an *overall* Japanese strategy has been remarkably muted. This reticence reflects a number of problems for Japanisation. First, the industrial relations, paternalism and local initiatives of the Japanese firms are dependent on their high profitability and expectations of stability. Most British-owned manufacturing firms tend to be less willing to commit funds in this way and to tie themselves down to the locality.

Second, it is hard to achieve the industrial relations regime of the Japanese plants in Britain, let alone that of factories in Japan. The intensity of work and dictatorial eliciting of cooperation in Japan have been produced by cumulative defeats of the trade union movement from the late 1940s to the present (Ichiyo, 1987); a comparable turn has not (yet) taken place in Britain, and there is resistance to moves towards such a work regime. Japanese transnationals have been able to impose a lightened version in their British plants because of the promise of stable jobs; and it is not yet clear whether this regime will remain unchallenged as the workforce matures (Garrahan and Stewart, 1992). The non-Japanese firms which have got the farthest with Japanisation are in cars and consumer electronics, which have been able to use the threat of domestic Japanese competition.

Third, existing patterns of production and welfare in Britain cut across Japanisation outside the individual workplace. The Nissan and Honda plants in England are using the British and European system of *non*-local subcontractors (Hudson and Sadler, 1992). Partly because of the more extensive welfare state in Britain, they have not intervened into local social life.

Fourth, large firms in Japan provide benefits only to their employees and thus tend to create a local dual society; this is at odds with consensus local initiatives in Britain which are integrationist in aspiration if not in effect. This reflects a profound difference in the relation between production and society in Japanese and British policy: broadly put, the British state eschews the planning of production but plans the social (welfare, town planning), with the result that consensus local economic initiatives are to a large extent a form of locality-wide welfare; in contrast, Japanese practice is to plan production and neglect the social except in its immediate connections with production, so that local economic initiatives directly serve the company. These are very different models of local community.

Fifth, the Japanese model involves not only the plant and locality, but also strong nation-state planning and protection of companies from takeover threats by the holding company system. The British Right is of course opposed to such practices, and even the strongest versions of the Centre do not approach them. British companies embarking on a thorough Japanese strategy at plant and local level would not have the state protection from raiders which is enjoyed by their Japanese counterparts. Once again, if local consensus strategy is to be carried through effectively it opens a Pandora's box.

Local action and economic crisis

Earlier we argued that for the foreseeable future world capitalism, and Britain in particular, will be faced with high rates of unemployment and low rates of profit and productive investment (pp. 192–3). Commentators on local economic policy have two contrary views on its relevance to this continuing crisis. The first is that local economic initiatives deal with the effects of crisis rather than its causes. Economic stagnation is seen as originating largely in processes which local economic initiatives cannot ameliorate, such as oil price rises (Cooke, 1989a, p. 15), demand management (Moore and Richardson, 1989, pp. 9–10; Keating and Boyle, 1986), or rapid technical change (Todd, 1984, p. 1.). Initiatives are then judged by their effectiveness or otherwise in dealing with the symptoms of crisis, such as the spatial and social incidence of unemployment (Howl, 1985, p. 73).

But the crisis is not simply an external context: local economic initiatives are about social relations, and these are integral to the crisis. The crisis arises most fundamentally from private control over investment, the control of the workplace by capital, and the dependence of both capital and labour on these structures for their survival and reproduction (Mandel, 1978b; Harvey, 1982); local economic policy is centrally concerned with these processes. In the course of the crisis, social groups compete to displace its burdens and 'cures' on to others; local economic policy participates actively in these conflicts. Thus whether or not local economic initiatives contribute to ending economic stagnation, they are undoubtedly about the reshaping of social relations within it, and about the *terms* under which it might be resolved.

The second popular view is that local economic policy can make an important contribution to overcoming the crisis. For the Centre and modernising Left, local collaboration between capital and labour can be the core of a New Deal to lift the economy out of depression (Cooke and Scott, 1988). All main political currents assume that increasing the competitiveness, efficiency and technological dynamism of each local economy separately would revive the national economy, and that an autonomous revival of each national economy would in aggregate restore world economic growth (Therborn, 1986).

But the immediate effects of such increases in efficiency are to lower prices and to redistribute a *given* amount of profit between local economies or countries. In electronics, for example, increases in efficiency increase the profits of the firms and regions which achieve them but at the expense of others; to the extent that these increases are generalised, they reduce world prices but do not increase total world profits. Similarly, in an industry with little international trade such as personal insurance or sausage manufacture, increases in efficiency redistribute profits between localities and tend to lower national prices but do not increase aggregate national profits. In locally traded and organised sectors such as solicitors or small scale building, increases in efficiency benefit the firms carrying them out and lower local prices but do not raise the overall rate of profit of the local sector. Yet at each spatial level an increase in the overall rate of profit is a necessary condition for a new wave of growth.

For some commentators, accelerated technical change is the key to fundamental economic revival, and local policy has a crucial role to play in achieving this (Hall, 1985a). But the link between the rate of technical innovation and upward long waves of the economy is empirically unclear (Freeman *et al*, 1982). More fundamentally, while technical innovations can give high profits to the particular firm or region, they do not necessarily raise the overall rate of profit (Mandel, 1978b, pp. 137–46).

These criticisms suggest how different theories of economic crisis lead to different views of the potential of local economic policy (Massey and Allen, 1988, Introduction; Beauregard, 1989a). We believe that marxist theory offers the best guide here. Within this approach technical change, increases in efficiency and reductions in price do affect profit rates, but through more complex mechanisms than in the views just criticised. Whereas the latter extrapolate from the profitability of the firm to that of the locality to that of the nation, the characteristic viewpoint of a competitor, the marxist approach considers mechanisms at the level of 'whole economies'. The only completely closed economy is that of the world; we can enquire what effects the local initiatives being carried out throughout the dominant countries might have on world economic revival. But the mechanisms we shall consider operate to some extent within the partially closed economies of nations and localities, and affect the profitability of those units. At these different levels, one can identify three broad types of effect of local economic policy on profitability and growth (Gough, 1986b).

● The first concerns the direct relations between capital and labour. Local cooperation of labour with capital can raise the share of value added going to capital, and hence the rate of profit. Collaborative industrial relations and community enterprises encourage moderation in wage demands, a more intense rate of work, and higher quality work. Labour market policies help to hold down wages and sometimes increase value added. Community initiatives can reduce the frictional costs of capital movements in and out of localities. However, strengthening local socialisation can, under some circumstances, strengthen labour's demands and bargaining power against capital (p. 257), and thus cause wages and benefits to eat into profits.

● A second set of effects revolves around labour productivity. The strengthening of local socialisation can raise productivity, which, if it is generalised, reduces prices in real terms. In locally marketed sectors, such as most consumer and business services, these productivity increases can reduce local prices; in more widely marketed sectors, such as manufacturing, they have an impact on prices only if carried out in many localities. Price reductions in consumption goods and services have a positive impact on the rate of profit by helping to hold down real wages. Price reductions in the goods and services bought by firms reduce the capital sunk in production, and thus, for given amount of profit, raise the rate of profit. If the commodities in question are locally marketed, then this boost to profits is local. Thus productivity rises made possible by local policy can have a positive impact on profits either locally or more widely.

However, most of the productivity-raising methods promoted by local initiatives increase the capital employed relative to the profits made from workers. This is true of improved infrastructures, machinery and buildings, and also of knowledge investments such as R&D and training amortised over long periods. An intensified socialisation of production more often than not raises the capital sunk in production relative to number of workers employed, and hence tends to reduce the profit rate.

The net effect on profit rates and growth of the productivity increases promoted by local initiatives is thus far from clear. This shows the need to consider not merely the efficiency and productivity of the economy but its social relations and overall economic articulation.

● A third set of effects concerns the relation between rates of profit and the rate of investment. A long period of low profit produces an excess of finance seeking profitable investment; local economic policy can help to open up new sectors of investment. For example, in the early 1980s the banks, having burnt their fingers in Third World investment, turned to domestic small firms as a field for investing their excess funds, initiating the Enterprise Agencies as a means to stimulate them. Local initiatives have since played an important role in making small firms a more attractive field of investment. In the 1980s local property and area strategies also facilitated the banks in their stampede into commercial property, amounting to £40bn by 1990. In both cases, however, excess money capital was shortly converted into excess productive capacity, reflected in the consequent attrition of small firms and property developers and the large losses sustained by the banks. We see here how local economic initiatives do not merely react to the crisis but actively contribute to it.

These examples show that it is not enough merely to open up new fields of investment; the impact of that investment on profitability is crucial. We noted in Chapter 6 that the small firms and community enterprises supported by local initiatives tend to have a lower than average rate of profit. We argued that Right and Centre policies tend to have different effects on the rate of profit and investment behaviour of these enterprises. The Right encourages extensive investment which maintains a low rate of profit among small enterprises, while Centre policies can stimulate intensive investment in at least some types of small enterprise, and thus move them to higher rates of profit. At the same time, the Right increases the profits of risk-averting sectors of capital such as landowners, property and private monopolies, which tend to have a low rate of productive investment.

These different impacts of Right and Centre initiatives on the divide between high and low profit parts of the economy can affect the propagation of the crisis. The Right tends to construct an economy divided between a sector of small enterprises with high extensive investment and low profits, and a sector of privileged industries with a low rate of productive investment but high profits. This benefits the latter sector, through distributing to it a higher proportion of aggregate profits. But higher profits only stimulate fundamental recovery if they lead to faster increases in productivity and price reductions. The Right, on the contrary, often benefits sectors with a low propensity to productive investment; it therefore tends to perpetuate stagnation in the form of excess finance and low productivity increases.

Centre initiatives, in contrast, tend to produce greater movement and fluidity between the low-profit small enterprises and the rest of the economy, a higher overall rate of productive investment, and thus a dynamic effect on the rate of profit via price reductions. Centre strategy, then, where it is successful, produces a segment of the economy with high profits *and* a high rate of productive investment. If this were sufficiently large, it could have a stimulating effect on the economy as a whole (Mandel, 1978b, chs 3 and 8); if not, the main effect of Centre local initiatives is to stimulate cyclical excess productive investment in profitable sectors and areas and thus exacerbate uneven development (pp. 132, 249–50). The Centre then tends to perpetuate stagnation in the form of exaggerated cycles of overcapacity in dynamic sectors and areas.

In the three types of effect we have considered, then, consensus local economic policy can have some recuperative effects on the rate of profit and investment in the long term; but these are offset by their tendency to raise the quantity of sunk capital, to stimulate overproduction and uneven development, and to strengthen labour in the distribution of value added.

Although this discussion of crisis barely skims the surface, we hope to have established two simple points. First, local initiatives do not merely occur in the 'context' of crisis, but contribute to its propagation and form. Some commentators understand that the social relations of local economic initiatives are important from a sociological or political point of view (e.g. Moore and Richardson, 1989); but they are also integral to the accumulation of capital and its crisis tendencies. Second, the aggregate effect of local initiatives on the employment crisis cannot be assessed without some theory of this crisis. In particular, it cannot be assumed that increases in efficiency, productivity or competitiveness necessarily contribute to long term economic recovery. The processes by which these are achieved have negative as well as positive effects for capital and growth.

Political tensions and local conditions

Consensus local economic initiatives, then, have deeper problems than appear at first sight. The problems of local economic policy are often pictured as being essentially ones of conflict between different social groups: the literature on growth coalitions and city centre regeneration, for example, typically sees their problems as lying in conflicts between business and the poor (Molotch, 1976; Mackintosh and Wainwright, 1987, ch. 12). In this part of the book we have tried to show that the problems rest on contradictions, which may take the form of conflicts between different groups but are also often dilemmas for a single group. We have argued that consensus initiatives, no less than those of the Left and Right, involve many contradictions, and these produce tensions and uncertainties for capital.

For this reason the consensus approach may not remain dominant; local economic strategies of the Right and Left may regain support. Whether they do so depends partly on the conditions in particular localities, which give promise – though no guarantee of success – to different strategies. These conditions need to be analysed case by case; but some examples may indicate the issues that need consideration.

The Right's strategy can shake out old institutional forms which block new lines of development; its policy in London Docklands may be seen in this way. In areas which lack an integrated local economy and which rely on cost competition, the Right may hold costs down, but only if there are no bottlenecks in the supply of labour, infrastructure or land; the attraction of electronics assembly work to south Wales is perhaps an example. Conversely, Centre strategy is relevant where there are such bottlenecks; and as Glasgow suggests, the Centre may be able to change old institutional structures by constructing alternatives rather than using *only* market threats and demolition as the the Right does. Centre policies have promise in areas with established industries which cannot ignore local socialisation, such as tourism; and in areas with potential growth sectors where new local interconnections need establishing, as in Consett's environmental services complex. The stronger policies for socialisation of the modernising Left have promise in areas where social-isation has been most ruinously neglected, as in London manufacturing and London infrastructure or, in a different sense, in branch plant economies. In all these areas, however, capital may need to use, and establish some balance between, the disciplinary policies of the Right and the socialisation of the Centre–Left.

Given British traditions, in growth areas two rather bland forms of intervention have had appeal: either to provide for growth with property and housing, as in Swindon and Peterborough; or to restrict it selectively in order to avoid inflationary pressures and demands for more infrastructure, as in much of the South-east. These economies could be strengthened by more far-reaching Centre policies such as planning within and between regions and sectoral and technological policies; but these pose political risks which in times of high growth appear unnecessary.

Local politics is also important. Distinctively Right policies have been most strongly pursued in areas like Wandsworth dominated, through their residential composition, by the ideas of the City. Other Tory areas incline to Centre–Right policies: the interventionist housing policies of farmer-dominated shires (Dickens *et al.*, 1985); the old paternalism of some country towns (Bagguley *et al.*, 1990); the economic planning of tourist towns (Buck *et al.*, 1989); and the 'good environment' planning traditions of Home Counties Conservatism which, in part, prevents the Sun Belt from pursuing the unrestricted growth of Italian or Japanese boom areas. The most extensive Centre strategies have been developed in Labour strongholds such as central Scotland, south Wales and north east England. There, the Labour councils and the unions have had the authority to deliver the collaboration of workers and residents with the economic restructuring which is essential to this strategy. Where the unions have been strongest they may play a role in pushing economic agencies towards high socialisation strategies; this may partly explain the interventionism of the Scottish Development Agency (and some of the Rust Belt States in the US). Where this organic Labourism is absent, most clearly in London and Liverpool, both Right and distinctively Left strategies have space.

This sketch suggests that local economic conditions and political traditions will lend support to Right and Left strategies as well as the Centre. However, the possibilities for winning support for any of these strategies and implementing them successfully will depend on how their endemic problems are manifested and understood and on how they mesh with national developments; we now turn to these issues.

The political future of local economic initiatives

The symbiotic combination of consensus local initiatives and disciplinarian national government which has marked the 1980s may continue, but it will, at the least, come under increasing strains. European integration and worsening balance-of-payments problems will on the one hand increase the propensity of British capital to look overseas, and on the other will intensify demands from labour and from sections of capital to combat domestic decline by addressing national and local socialisation – pressures reflected in the demise of Thatcher. These contrary pressures are reinforced by the contradictions of consensus local initiatives them- selves. The benefits of these initiatives are highly uneven as between sector, social group and area, eliciting demands for further action from the losers. There is constant pressure to deepen and widen these initia- tives to make them more effective; yet the conflicts and demands that deeper intervention produces make for caution; if they erupted in many localities, the consensus could retreat to the right.

There are therefore other possibilities than a continuation of the present local consensus. The first, discussed in Chapter 9, is a shift to the right. This could occur under a government (of whatever party) with a renewed Thatcherite strategy centred on capital export, the City, and domestically oriented consumer goods and services. Local agencies seeking to continue an interventionist path would be hamstrung by lack of central government funding and further restrictions on local govern- ment powers, and increasingly discredited by failures. It is possible, however, that in this situation some sections of capital would step up their local initiatives. Sectors dependent on the home market, the prime supporters of the Enterprise Agencies, might increase their contribu- tions in the face of the political instability threatened by widening pauperisation. Some large manufacturing firms – US and Japanese transnationals, old paternalist British firms – might intensify initiatives in their localities in order to compensate for the decline of national economic and social infrastructure. The isolation of these initiatives would tend to increase labour's commitment to them, but would also limit their effectiveness. Worsening poverty might encourage more bottom-up community businesses; but lack of resources would ensure their ghettoisation, and might discredit them. Consensus local policy would thus be marginalised.

An alternative possibility is that intensifying economic difficulties will produce more strongly interventionist local economic policy. This is possible under a Right–Centre government such as Major's (p. 00), but would go further under a Centre–Left government which addressed socialisation more strongly, attempting to deal with the legacy of neo- liberalism. In the latter case, local authorities might obtain greater powers to undertake economic initiatives, and economic powers could be devolved to a Scottish Assembly and new regional authorities. Busi- ness might decrease its involvement on the grounds that the state was doing its job again. But it is likely that there would be continuing high national unemployment and increasing regional and local differentiation within a European framework. The strengthened local agencies would be buffeted by demands from capital and labour. There would be a temptation to try to sidestep these pressures by introducing a mayoral-type system into local government, by making the regional and local economic agencies indirectly or non-elected, by fragmenting their operations to sub-agencies, and by handing their control to business executives and union officials. But five to ten years' experience of such a regime would produce enormous political tensions.

Such a national revival of the Centre, and the restoration and extension of powers of local and regional government, could give renewed life to the local Left. The weakening of the union, women's and black movements and the decline of offensive campaigns around housing and social welfare have played a central part in the development of consensus local economic policy. But the failure of years of austerity and restructuring to meet its promises may precipitate renewed offensives, which would be locally uneven and in many cases locally organised. This, together with the failures of milder intervention, could feed into a renewed Left modernising project, which might be backed by sections of capital. It would however be faced with stronger capital mobility and international linkages than before, and with obstruction by the EC. Alternatively, a renewed popular offensive could take the form of socialist local initiatives of the kind discussed in Chapter 8, centred on increasing popular power rather than modernisation.

We cannot, then, take for granted a future of local economic initiatives in their present form (contrary to Benington, 1986). While local and central government and other actors will continue to take actions with local economic effects and aims, these may differ from the current consensus initiatives as much as the latter do from local government policies of the 1960s. It is not merely a matter of more or less interventionist localities (Cooke, 1989a): the aims, economic mechanisms and organisational form of local initiatives are all up for grabs. Local economic policy is shaped by, and shapes, the relations between the classes and relations within the classes; it therefore remains open to struggle and to conscious political strategy.

Bibliography

C. Abbott, *The New Urban America* (Chapel Hill: Univ. of N. Carolina Press, 1981).

Advisory Council on Science and Technology, *The Enterprise Challenge* (London: HMSO, 1990).

M. Aglietta, *A Theory of Capitalist Regulation* (London: NLB, 1979).

M. Allan, M. Fenton and A. Flockhart, *Creating a Local Economic Development Network* (Glasgow: Planning Exchange, 1985).

J. Allen, 'Towards a post-industrial economy?', in D. Massey and J. Allen (eds), *The Economy in Question* (Milton Keynes: Open Univ. Press, 1988).

S. Allen and C. Wolkowitz, *Homeworking: myths and realities* (London: Macmillan, 1987).

P. Ambrose and B. Colenutt, *The Property Machine* (Harmondsworth: Penguin, 1975).

A. Amin, 'Flexible specialisation and small firms in Italy', *Antipode*, 21 (1989) 134–34.

A. Amin and J. Goddard (eds) *Technological Change, Industrial Restructuring and Regional Development* (London: Allen & Unwin, 1986).

A. Amin and K. Robins, 'The re-emergence of regions?: the mythical geography of flexible accumulation', *Society and Space*, 8 (1990) 7–34.

A. Amin and I. Smith: 'The internationalisation of production and its implications for the UK', in Amin and Goddard 1986.

S. Amin, *Accumulation on a World Scale* (Hassocks: Harvester, 1974).

J. Anderson, 'Some contradictions in the urban policy of the New Right', *ISA. Conference, Trends and Challenges of Urban Restructuring*, Rio de Janeiro (1988).

P. Anderson, 'The figures of descent', *New Left Rev.*, 161 (1987) 20–77.

V. Andreff, 'The international centralization of capital and the reordering of world capitalism', *Capital and Class*, 22 (1984) 58–80.

Archbishop of Canterbury's Commission on Urban Priority Areas, *Faith in the City* (London: Church Housing Publishing, 1985).

H. Armstrong and S. Fildes, *District Council Industrial Development Units and Regional Industrial Policy* (Oxford: Pergamon, 1988).

P. Armstrong, A. Glyn and J. Harrison, *Capitalism since 1945* (Oxford: Blackwell, 1991).

D. Ashton, F. Green and M. Hoskins, 'The training system of British capitalism', in F. Green (ed.) *The Restructuring of the UK Economy* (Hassocks: Harvester, 1989).

Association of British Chambers of Commerce, *A Tale of Four Cities: business responsibility in action* (London: ABCC, 1989).

Association of County Councils, Association of District Councils and Association of Metropolitan Authorities, *Stimulating Local Enterprise* (London: ACC, 1988).

Association of District Councils, *A Blueprint for Urban Areas* (London: ADC, 1987).

P. Bagguley *et al.*, *Restructuring: place, class and gender* (London: Sage, 1990).

J. Baker, *Arguing for Equality* (London: Verso, 1987).

E. Banfield, *The Unheavenly City Revisited* (Boston: Little Brown, 1974).

R. Banham, P. Barker, P. Hall and C. Price, 'Non-plan: an experiment in freedom,' *New Society*, 13 (1969) 442–3.

M. Banks *et al.*, *Careers and Identities* (Milton Keynes: Open Univ. Press, 1991).

T. Barnekov, R. Boyle and D. Rich, *Privatisation and Urban Policy in Britain and the US* (Oxford: OUP, 1989).

M. Barrett and M. McIntosh, *The Anti-Social Family* (London: NLB, 1982).

K. Basset, M. Boddy, M. Harloe and J. Lovering, 'Living in the fast lane: economic and social change in Swindon', in Cooke 1989b (1989).

A. Batkin, 'The impact of local authorities on Labour Party economic policy', *Local Economy*, 2 (1987) 14–24.

R. Beauregard, 'Space, time and economic restructuring', in Beauregard 1989b (1989a).

R. Beauregard (ed.) *Economic Restructuring and Political Response* (Newbury Park: Sage, 1989b).

F. Bechofer and B. Elliott (eds) *The Petit Bourgeoisie* (London: Macmillan, 1981).

J. Benington, 'Interview', *Critical Social Policy*, 9 (1984) 69–87.

J. Benington, 'Local economic strategies: paradigms for a planned economy?', *Local Economy*, 1 (1986) 7–25.

A. Bennett and S. Smith-Gavine, 'The percentage utilisation of labour index (PUL)', in D. Bosworth and D. Heathfield (eds) *Working Below Capacity* (London: Macmillan, 1987).

R. Bennett (ed.) *Decentralisation, Local Government and Markets* (Oxford: Clarendon, 1990).

R. Bennett, *Attaining quality: the agenda for local business services in the 1990s*, Dept. of Geog. Research Paper, LSE, 1991.

R. Bennett and G. Krebs, *Local Economic Development: public–private partnership initiatives in Britain and Germany* (London: Bellhaven, 1991).

H. Berndt, *New Rulers in the Ghetto* (Westport Conn.: Greenwood Press, 1977).

M. Best, 'Strategic planning and industrial policy', *Local Economy*, 1 (1986) 65–77.

M. Best, *The New Competition: institutions of industrial restructuring* (Cambridge: Polity, 1990).

H. Beynon, 'False hopes and real dilemmas; the politics of the collapse of British manufacturing', *Critique*, 16 (1983) 1–22.

H. Beynon *et al.*, 'It's all falling apart here: coming to terms with the future of Teeside', in Cooke 1989b (1989).

F. Bianchini, 'Cultural policy and urban development', *ISA Conference, Urban Change and Conflict*, Lancaster (1991).

F. Bianchini, M. Fisher, J. Montgomery and K. Worpole, *City Centres, City Cultures* (Manchester: CLES, 1991) 2nd edn.

R. Bingham and J. Blair (eds) *Urban Economic Development* (Beverly Hills: Sage, 1984).

R. Bingham, E. Hill and J. White (eds) *Financing Economic Development* (Beverly Hills: Sage, 1990).

D. Birch, *The Job Generation Process* (Cambridge Mass.: 1979).

S. Birley and S. Bridges, 'Small firms/ new firms: a strategy for Northern Ireland', *9th UK Small Firms Conference*, Gleneagles (1986).

P. Blackburn and R. Sharpe (eds) *Britain's Industrial Renaissance?* (London: Routledge, 1988)

P. Blair, 'Trends in local autonomy and democracy', in R. Batley and G. Stoker (eds) *Local Government in Europe* (London: Macmillan, 1991).

B. Bluestone and B. Harrison, *The Deindustrialisation of America* (New York: Basic Books, 1982).

B. Bluestone and B. Harrison, *The Dark Side of Labour Market 'Flexibility'* (Geneva: ILO, 1987).

W. Bonefeld and J. Holloway, *Post-Fordism and Social Form* (London: Macmillan 1991).

R. Botham, 'Local Authority employment subsidies', *The Planner*, 69 (1983) 165–7.

L. Bown, 'Initiatives for employment', Proc. of the Summer School, *The Planner*, 72 (1986) 7–10.

R. Boyle, '"Leveraging" urban development', *Policy and Politics*, 13 (1985) 175–210.

H. Braverman, *Labour and Monopoly Capitalism* (New York: Monthly Review Press, 1974).

T. Brindley, Y. Rydin and G. Stoker, *Remaking Planning* (London: Unwin Hyman, 1989).

S. Brownill, *Developing London's Docklands* (London: Chapman, 1990).

I. Bruegel, 'Local economic strategies and service employment', *Local Economy*, 1 (1987) 17–28.

I. Brunskill and R. Minns, 'Local financial markets', *Local Economy*, 3 (1989) 295–305.

S. Brusco, 'Small firms and industrial districts: the experience of Italy', in D. Keeble and E. Wever (eds) *New Firms and Regional Development in Europe* (London: Croom Helm, 1980).

P. Buchanan, 'Urban design guidelines in London Docklands', *Arch. Rev.*, 1106 (1989) 39–44.

N. Buck and I. Gordon, 'The beneficiaries of employment growth: an analysis of the experiences of disadvantaged groups in expanding labour markets', in Hausner 1987a (1987).

N. Buck, I. Gordon, C. Pickvance and P. Taylor-Gooby, 'The Isle of Thanet: restructuring and municipal conservatism', in Cooke 1989b (1989).

N. Buck, I. Gordon and K. Young, *The London Employment Problem* (Oxford: Clarendon, 1986).

R. Burgess, 'Self-help housing advocacy: a curious form of radicalism', in P. Ward (ed.) *Self-help Housing – a Critique* (London: Mansell, 1982).

P. Burns and J. Dewhurst, 'Small business in Europe', in Burns and Dewhurst 1986c (1986a).

P. Burns and J. Dewhurst, 'Great Britain and Northern Ireland', in Burns and Dewhurst 1986c (1986b).

P. Burns and J. Dewhurst (eds) *Small Business in Europe* (London: Macmillan, 1986c).

R. Burrows (ed.) *Deciphering the Enterprise Culture* (London: Routledge, 1991).

R. Burrows, N. Gilbert and A. Pollert, *Fordism and Flexibility* (London: Macmillan, 1992).

Business in the Community, 'Redundancy – guide to good practice', *Business in the Community Magazine*, 6 (1987) 8–11.

B. Bye and J. Beattie, *Local Economic Planning and the Unions* (London: Workers Ed. Assoc., 1982).

Cabinet Office, *Action for Cities* (London: HMSO, 1988).

M. Camina, *Local Authorities and the Attraction of Industry* (Oxford: Pergamon, 1974).

M. Campbell, 'Introduction', in Campbell 1990b (1990a).

M. Campbell (ed.) *Local Economic Policy* (London: Cassell, 1990b).

M. Campbell *et al.*, 'The economics of local jobs plans', *Local Economy*, 1 (1987) 81–91.

M. Castells, *The Urban Question* (London: Arnold, 1977).

M. Castells, *The Informational City* (Oxford: Blackwell, 1989).

J. Cater and T. Jones, *Social Geography* (London: Arnold, 1989).

R. Caves, 'Productivity differences among industries', in R. Caves and L. Krause (eds) *Britain's Economic Performance* (Washington DC: Brookings Inst. 1980).

Centre for Alternative Industrial & Technological Systems, *Employee Share Ownership* (London: CAITS, 1987).

Centre for Employment Initiatives, *Local Employment Initiatives* (Luxembourg: Commission for European Communities, 1985).

Centre for Local Economic Studies, *Enterprise Boards* (Manchester: CLES, 1987a).

Centre for Local Economic Studies Black Employment Group, *Jobs for Black People* (Manchester: CLES, 1987b).

D. Cesarani, 'Massacre beyond Aldgate', *Times Higher Ed. Supp.*, 1 July 1988.

J. Chandler and P. Lawless, *Local Authorities and the Creation of Employment* (Aldershot: Gower, 1985).

P. Cheshire and D. Hay, *Urban Problems in Europe* (London: Unwin Hyman, 1988).

A. Church and J. Hall, 'Local initiatives for economic regeneration', in D. Herbert and D. Smith (eds) *Social Problems and the City* (Oxford: OUP, 1989).

Civic Trust, *Regeneration – new forms of community partnership* (London: Civic Trust, 1989).

P. Clark, 'Working with people', *Radical Science Jnl.*, 13 (1983) 100–4.

S. Clarke, *Keynsianism, Monetarism and the Crisis of the State* (Aldershot: Elgar, 1988).

S. Clarke, 'New utopias for old: Fordist dreams and post-Fordist fantasies', *Capital and Class*, 42 (1990) 131–53.

J. Coakley, 'The internationalisation of bank capital', *Capital and Class*, 23 (1984) 107–20.

A. Cochrane (ed.) *Developing Local Economic Strategies* (Milton Keynes: Open Univ. Press, 1987).

A. Cochrane, 'In and against the market?: the development of socialist economic strategies in Britain, 1981–1986', *Policy and Politics*, 16 (1988) 159–68.

A. Cochrane, 'Restructuring local politics: Sheffield's economic policies in the 1980s', *ISA Conference, Urban Change and Conflict*, Lancaster (1991).

C. Cockburn, *The Local State* (London: Pluto, 1977).

C. Cockburn, *Brothers: male dominance and technological change* (London: Pluto, 1983).

B. Colenutt and S. Tansley, *Urban Development Corporations: Interim Report* (Manchester: CLES, 1989).

B. Colenutt and S. Tansley, *Inner City Regeneration: a local authority perspective* (Manchester: CLES, 1990).

C. Collinge, *Investing in the Local Economy* (London: Community Projects Foundation, 1983)

Community Development Project, *The Costs of Industrial Change* (London: CDP, 1977).

Confederation of British Industry, *Initiatives beyond Charity* (London: CBI, 1988).

Confederation of British Industry, *Competing with the World's Best* (London: CBI, 1991).

Conference of Mayors, *Rebuilding America's Cities* (Cambridge, Mass: Ballinger, 1986).

R. Cook Benjamin, 'From waterways to waterfronts: public investment for cities 1815–1980', in Bingham and Blair 1984.

P. Cooke, 'Workers' plans: an alternative to entrepreneurialism?', *Int. Jnl. Urb. Reg. Res.*, 8 (1984) 421–37.

P. Cooke, 'Locality, economic restructuring and world development', in Cooke 1989b (1989a).

P. Cooke (ed.) *Localities* (London: Unwin Hyman, 1989b).

P. Cooke and A. Scott, 'The new geography and sociology of production', *Space and Society*, 6 (1988) 241–4.

Coopers and Lybrand Deloitte and BiC with the CBI, *Local Support for Enterprise* (London: Coopers Lybrand, 1991).

N. Costello, J. Michie and S. Milne, *Beyond the Casino Economy* (London: Verso, 1989).

C. Couch, 'Inner areas development agencies', *Town and Country Planning*, 45 (1977) 436–8.

C. Couch, 'Germans take long view with urban renewal park', *Planning*, 917 (1991) 18–19.

A. Coulson, 'Evaluating local economic policy', in Campbell 1990b (1990).

A. Coupland, 'Planning gain: the Boston version', *Planning*, 792 (1988) 10–11.

Coventry, Liverpool, Newcastle and Tyneside Trades Councils, *State Interven-*

tion in Industry: a workers' inquiry (Newcastle-upon-Tyne: Coventry Trades Council, 1980).

K. Cox and A. Mair, 'Urban growth machines and the politics of local economic development' *Int. Jnl. Urb. Reg. Res.*, 13 (1989a) 137–46.

K. Cox and A. Mair, 'Levels of abstraction in locality studies', *Antipode*, 21 (1989b) 121–32.

P. Cressey and J. MacInnes, 'Voting for Ford: industrial democracy and the control of labour', *Capital and Class*, 11 (1980) 5–33.

E. Crowther-Hunt and L. Billinghurst, *Inner Cities, Inner Strengths* (London: Industrial Society, 1990).

M. Danson, G. Lloyd and D. Newlands, *The Role of Regional Development Agencies in Economic Regeneration* (London: Kingsley, 1991).

P. Davey, 'Authority and freedom', *Arch. Rev*, 1002 (1980) 75–7.

J. Davies, 'From municipal socialism to . . . municipal capitalism?', *Local Govt. Stud.*, 14 (1988) 19–22.

T. Davies and C. Mason, *Government and Local Labour Market Policy Implementation* (Aldershot: Gower, 1984).

T. Davies and C. Mason, *Shutting out the inner city worker*, SAUS Occ. Paper 23, Univ. of Bristol (1986).

M. Davis, S. Hiatt and M. Sprinker (eds) *Left at the Doorstep: the radical politics of place in America* (London: Verso, 1989).

M. Dear and A. Scott, *Urbanization and Urban Planning in Capitalist Society* (London: Methuen, 1981).

Department of the Environment, *Tourism and the Inner City* (London: HMSO, 1990).

P. Devine, *Democracy and Economic Planning* (Cambridge: Polity, 1988).

P. Dickens, *One Nation? social change and the politics of locality* (London: Pluto, 1988).

P. Dickens, S. Duncan, M. Goodwin and F. Gray, *Housing, States and Localities* (London: Methuen, 1985).

A. Dobson, *Green Political Thought* (London: Unwin Hyman, 1990).

Docklands Consultative Committee, *The Docklands Experiment* (London: DCC, 1990).

P. Donnel, 'Local discretion: the CDBG approach', in Bingham and Blair (1984).

D. Donnison and P. Soto, *The Good City* (London: Heinemann, 1980).

D. Donnison and A. Middleton (eds), *Regenerating the Inner City* (London: Routledge & Kegan Paul, 1987).

M. Douglass, 'The transnationalization of urbanization in Japan', *Int. Jnl. Urb. Reg. Res.*, 12 (1988) 425–54.

H. Duffy, 'Phoenix: enthusiasm in search of funds', *Financial Times* 24 Feb. 1987.

H. Duffy, 'Stitches in time for Nottingham', *Financial Times* 8 Aug. 1989.

S. Duncan and M. Goodwin, *The Local State and Uneven Development* (Cambridge: Polity, 1988).

M. Dunford and D. Perrons, *The Arena of Capital* (London: Macmillan 1983).

C. Dutton 'Sustaining regeneration on the eastern seaboard', *Planning*, 924 (1991) 14–15.

The Economist, 'When cities smile again', 306 (1988) 15–16.

The Economist, Thatcher-upon-Tyne, 311 (1989) 20.

C. Edwards, 'Still an experiment: some issues affecting the credibility of co-operatives as businesses', *14th UK Small Firms Conference*, Blackpool, (1991).

A. Eisenschitz and D. North, 'The London industrial strategy: socialist transformation or modernising capitalism?', *Int. Jnl. Urb. Reg. Res.*, 10 (1986) 419–40.

T. Elkin, D. McLaren and M. Hillman, *Reviving the City* (London: Friends of the Earth, 1991).

J. Ermisch and D. Maclennan, 'Housing policies, markets and urban economic change', in Hausner 1987a (1987).

J. Esser and J. Hirsch, 'The crisis of Fordism and the dimensions of a "post-Fordist" regional and urban structure', *Int. Jnl. Urb. Reg. Res.*, 13 (1989) 417–37.

Estates Gazette, Editorial, 'Zones of doubt', 255 (1980) 507.

D. Etherington, 'Local economic strategies and area based initiatives: another view of improvement areas', *Local Economy*, 2 (1987) 31–7.

N. Falk, 'Growing new firms; the role of the social entrepreneur', *Built Env.*, 4 (1978a) 204–12.

N. Falk, *Think Small: enterprise and the economy* (London: Fabian Soc., 1978b).

C. Fanning, *Renewing the Local Economy* (Cork: Cork Univ. Press, 1986).

Financial Times, 'Pension fund's progress', Supplement, 2 Nov. 1984, viii.

Financial Times, 'Call for locally based plan to help Ulster's economy', 20 Sept. 1988 (1988).

B. Fine and L. Harris, *The Peculiarities of the British Economy* (London: Lawrence & Wishart, 1985).

D. Finn, *Training without Jobs* (London: Macmillan, 1987).

M. Folin, 'The production of the general conditions of social production and the role of the state', in M. Harloe and E. Lebas (eds) *City, Class and Capital* (London: Arnold, 1981).

J. Forrester, 'Planning under the dynamic influences of complex social systems', in Jantsch 1969.

S. Fothergill and G. Gudgin, *Unequal Growth* (London: Heinemann, 1982).

S. Fothergill, S. Monk and M. Perry, *Property and Industrial Development* (London: Hutchinson, 1987).

C. Freeman, *Innovation in Small Firms* (London: HMSO, 1971).

C. Freeman, *Technology Policy and Economic Performance* (London: Pinter 1987).

C. Freeman, J. Clark and L. Soete, *Unemployment and Technical Innovation* (London: Pinter, 1982).

B. Frieden, 'Center city transformed: planners as developers,' *Jnl. of the American Planning Assoc.*, 56 (1990) 423–8.

A. Friedman, *Industry and Labour* (London: Macmillan, 1977).

A. Friedman, 'Developing the managerial strategies approach to the labour process', *Capital and Class*, 30 (1986) 97–124.

K. Fujita, 'The technopolis: hi-tech and regional development in Japan', *Int. Jnl. Urb. Reg. Res.*, 12 (1988) 566–94.

Furniture, Timber and Allied Trade Union, *Beneath the Veneer* (London: FTAT/LSPU, 1986).

A. Gamble, *Britain in Decline* (London: Macmillan, 1981).

H. Gans, 'Deconstructing the underclass', *Jnl. of the American Planning Assoc.*, 56 (1990) 271–7.

G. Gappert (ed.) *The Future of Winter Cities* (Beverly Hills: Sage, 1987).

P. Garrahan and P. Stewart, *The Nissan Enigma* (London: Mansell, 1992).

M. Geddes, 'Social audits and social accounting in the UK: a review', *Reg. Stud.*, 22 (1988a) 60–3.

M. Geddes, 'The capitalist state and the local economy: "restructuring for labour" and beyond', *Capital and Class*, 35 (1988b) 85–120.

C. Gerry, 'The working class and small enterprises in the UK recession', in N. Redclift and E. Mingione (eds) *Beyond Employment* (Oxford: Blackwell, 1985).

M. Giaoutzi, P. Nijkamp and D. Storey, *Small and Medium Sized Enterprises and Regional Development* (London: Routledge, 1988).

D. Gibbs with A. Tickell and C. Gentle, *Banking on Success* (Manchester: CLES, 1989).

A. Gifford, *Loosen the Shackles: first report of the Liverpool 8 inquiry into race relations in Liverpool* (London: Karia, 1989).

R. Giloth, 'Beyond common sense: the Baltimore renaissance', *Local Economy*, 4 (1990) 290–7.

A. Glyn, 'The economic case against pit closures', in D. Cooper and T. Hopper (eds) *Debating Coal Closures* (Cambridge: CUP, 1988).

J. Goddard, *The geography of the information economy*, PICT Policy Research Paper, Univ. of Newcastle-upon-Tyne (1990).

J. Goddard and S. Gillespie, 'Advanced telecoms and regional economic development', in B. Robson (ed.) *Managing the City* (London: Croom Helm, 1987).

R. Goodman, *The Last Entrepreneurs* (New York: Simon & Schuster, 1979).

M. Goodwin and S. Duncan, 'The local state and local economic policy: political mobilisation or economic regeneration', *Capital and Class*, 27, 1986, 14–36.

D. Gordon, 'Class struggle and the stages of urban development', in D. Perry and A. Watkins (eds) *The Rise of the Sunbelt Cities* (Beverly Hills: Sage, 1978).

A. Gorz (ed.) *The Division of Labour* (Hassocks: Harvester, 1976).

A. Gorz, *Farewell to the Working Class* (London: Pluto, 1982).

I. Gough, *The Political Economy of the Welfare State* (London: Macmillan, 1979).

J. Gough, 'The purpose of local industrial policy', *Local Economy*, 1 (1986a) 69–76.

J. Gough, 'Industrial policy and socialist strategy: restructuring and the unity of the working class', *Capital and Class*, 29 (1986b) 58–82.

J. Gough, 'Structure, system and contradiction in the capitalist space economy', *Society and Space*, 9 (1991a) 433–49.

J. Gough, *Towards research on infrastructures* Sheffield Univ. Management School Discussion Paper (1991b).

J. Gough, 'Where's the value in post-Fordism?', in Burrows 1992 (1992a).

J. Gough, 'Worker's competition, class relations and space', *Society and Space*, 10 (1992b).

J. Gough and M. Macnair, *Gay Liberation in the Eighties* (London: Pluto, 1985).

J. Graham and R. Ross, 'From manufacturing-based industrial policy to service-based employment policy?: industrial interests, class politics and the "Massachusetts miracle"', *Int. Jnl. Urb. Reg. Res.*, 13 (1989) 121–36.

C. Gray, 'Growth-orientation and the small firm' *14th UK Small Firms Conference*, Blackpool, (1991).

Greater London Council, 'What's different about our plan?', *Jobs for a Change*, (Sept. 1983a) 5.

Greater London Council, *Small Firms and the London Industrial Strategy*, Economic Policy Group Document 4 (London: GLC, 1983b).

Greater London Council, *London Industrial Strategy* (London: GLC, 1985a).

Greater London Council, *Strategy for the London Clothing Industry: a debate*, Economic Policy Group Document 39 (London: GLC, 1985b).

Greater London Council, *Technology Networks: a review*, Industry and Employment Cttee. paper (London: GLC, 1985c).

Greater London Council, *London Labour Plan* (London: GLC, 1986a).

Greater London Council, *The London Financial Strategy* (London: GLC, 1986b).

Greater London Council, *Textiles and Clothing: sunset industries?* (London: GLC, 1986c).

F. Green (ed.) *The Restructuring of the UK Economy* (Hassocks: Harvester, 1989).

R. Green (ed.) *Enterprise Zones* (Beverly Hills: Sage, 1991).

D. Gregory and J. Urry (eds) *Social Relations and Spatial Structures* (London: Macmillan, 1985).

R. Griffiths, 'Planning in retreat?: town planning and the market in the eighties', *Planning Practice and Research*, 1 (1986) 3–7.

B. Groom, 'New jobs: the battle to keep communities alive', *Financial Times*, 30 Jan. 1985.

G. Gudgin *et al.*, *Job Generation and Manufacturing Industry 1973–1986* (London: Northern Ireland Economic Research Centre, 1986).

A. Guild, 'The community approach raises confidence', *Financial Times*, 18 Oct. 1988.

J. Habermas, *Legitimation Crisis* (London: Heinemann, 1976).

G. Hadley, 'Enterprise Zones in Britain', *Planning Bull.*, 27 (1984) 34–8.

P. Hall, 'Green fields and grey areas', *Proc. Royal Town Planning Institute's Annual Conference*, London (1977) 1–6.

P. Hall, 'The geography of the fifth Kondratieff' in Hall and Markusen, 1985 (1985a).

P. Hall, 'Waterfronts: a new urban frontier', *Consazio Venezia Nuova Conference, Cities on Water*, Venice (1991).

P. Hall and A. Markusen, *Silicon Landscapes* (Winchester Mass. : Allen & Unwin, 1985).

P. Hall, R. Thomas, G. Gracey and R. Drewett, *The Containment of Urban England* (London: Allen & Unwin, 1973).

S. Hall, 'Authoritarian populism: a reply', *New Left Rev.*, 151 (1985b) 115–24.

S. Hall and M. Jacques (eds) *New Times* (London: Lawrence & Wishart, 1989).

I. Hamilton Fazey, 'Taking out the risks', *Financial Times* Supplement, 8 Oct. 1988.

M. Harloe (ed.), *Captive Cities* (Chichester: Wiley, 1977).

M. Harloe, C. Pickvance and J. Urry (eds) *Place, Policy and Politics* (London: Unwin Hyman, 1990).

N. Harris, 'What to do with London? the strategies of the GLC 1981–6', *Int. Socialism*, 2 (1986) 113–34.

B. Harrison and B. Bluestone, 'Wage polarisation in the US and the "flexibility" debate', *Cam. Jnl. of Econ.*, 14 (1990) 351–73.

D. Harvey, *The Limits to Capital* (Oxford: Blackwell, 1982).

D. Harvey, 'The geopolitics of capitalism', in Gregory and Urry 1985.

D. Harvey, 'Flexible accumulation through urbanisation: reflections on "postmodernism" in the American city', *Antipode*, 19 (1987) 260–86.

D. Harvey, *The Condition of Postmodernity* (Oxford: Blackwell, 1989).

G. Haughton and J. Peck, 'Skill Audits – a framework for local economic development', *Local Economy*, 3 (1988) 11–19.

G. Haughton, J. Peck and S. Steward, 'Local jobs and local houses for local workers', *Local Economy*, 2 (1987) 201–8.

G. Haughton and P. Roberts, 'Government urban economic policy 1979–1989: problems and potential', in Campbell 1990a (1990).

H. Hausermann and T. Kramer-Badoni, 'The growth of regional inequality in the Federal Republic of Germany', in M. Gottdiener and N. Komninos (eds) *Capitalist Development and Crisis Theory* (London: Macmillan, 1989).

V. Hausner (ed.) *Critical Issues in Urban Economic Development*, vol. I (Oxford: Clarendon, 1986).

V. Hausner (ed.) *Critical Issues in Urban Economic Development*, vol. II (Oxford: Clarendon, 1987a).

V. Hausner (ed.) *Urban Economic Development: five city studies* (Oxford: Clarendon, 1987b).

K. Hayton, 'Getting people into jobs', *Local Economy*, 3 (1989) 279–93.

M. Heafey, 'Barriers to the enterprise culture: new firm formation in the merchant city area of Glasgow', *Planning Outlook*, 32 (1989) 35–42.

A. Heal, 'BP's corporate responsibility programme', in *PTRC Conference, Regional and Local Economic Strategies*, London (1982) 35–44.

M. Hechter, *Internal Colonialism* (London: Routledge & Kegan Paul, 1975).

S. Hegarty, 'Inner city aid: the figures behind the hype, *Public Finance and Accountancy*, 9 Jan. 1988, 7–10.

W. Hendon and D. Shaw, 'The arts and urban development', in Gappert 1987.

T. Herrmann and K. Ward, 'Can there be a local economic strategy'?, *Community Dev. Jnl.*, 24 (1989) 157–60.

R. Hewison, *The Heritage Industry* (London: Methuen 1987).

J. Hirst, 'Mediocre, to say the least!', *New Statesman and Society*, 1 (1988) 25.

P. Hirst and J. Zeitlin (eds) *Reversing Industrial Decline?* (Oxford: Berg, 1989).

HMSO, *The Conduct of Local Authority Business* Cmnd. 433 (London, 1988).

G. Hodgson, *The Democratic Economy* (Harmondsworth: Penguin, 1984).

P. Hoggett and R. Hambleton, 'Beyond bureaucratic paternalism', in Hoggett and Hambleton 1987b (1987a).

P. Hoggett and R. Hambleton (eds) *Decentralisation and democracy*, SAUS Working Paper 28, Univ. of Bristol (1987b).

S. Holland, *Capital versus the Regions* (London: Macmillan, 1976).

J. Holloway, 'The red rose of Nissan', *Capital and Class*, 32 (1987) 142–64.

R. Hopkins, 'Industrial Wales and the enterprise culture: the community development aspect', *Community Dev. Jnl.*, 24 (1989) 55–61.

J. Howells and A. Green, *Technical Innovation, Strategic Change and the Location of UK Services* (Aldershot: Avebury, 1988).

D. Howl, 'Towards a people-based approach to local economic planning', in Wilmers and Bourdillon 1985.

B. Hoyle, D. Pitt and M. Hussain (eds) *Revitalising the Waterfront* (London: Bellhaven, 1988).

R. Hudson, 'Producing an industrial wasteland: capital, labour and the state in north-east England', in Martin and Rowthorn 1987.

R. Hudson and J. Lewis (eds) *Regional Planning in Europe* (London: Pion, 1982).

R. Hudson and D. Sadler, ' "Just-in-time" production and the European automotive components industry', Discussion Paper, Univ. of Durham, (1992).

P. Hughes and N. McCarthy, 'Cable technology', *Capital and Class*, 19 (1983) 5–17.

W. Hutton, 'Creeping paranoia threatens economy', *Guardian*, 13 June 1990.

R. Hyman and J. Elger, 'Job controls, the employers' offensive and alternative strategies', *Capital and Class*, 15 (1981) 115–49.

M. Ichiyo, *Class Struggle and Technological Innovation in Japan since 1945* (Amsterdam: Int. Inst. for Res. and Educ., 1987).

I. Illich, *Deschooling Society* (Harmondsworth: Penguin, 1973).

I. Illich, *The Right to Useful Unemployment and its Professional Enemies* (London: Boyars, 1978).

G. Ingham, *Capitalism Divided?: the City and industry in British social development* (London: Macmillan, 1984).

INSEAD, *Factories of the Future* (Fontainbleau: INSEAD, 1991).

M. Itoh, *Value and Crisis* (London: Pluto, 1980).

J. Jacobs, *The Death and Life of Great American Cities* (Harmondsworth: Penguin, 1965).

M. Jacobs, 'Community Businesses: are their aims confused?', *Local Economy*, 1 (1986) 29–34.

F. James, 'Urban economic development: a zero sum game?', in Bingham and Blair 1984.

E. Jantsch (ed.) *Perspectives on Planning* (Paris: OECD, 1969).

C. Jenkins and B. Sherman, *The Leisure Shock* (London: Eyre Methuen, 1981).

R. Jenkins, 'Divisions over the international division of labour', *Capital and Class*, 22 (1984) 28–57.

R. Johnson, 'The state, the region and the division of labour', in A. Scott and M. Storper (eds) *Production, Work and Territory* (Boston: Allen & Unwin, 1986).

R. Johnson and A. Cochrane, *Economic Policy Making by Local Authorities in Britain and West Germany* (London: Allen & Unwin, 1981).

D. Johnstone, *The Role of Local Authorities in Promoting Local Employment Initiatives* (Luxembourg; Commission of European Communities, 1985).

D. Johnstone, K. Hayton, R. Macfarlane and C. Moore, *Developing Businesses; good practice in urban regeneration* (London: HMSO, 1988).

K. Joseph, 'The quest for common ground', in K. Joseph (ed.) *Stranded on the Middle Ground* (London: Centre for Policy Stud., 1976).

D. Judd and M. Parkinson, *Leadership and Urban Regeneration* (Beverly Hills: Sage, 1990).

A. Kaletsky, 'Why every Chrysler has a $700 health bill', *Financial Times*, 1 Sept. 1989.

A. Kantrow (ed.), *Sunrise . . . Sunset: challenging the myth of industrial obsolescence* (New York: Wiley, 1985).

S. Katz and M. Mayer, 'Gimme Shelter: self help housing struggles within and against the state in New York City and West Berlin', *Int. Jnl. Urb. Reg. Res.*, 9 (1985) 15–46.

R. Keating and M. Boyle, *Remaking Urban Scotland* (Edinburgh: Edinburgh Univ. Press, 1986).

M. Keith and A. Rogers (eds) *Rhetoric and Reality in the Inner City* (London: Mansell, 1991).

R. King, 'Corporatism and the local economy', in W. Grant (ed.) *The Political Economy of Corporatism* (London: Macmillan, 1985).

R. Kirwan, 'Local fiscal policy and inner city economic development', in Hausner 1986.

C. Knevitt, *Community Enterprise* (London: *The Times*/ Gulbenkian Foundation, 1986a).

C. Knevitt, 'Community Enterprise', in Knevitt 1986a (1986b).

N. Krumholz, 'City planning for greater equity', *Jnl. of Arch. and Planning Res.*, 1 (1986) 327–37.

Labour Party, *Modern Manufacturing Strength* (London: Labour Party, 1991a).

Labour Party, *Devolution and Democracy* (London: Labour Party, 1991b).

P. Lawless, *Britain's Inner Cities* (London: Paul Chapman, 1989) 2nd edn.

R. Layard, D. Metcalf and R. O'Brien, 'A new deal for the long-term unemployed', in P. Hart (ed.) *Unemployment and Labour Market Policies* (Aldershot: Gower, 1986).

W. Lazonick, *Comparative Advantage on the Shopfloor* (Boston: Harvard Univ. Press, 1991).

C. Leadbeater, 'Training at Jaguar: an investment not a cost', *Financial Times*, 24 June 1987.

C. Leadbeater and J. Lloyd, *In Search of Work* (Harmondsworth: Penguin, 1987).

R. Leigh and D. North, 'Innovation Centres: the policy options for local authorities', *Local Economy*, (1986) 45–56.

R. Leigh, D. North, K. Escott and J. Gough, *Monitoring Manufacturing Employment Change in London 1976–81*, vol. 1 (London: Middx. Poly., 1982).

C. Leo, 'Urban hierarchy and the power of the local state', *ISA Conference, Urban Change and Conflict*, Lancaster (1991).

L. Levidow, 'We won't be fooled again?: economic planning and left strategies', *Radical Science Jnl.*, 13 (1983) 28–38.

R. Levitas, 'Introduction', in R. Levitas (ed.) *The Ideology of the New Right* (Cambridge: Polity, 1986).

C. Leys, 'Thatcherism and manufacturing: a question of hegemony,' *New Left Rev.*, 151 (1985) 5–25.

A. Lipietz, *Mirages and Miracles* (London: Verso, 1987).

J. Lloyd, 'Misty eyes on 19th century charity', *Financial Times*, 4 May 1988.

J. Logan and H. Molotch, *Urban Fortunes* (Berkeley: Univ. of Calif. Press, 1987).

J. Lojkine, 'Big firms' strategies, urban policy and urban social movements', in Harloe 1977.

London Conference of the Socialist Economists Group, *The Alternative Economic Strategy* (London: CSE, 1980).

J. Lovering, 'The local economy and local economic strategies', *Policy and Politics*, 16 (1988) 145–57.

A. McArthur and A. McGregor, 'Local employment and training initiatives in the national manpower policy context', in Hausner 1987a (1987).

R. McArthur, 'Locality and small firms', *Society and Space*, 7 (1989) 197–210.

J. McDermott, 'Free enterprise and socialised labour', *Science and Society*, 55 (1991) 388–416.

R. MacDonald, 'Runners, fallers and plodders: youth and the enterprise culture', *14th UK Small Firms Conference* Blackpool, (1991).

R. MacDonald and F. Coffield, *Risky Business?* (Lewes: Falmer Press, 1991).

S. McKellar, 'The enterprise of culture', *Local Work*, 8 (1988) 14–17.

S. Mackenzie and D. Rose, 'Industrial change, the domestic economy and home life', in J. Anderson, S. Duncan and R. Hudson (eds) *Redundant Spaces in Cities and Regions?* (London: Academic Press, 1983).

M. Mackintosh, 'Planning the public sector: an argument from the case of transport in London', in Cochrane 1987.

M. Mackintosh and H. Wainwright, *A Taste of Power* (London: Verso, 1987).

A. MacLeary and G. Lloyd, 'Enterprise Zones: a step forward?', *Estates Gazette*, 255 (1980) 149–50.

S. Maddock, 'New values in business, a necessity not a luxury: community enterprise in the small business sector', *14th UK Small Firms Conference*, Blackpool (1991).

M. Maguire, 'Work, locality and social control', *Work, Employment and Society*, 2 (1988) 71–87.

E. Malecki and P. Nijkamp, 'Technology and regional development', *Env. and Planning*, 6 (1988) 383–400.

E. Mandel, *The Second Slump* (London: NLB, 1978a).

E. Mandel, *Late Capitalism* (London: Verso, 1978b).

Manpower Services Commission, *Young People and Work* (London: HMSO, 1977).

O. Marriot, *The Property Boom* (London: Hamilton, 1967).

D. Marsh, 'Why the market is a fickle ally', *Financial Times*, 28 July 1981.

A. Marshall, *Principles of Economics* (London: Macmillan, 9th ed. 1961).

J. Marshall, *Services and Uneven Development* (Oxford: OUP, 1988).

R. Martin and B. Rowthorn (eds) *The Geography of Deindustrialisation* (London: Macmillan, 1987).

S. Martin, 'New jobs in the inner city: the employment impacts of projects assisted under the Urban Development Grant programme', *Urb. Stud.*, 26 (1989) 627–38.

S. Martin, 'City grants, Urban Development Grants, and Urban Regeneration Grants', in Campbell 1990b (1990).

H. Martinos and E. Humphreys, 'European Perspectives on Urban Economic and Employment Regeneration', *Innovation Development Planning Group Conference, Economic Regeneration in Urban Areas*, Sheffield (1990).

C. Mason, 'Explaining recent trends in new firm formation in the UK: some evidence from South Hampshire', *Reg. Stud.*, 23 (1990) 371–376.

C. Mason, and R. Harrison, 'A strategy for closing the small firms' finance gap', *14th UK Small Firms Conference* Blackpool, (1991).

D. Massey, *Spatial Divisions of Labour* (London: Macmillan, 1984).

D. Massey, 'The legacy lingers on: the impact of Britain's international role on its internal geography', in Martin and Rowthorn 1987 (1987a).

D. Massey,'Equal opportunities: the GLEB experience', in Cochrane 1987 (1987b).

D. Massey and J. Allen (eds) *Uneven Re-development* (London: Hodder & Stoughton, 1988).

D. Massey and R. Meegan, *The Geography of Industrial Reorganisation*, (Oxford: Pergamon, 1979).

D. Massey and R. Meegan, *The Anatomy of Job Loss* (London: Methuen, 1982).

D. Massey and R. Meegan (eds) *Politics and Method* (London: Methuen, 1985).

D. Massey, D. Wield and P. Quintas, *High-Tech Fantasies* (London: Routledge, 1992).

P. Mattera, *Off the Books* (London: Pluto, 1985).

J. Mawson and D. Miller, 'Interventionist approaches in local employment and economic development', in Hausner 1986a (1986).

R. Meegan, 'Paradise postponed: the growth and decline of Merseyside's outer estates', in Cooke 1989b (1989).

P. Meyer and R. Boyle, 'Lessons from the USA and directions for British local economic development efforts', *Local Economy*, 4 (1990) 317–21.

A. Middleton, 'The burden in the haystack', *Planning*, 633 (1985) 6–7.

S. Miller and D. Tomaskovic-Devey, *Recapitalising America* (Boston: Routledge & Kegan Paul, 1983).

L. Mills and K. Young, 'Local authorities and economic development', in Hausner 1986.

N. Mobbs, *Inner City Challenge* (London: Aims of Industry, c. 1987).

V. Mole and D. Elliott, *Enterprising Innovation* (London: Pinter, 1987).

H. Molotch, 'The city as a growth machine', *Am. Journal of Sociology*, 82 (1976) 309–32.

B. Moore and P. Townroe, *Urban Labour Markets* (London: HMSO, 1990).

C. Moore and S. Booth, 'The Scottish Development Agency: market consensus, public planning and local enterprise', *Local Economy*, 1 (1986) 7–19.

C. Moore and J. Pierre, 'Partnership or privatisation? The political economy of local economic restructuring', *Policy and Politics*, 16 (1988) 169–78.

C. Moore and J. Richardson, *Local Partnership and the Unemployment Crisis in Britain* (London: Unwin Hyman, 1989).

K. Morgan; 'Re-industrialisation in peripheral Britain', in Martin and Rowthorn 1987.

K. Morgan and A. Sayer, *Micro-circuits of Capital* (Cambridge: Polity, 1988).

H. Morison, *The Regeneration of Local Economies* (Oxford: Clarendon, 1987).

M. Mowbray, 'Localism and austerity: the political economy of community welfare services', *Community Dev. Jnl.*, 18 (1983) 238–46.

M. Moynagh, *Making Unemployment Work* (Tring: Lion, 1985).

G. Mulgan, 'The power of the weak', *Marxism Today*, 32 (1988) 24–31.

G. Mulgan, 'The changing shape of the city', in Hall and Jacques (1989).

R. Muller and A. Bruce, 'Local government in pursuit of an industrial strategy,' *Local Govt. Stud.*, 7 (1981) 3–18.

F. Murray, 'The decentralisation of production – the decline of the mass-collective worker?', *Capital and Class*, 19 (1983b) 74–99.

F. Murray, 'Flexible specialisation in the Third Italy', *Capital and Class*, 33 (1987) 84–95.

R. Murray, 'Pension funds and local authority investments', *Capital and Class*, 20 (1983a) 89–102.

R. Murray, 'Bennetton Britain: the new economic order', *Marxism Today*, 29 (1985) 28–32.

R. Murray, *Crowding Out: boom and crisis in the South East* (Stevenage: South East Economic Development Strategy, 1989).

R. Nabarro, R. Davies, C. Cobbold and N. Galley, *Local Enterprise and the Unemployed* (London: Calouste Gulbenkian Foundation, 1986).

J. Nash, 'Training designs "stolen"', *Times Ed. Supp.* 21 Feb. 1992.

National Audit Commission, *Urban Regeneration and Economic Development: the local government dimension* (London: HMSO, 1989).

National Audit Office, *Regenerating the Inner Cities* (London: HMSO, 1990).

M. Neary, *The politics of policy: post-Fordism, the informal economy and the local state*, MA Dissertation (London: Middx. Poly., 1989).

W. Neill, 'Industrial policy in Detroit: the search for a new regional development model in the home of Fordism', *Local Economy*, 6 (1991) 250–71.

H. Newby, *The Deferential Worker* (London: Allen Lane, 1977).

Newham Docklands Forum, *The People's Plan for the Royal Docks* (London: NDF/GLC, 1983).

I. Newman, 'Locally relevent job creation in the UK', *Community Dev. Jnl.*, 24 (1989) 120–6.

S. Newton and D. Porter, *Modernisation Frustrated* (London: Unwin Hyman, 1988).

T. Nichols, *The British Worker Question* (London: Routledge & Kegan Paul, 1986).

P. Nolan and K. O'Donnell, 'Taming the market economy?: a critical assessment of the GLC's experiment in restructuring for labour', *Cam. Jnl. of Econ.*, 11 (1987) 251–63.

R. Oakey, *High Technology Small Firms* (London: Pinter, 1984).

R. Oakey, 'Government policy towards high technology', in J. Curran and R. Blackburn (eds) *Paths of Enterprise; the future of small business* (London: Routledge, 1991).

OECD, *Community Business Ventures and Job Creation* (Paris: OECD, 1984a).

OECD, *Education, Urban Development and Local Initiatives* (Paris: OECD, 1984b).

OECD, *Creating Jobs at the Local Level* (Paris: OECD, 1985).

OECD, *Women, Local Initiatives and Job Creation* (Paris: OECD, 1986).

OECD, *New Roles for Cities and Towns* (Paris: OECD, 1987).

OECD, *The Role of Large Firms in Local Job Creation* (Paris: OECD, n.d.).

N. Oliver and B. Wilkinson, *The Japanisation of British Industry* (Oxford: Blackwell, 1988).

Open University, *Introduction to Sociology, Block 3, Comparison and Change; Unit 20 Community* (Milton Keynes: Open Univ. Press, 1980).

E. Oxford, *Work that Works* (Chicago: Northeast Midwest Inst., 1987).

H. Ozbekhan, 'Toward a general theory of planning', in Jantsch 1969.

PA Cambridge Economic Consultants, *An Evaluation of the Enterprise Zone Experiment*, (London: HMSO, 1987).

J. Palmer and H. Wainwright, 'Plans, cooperatives and the struggle for socialism', *Socialist Rev.* (Oct. 1983) 15–17.

J. Panet-Raymond, 'Community groups in Quebec: from radical action to voluntarism for the state?', *Community Dev. Jnl.*, 22 (1987) 281–6.

M. Parkinson and R. Evans, *Urban Development Corporations*, in Campbell 1990b (1990).

R. Paton, *Reluctant Enterpreneurs* (Milton Keynes: Open Univ. Press, 1989).

G. Pearce, 'Urban Development Grants show mixed performance', *Planning*, 761 (1988) 10–11.

Peat Marwick and McLintock, *The Local Impact of Canary Wharf* (London: unpublished, 1986).

J. Peck, 'The politics of training in Britain: contradictions in the TEC initiative', *Capital and Class*, 44 (1991) 23–34.

C. Pickvance, 'From "social base" to "social force": some analytical issues in the study of urban protest', in Harloe 1977.

D. Pignon and J. Querzola, 'Dictatorship and democracy in production', in Gorz 1976.

M. Piore and C. Sabel, *The Second Industrial Divide* (New York: Basic Books, 1984).

F. Piven and R. Cloward, 'The new class war in the United States', in Szelenyi 1984.

S. Pollard, *The Development of the British Economy 1914–67* (London: Arnold, 1969).

Pollert, A. (ed.) *Farewell to Flexibility?* (Oxford: Blackwell, 1991).

Prince Charles, 'Foreword', in Knevitt 1986.

PSMRC, *An Evaluation of the Urban Development Grant Programme* (London: HMSO, 1988).

D. Raffe, 'Can there be an effective youth unemployment policy?', in R. Fiddy (ed.) *In Place of Work* (Lewes: Falmer Press, 1983).

A. Rainnie, *Industrial Relations in Small Firms* (London: Routledge, 1989).

R. Ramtin, *Capitalism and Automation* (London: Pluto, 1990).

Red Notes, *Working Class Autonomy and the Crisis* (London: Red Notes/CSE Books, 1979).

R. Reich, *The Work of Nations* (New York: Simon & Schuster, 1991).

C. Rigg and M. Miller, 'Women and economic development', *Local Economy*, 6 (1991) 196–210.

Y. Roberts, 'Boys with the greenbacks', *New Statesman and Society*, 1 (1988) 14–17.

K. Robins, *Capital and Cable* (London: GLC, 1983).

K. Robins and F. Webster, 'Higher education, high tech, high rhetoric', *Radical Science Jnl.*, 18 (1985) 36–57.

K. Robins and F. Webster, 'Athens without slaves .. or slaves without Athens?', *Science as Culture*, 3 (1988) 7–53.

F. Robinson, J. Goddard and C. Wren, *Economic Development Policies: an evaluation study of the Newcastle metropolitan region* (Oxford: OUP, 1987).

P. Robinson, *The Unbalanced Recovery* (Oxford: Allan, 1988).

E. Rose (ed.) *New Roles for Old Cities* (Aldershot: Gower, 1986a).

E. Rose, 'The entrepreneurial city – the new frontier', in Rose 1986a (1986b).

S. Roweis, 'Urban planning in early and late capitalist societies', in Dear and Scott 1981.

S. Roweis and A. Scott, 'The urban land question', in Dear and Scott 1981.

B. Rowthorn, 'The past strikes back', in S. Hall and M. Jacques (eds) *The Politics of Thatcherism* (London: Lawrence & Wishart, 1983).

Royal Town Planning Institute, *How Effective is Local Economic Planning?* (London: RTPI, 1985).

J. Rubery, 'Structured labour markets, worker organisation and low pay', *Cam. Jnl. of Econ.*, 2 (1978) 17–36.

D. Ruccio, S. Resnick and R. Wolff, 'Class beyond the nation-state', *Capital and Class*, 43 (1991) 25–44.

V. Ruggiero, 'Technocity: symbolic Utopia and status panic', *Science as Culture*, 5 (1989) 87–99.

M. Rustin, 'Lessons of the London Industrial Strategy', *New Left Rev.*, 155 (1986) 75–85.

C. Sabel, 'Flexible specialisation and the re-emergence of regional economies', in Hirst and Zeitlin 1989.

C. Sabel, G, Herrigel, R. Deeg and R. Kazis, 'Regional prosperities compared: Massachusetts and Baden-Württemberg in the 1980s', *Economy and Society*, 18 (1989) 374–400.

D. Sadler, *The Global Region* (Oxford: Pergamon, 1992).

P. Saunders, 'Rethinking local politics', in M. Boddy and C. Fudge (eds) *Local Socialism?* (London: Macmillan, 1984).

A. Saxenian, 'The urban contradictions of Silicon Valley', *Int. Jnl. Urb. Reg. Res.*, 7 (1983) 237–62.

A. Saxenian, 'The Cheshire Cat's grin: innovation, regional development and the Cambridge case', *Economy and Society*, 18 (1989) 448–77.

A. Sayer, 'Post-Fordism in question' *Int. Jnl. Urb. Reg. Res.*, 13 (1989) 666–95.

A. Sayer and K. Morgan, 'A modern industry in a declining region: links between method, theory and policy', in Massey and Meegan 1985.

L. Scarman, *The Brixton Disorders, 10–12 April 1981, Report of an Inquiry*, Cmnd. 8427 (London: HMSO, 1981).

E. Schumacher, *Small is Beautiful* (London: Blond & Briggs, 1973).

A. Scott, 'Flexible production systems and regional development', *Int. Jnl. Urb. Reg. Res.*, 12 (1988) 171–86.

Segal, Quince, Wicksteed, *Encouraging Small Business Start-ups and Growth* (London: HMSO, 1988).

J. Sellgren, 'Local economic development and local initiatives in the mid-1980s', *Local Govt. Stud.*, 13 (1987) 51–68.

R. Selucky, *Marxism, Socialism and Freedom* (New York: St Martin's Press, 1979).

E. Sheppard and T. Barnes, *The Capitalist Space Economy* (London: Unwin Hyman, 1990).

A. Sills, G. Taylor and P. Golding, *The Politics of the Urban Crisis* (London: Hutchinson, 1988).

D. Smith, ' "Not getting on, just getting by": changing prospects in South Birmingham', in Cooke 1989b (1989).

L. Smith and J. Carr, 'Contract compliance and equal opportunity', *Local Economy*, 1 (1986) 35–44.

M. Smith, *City, State and Market* (Oxford: Blackwell, 1988).

N. Smith, *Uneven Development* (Oxford: Blackwell, 1984).

G. Solinas, 'Labour market segmentation and workers' careers: the case of the Italian knitwear industry', in R. Pahl (ed.) *On Work* (Oxford: Blackwell, 1988).

H. Steedman and K. Wagner, 'Productivity, machinery and skills: clothing manufacturing in Britain and Germany', *Nat. Inst. Econ. Rev.*, 128 (1989) 40–57.

D. Storey and S. Johnson, 'Job generation in Britain: a review of recent studies', *Int. Small Bus. Jnl.*, 4 (1986) 29–46.

D. Storey and S. Johnson, *Job Generation and Labour Market Change* (London: Macmillan, 1987).

D. Storey, K. Keasey, R. Watson and P. Wynarczyk, *The Performance of Small Firms* (London: Croom Helm, 1987).

D. Storey and A. Strange, 'New Players in the "Enterprise Culture"?', *14th UK Small Firms Conference*, Blackpool (1991).

M. Storper and R. Walker, *The Capitalist Imperative* (Oxford: Blackwell, 1989).

D. Stout, 'De-industrialisation and industrial policy', in F. Blackaby (ed.) *De-industrialisation* (London: Heinemann, 1981) 2nd edn.

C. Stubbs and J. Wheelock, *A Woman's Work in the Changing Local Economy* (Aldershot: Avebury, 1990).

D. Swartz, 'The eclipse of politics: the Alternative Economic Strategy as socialist strategy', *Capital and Class*, 13 (1981) 102–13.

T. Symonds, 'TECs faulted over basic skills training', *Financial Times*, 10 Jan. 1991.

I. Szelenyi (ed.) *Cities in Recession* (New York: Sage, 1984).

W. Tabb and S. Yokota, 'Capital versus the regions: the case of post-war Japan', *ISA Conference, Urban Change and Conflict*, Lancaster (1991).

D. Taylor, 'Citizenship and social power', *Crit. Social Policy*, 26 (1989) 19–31.

G. Therborn, *Why Some People are More Unemployed than Others* (London: Verso, 1986).

G. Therborn, 'The two-thirds, one-third society', in Hall and Jacques 1989.

W. Thompson and P. Thompson, 'Alternative paths to the revival of industrial cities', in Gappert 1987.

A. Thornley, *Urban Planning under Thatcherism* (London: Routledge, 1991).

N. Thrift, 'The geography of international disorder', in Massey and Allen 1988.

G. Todd, *Creating New Jobs in Europe* (London: Economist Intelligence Unit, 1984).

J. Tomlinson, *The Unequal Struggle: British society and the capitalist enterprise* (London: Methuen, 1982).

P. Totterdill, *Sunset Industries: industrial policy and the regeneration of British manufacturing'*, Local Econ. Policy Rev. 2, Univ. of Technology (Loughborough, 1990a).

P. Totterdill, *Restructuring Retailing* (Manchester: CLES, 1990b).

P. Townroe and P. Brenton, 'Local authority aid to small firms in neighbouring areas', *Local Economy*, 2 (1987) 169–80.

A. Townsend and F. Peck, 'An approach to the analysis of redundancies in the UK (post-1976)', in Massey and Meegan 1985.

Trades Union Congress, *Trade Unions in the Cities* (London: TUC, 1988).

J-J Turkie, *An examination into the role of the state in the development of Canary Wharf*, MA Dissertation, Middx. Poly., 1991.

I. Turok, 'Evaluation and understanding in local economic policy', *Urb. Stud.*, 26 (1989) 587–606.

I. Turok and U. Wannop, *Targeting Urban Economic Employment Initiatives* (London: HMSO, 1989).

J. Urry, 'Social relatiòns, space and time', in Gregory and Urry 1985.

H. Wainwright and D. Elliot, *The Lucas Plan* (London: Allison & Busby, 1982).

R. Waldinger, H. Aldrich and R. Ward, *Ethnic Entrepreneurs* (Beverly Hills: Sage, 1990).

R. Walker, 'Two sources of uneven development under advanced capitalism: spatial differentiation and capital mobility', *Rev. Rad. Pol. Econ.* 10 (1978) 28–37.

London Borough of Wandsworth, *Prosperity or Slump?* (London: LBW., 1976).

U. Wannop, 'Stimulating local enterprise: GEAR and the urban projects of the Scottish Development Agency', in Rose 1986a (1986).

M. Ward, *Job Creation by the Council* (Nottingham: Instit. of Workers Control, n.d.).

S. Ward, 'Local industrial promotion and development policies 1899–1940', *Local Economy*, 5 (1990) 100–18.

A. Warde, 'The homogenisation of space?', in H. Newby *et al.* (eds) *Restructuring Capital* (London: Macmillan, 1985).

A. Warde, 'Industrial restructuring, local politics and the reproduction of labour power', *Society and Space*, 6 (1988) 75–95.

S. Watson, 'Gilding the smokestacks: the new symbolic representation of deindustrialised regions', *Society and Space*, 9 (1991) 59–70.

C. Weaver, 'The limits of economism: towards a political approach to regional development and planning', in Hudson and Lewis 1982.

M. White, 'Encouraging product innovation in small firms', *Policy Studies*, 9 (1988) 21–34.

A. Whyatt, 'The prospects for local economic and employment policy', *Local Economy*, 3 (1988) 126–31.

Widdicombe Inquiry, *The Conduct of Local Authority Business*, Cmnd. 9797 (London: HMSO, 1986).

P. Wiggins and P. Snell, *Food is Work* (Manchester; CLES, 1986).

K. Williams, T. Cutler, J. Williams and C. Haslam, 'The end of mass production?', *Economy and Society*, 16 (1987) 405–39.

K. Williams, J. Williams and C. Haslam, 'The hollowing out of British manufacturing and its implications for policy', *Economy and Society*, 19 (1991a) 456–490.

K. Williams, J. Williams and C. Haslam, 'Look before you leap: the implications of EMU for the future of the EC', in A. Amin and M. Dietrich (eds) *Towards a New Europe* (Aldershot: Elgar, 1991b).

K. Williams, J. Williams and D. Thomas, *Why are the British Bad at Manufacturing?* (London: Routledge & Kegan Paul, 1983).

P. Wilmers and B. Bourdillon (eds) *Managing the Local Economy* (London: Geobooks, 1985).

Wilson Committee, *Report of the Committee to Review the Functioning of Financial Institutions* Cmnd. 7937 (London: HMSO, 1980).

S. Windass (ed.) *Local Initiatives in Great Britain: vol. 1 Economic* (Oxford: New Foundations for Local Initiative Support, 1982).

J. Wolch, 'The shadow state: transformation in the voluntary sector', in J. Wolch and M. Dear (eds), *The Power of Geography* (Boston: Unwin Hyman, 1989).

E. Wood, *The Pristine Culture of Capitalism* (London: Verso, 1991).

S. Wood (ed.) *The Transformation of Work?* (London: Unwin Hyman, 1989).

S. Woolcock, M. Hodger and K. Schreiber, *Britain, Germany and 1992* (London: Pinter, 1991).

I. Wray, 'Selling brainpower–not hamburgers', *Business in the Community Magazine*, 7 (1987/8) 21.

P. Wright, *On Living in an Old Country* (London: Verso, 1985).

C. Wright Mills, *The Sociological Imagination* (Harmondsworth: Penguin 1970.

K. Young and C. Mason (eds) *Urban Economic Development* (London: Macmillan, 1983).

Index